What a Body Remembers

What a Body Remembers

A Memoir of Sexual Assault and Its Aftermath

KAREN STEFANO

A Vireo Book | Rare Bird Books
Los Angeles, Calif.

This is a Genuine Vireo Book

A Vireo Book | Rare Bird Books
453 South Spring Street, Suite 302
Los Angeles, CA 90013
rarebirdbooks.com

For more information, address:
A Vireo Book | Rare Bird Books Subsidiary Rights Department
453 South Spring Street, Suite 302
Los Angeles, CA 90013

Set in Minion

Printed in the United States

10 9 8 7 6 5 4 3 2 1

Publisher's Cataloging-in-Publication Data

Names: Stefano, Karen, author.
Title: What a Body Remembers: A Memoir of Sexual Assault
and its Aftermath / Karen Stefano.
Description: First Trade Paperback Original Edition |
A Genuine Vireo Book | New York, NY; Los Angeles, CA:
Rare Bird Books, 2019.
Identifiers: ISBN 9781947856950
Subjects: LCSH Stefano, Karen. | Rape Victims—Biography. |
Post-traumatic Stress Disorder—Patients. | Rape—Investigation. |
BISAC BIOGRAPHY & AUTOBIOGRAPHY / Personal Memoirs
Classification: LCC HV6561 .S73 2019 | DDC 364.1/532/092—dc23

For my assailant.

How she might have done things differently. But didn't.
How it is too late to change things now. How it isn't.

—Larry Levis, "Elegy with a Darkening Trapeze Inside It"

Say there-is-nothing-I-won't-do-to-live.

—Alan Shapiro, "Sunflower"

CHAPTER 1

July 27, 1995, Superior Court Department 12,
San Diego, California

THE COURTROOM HOLDS A palpable edge, even before the judge takes the bench and trial begins. Nerves. Expectancy. Fear of losing control. I always dreaded trial, fretted about it, wore myself out trying to anticipate all that might go wrong, where the prosecutor might trip me up, destroy me. But the moment Judge Hirsch opens the door from his chambers and the bailiff's voice booms, "Please remain seated and come to order!" the angst evaporates. Battle has begun.

We've already impaneled the jury and they sit in the box, twelve of them and two alternates, dutifully gripping notepads and pens. They look at me, steal glances at my client. They are curious, ready for the show to begin.

The deputy district attorney goes first with his opening statement: A brutal assault in broad daylight in a bank parking lot. Female victim pistol whipped with a .45 automatic. Facial injuries. Purse wrenched from shoulder and attacker fled. Victim called 911, described her assailant. Black male, late twenties, muscular, six foot two, or three. Fled in a white Buick. My client,

Dwayne Sayers, is stopped two hours later in a car meeting this description. On the passenger seat sits this woman's purse minus her wallet and a few other items. Dwayne is arrested.

My opening statement is more vague. As a criminal defense attorney, I cannot tell the jury that "the evidence will show..." and then fail to deliver. As a criminal defense attorney, I can never quite be certain what the judge will let me get away with. In this trial, I know my client can't testify. This is for two reasons. One, he is likely guilty and ethical rules prohibit an attorney from putting on perjured testimony. I don't know for a fact that Dwayne is guilty. I haven't asked. I don't ask that question. I don't care. All I care about is convincing a jury to see reasonable doubt. The other reason Dwayne can't testify is that he has prior convictions for similar crimes. If he testifies the DA is allowed to impeach his credibility as a witness by bringing up those prior assaults. Once the jury hears about them, they will assume he is guilty. No question.

Dwayne has served time in the toughest prisons in California—Folsom, San Quentin, Pelican Bay. He's been in custody five months, held on $250,000 bail, which he has no chance of posting. Because it would be prejudicial for the jury to see Dwayne in his county jail uniform, I have obtained a "Dress Out Order," requiring the San Diego County Sheriff's Department to dress Dwayne in the clothes I have provided: tan khakis; long-sleeved, pastel yellow button-down; sweater-vest; loafers. Mr. Rogers clothes. Whenever I have the opportunity, I touch Dwayne's forearm. I lean in close and whisper in his ear. I do this for the benefit of the jury. I want to transmit the message that I am not afraid of this man. I want them to sense my client is harmless.

I expected Dwayne to be a difficult client, but he isn't. He understands that of all the people in this world I'm the only one on his side, the only one fighting for him. He likes me and knows

I'm a good lawyer, a lawyer working like hell for him in a difficult case. The night before this woman's assault, a man was robbed in the same neighborhood, at an ATM. The ATM had a camera. Seven photos show Dwayne holding a gun to the man's head, grabbing cash as the ATM spit it out, and the gun in these photographs is identical to the one described by the woman assaulted in the bank parking lot. I have managed to keep this out of evidence. This jury will never hear about that ATM robbery, will never see those photos, and this has impressed Dwayne immensely. On the charges of the assault of this woman, I might actually have a shot of winning. And winning matters deeply. Winning is everything because in some place inside me, a place I can't name, a voice screams, a ceaseless screeching, "*I dare you to knock this chip off my shoulder, motherfucker!*"

◆◆◆

ON THE SECOND DAY of trial, the victim testifies. She is blonde and petite like me, in her early thirties like me. She is pretty, earnest, likable, and I imagine her as someone with whom I might sit down on a summer evening, sipping wine, sharing stories of our lives. She describes what happened in the bank parking lot. When asked if the man who assaulted her is in the courtroom today she points to Dwayne and shudders. The DA says, "I have no further questions for this witness, Your Honor."

Now it's my turn.

Adrenaline shoots through my body as I stand for cross-examination. The sensation is pure, primal, and I feel how similar the coursing sense of power is to panic. I smooth the fabric of my skirt, pausing a few seconds for effect, for drama. I don't usually wear pink in a jury trial, but for this one I wear a soft rose suit and white blouse. I have colored my hair a lighter shade of blonde.

I want to juxtapose my innocence with Dwayne's Mr. T-sized physique. If this little blonde lady in pink isn't afraid of him, he must be innocent.

No testimony can convey the force and scale of an assault. The questions are not designed for that. The strategy of the prosecution is to simply lay out the pieces, to connect the dots, to create a sequence that makes it as easy as possible for a jury to see things their way. The strategy of the defense is the opposite: to raise questions, to undercut certainty, to create as much doubt in the minds of jurors as possible. On cross-examination, control is critical. You must permit the witness to answer only with a "Yes" or a "No," a response that you, as the framer of each question, dictate. Done correctly, a beat emerges, a rhythm, a song. Cross-examination is an art.

"When you described the man who assaulted you to the police, you didn't say anything about him having tattoos, did you?"

"No," she says, already sounding less confident than when the DA questioned her, when the narrative of the case was going her way.

I have already elicited testimony from the arresting officer indicating that my client has numerous tattoos on his arms, one of which, in two-inch cursive letters on his left forearm reads, *TRUST NO BITCH*. It's because of this tattoo that Dwayne will wear only long-sleeved shirts during trial.

"In fact, sitting here today, it's your recollection that the man who assaulted you didn't have any tattoos?"

She pauses, bites at her lower lip. "Yes, that's right."

I can tell she is confused, has no idea where I'm going with this, and that this blind spot disquiets her.

I drop the subject; I don't need her for anything else on this point. A good defense attorney doesn't try to get the witness to agree with the ultimate point. Instead, she uses the witness, takes what is needed, and moves along. Then she drives the point home in the closing argument. This one I will hit hard. The man who assaulted this victim had no tattoos. My client has many tattoos. This, I will argue, creates one of many inconsistencies in the facts, and these inconsistencies trigger reasonable doubt. And if a juror has reasonable doubt, that juror is obligated to vote not guilty, obligated to set my client free.

I will pound this point hard, even after I have Dwayne remove his shirt in the hallway outside Judge Hirsch's chambers during the last recess so I can inspect his tattoos for myself. All of the dark ink is nearly invisible against his black skin. Having Dwayne remove his shirt for the jury as demonstrative evidence would only make them see it from the victim's point of view: you can barely see the damn tattoos. In spite of this, I will smash my point home.

I move on to my next topic.

"The assault happened quickly, didn't it?"

"Yes," the victim says.

"You only saw the man who assaulted you for maybe a minute, correct?"

"Correct," she says, voice sheepish now.

"And you were scared while it happened, weren't you?"

"Yes, I was."

Enough. That's all I need. I pause, let this information linger in the ears of the jury, pick up a wax-coated Dixie cup on the defense table, fill it with water, let the tepid liquid slide down my throat, then crumple the thin paper in my hand. In closing, I will argue to the jury how fast the assault happened, how terror disarms the senses, how easy it becomes under such circumstances to make a mistake, how this alone should make these jurors give serious thought to whether there is reasonable doubt the man who perpetrated this brutal assault was in fact Dwayne Sayers.

It is uncharacteristic of me to be so confrontational unless I'm in court. I abhor conflict in my daily life, do everything possible to avoid it, even if that aversion turns me into a doormat. But it's a price almost worth paying because I don't know how to do conflict, don't know how to stand up for myself without feeling like a shrill, petty bitch. But in my rose-colored armor, inside the well of a courtroom, I get to play a role. I get to pretend. And more often than not when I pretend, people believe me.

As I continue my pummeling, that voice in my cold dark place tells me I'm evil, that I am on the wrong side, that this woman on the witness stand is hurting and my mauling is making her suffering worse.

I tell that voice to shut the fuck up, and though it quiets, the message still resonates, and I can't help but wonder how she feels. Whether she feels the same way I had.

CHAPTER 2

THIS IS THE STORY of the night I died.

The night of the footsteps, of the harmless, pale-haired man jogging down a sidewalk; the night I walked home from work in darkness; the night he turned into my hallway; the night our eyes locked and he showed me the knife in his hand.

This is the night that still possesses my body.

It was just a small tragedy.

And yet it wasn't.

It was like falling into a well. Distant and far away is a glimpse of light, but there's no way to reach it. You're still you, just not the same version. You're stuck and can't climb out, can't even begin to know how to get out, and though there are people up there, people who want to help, those people don't know how and you don't know how to let them. So you stay stuck. In that deep, dark, cold place that has swallowed you.

After the night of the footsteps, I wanted to feel the strength of others, wanted to use it, to make it mine until I could get my own strength back or contrive some new strain of that thing called stability, personal power. But I couldn't find it. Not in the lover I wore out with my clinging need, not in the mother who promised only to make it worse, not in the brilliance of the university where I pretended to belong, not in the department of gun-wearing, baton-toting cops among whom I orbited twenty-five hours each week. They were all strangers.

So in the days, weeks, months, years following my brief meeting with the man and his knife, I learned something. Something I didn't want to know: Beneath the narrative of our days there is another story, a story we don't get to write.

CHAPTER 3

May 29, 2014—Moving Day, San Diego, California

NEARLY EVERY INCH OF the seven hundred square feet of my new apartment is covered with boxes. My best friend, Janice, stands by my side, poised as she has been all day to take command in the event of my unraveling. The movers have gone and I have officially left the man with whom I've shared the last fourteen years. Now all that remains is the task of unpacking. The easy part, really.

In all the angst, I failed to label a single box, so I now have no way of getting to anything I need. Janice lifts a lid to begin unpacking, but it's a box of loose scattered photos, nothing that might prove useful in this moment, like toilet paper. She shuffles through images of my mother as a seven-year-old child: wide-eyed, face tilted up for the camera, standing next to a dustbowl Oklahoma house, wearing the expression of a girl who can never tell what might happen to her next. Janice returns them gently, carefully, then comes across another photo, stops for a long moment, and simply stares.

"Who's this?" she asks.

I peer over her shoulder. "That's me."

"Seriously?" Janice laughs.

It's no surprise that my best friend of twenty years doesn't recognize me. In the photo it's Spring 1984 and I am nineteen years old. My body is pale and soft, my teeth yellow, hair the color of dishwater. I wear purple Maybelline eyeshadow and haven't yet learned the tricks of lip liner, haven't yet been told that a woman is supposed to manage her eyebrows. Now, thirty years later, my face is leaner, my cheekbones more prominent, and my hair shimmers light blonde. Even more, my eyes are open now in a way they weren't then. The snapshot shows another version of me, a "before" shot in a gruesome mental makeover.

In the photo I'm smiling, smug, pointing with pride to the blue-and-gold shield-shaped patch on the arm of my khaki uniform: *University of California Police Department.* Pinned to my chest is a silver badge. My uniform is adorned with a black leather utility belt and leather cases that hold my police radio and Maglite flashlight, a tool so heavy it could serve as a club. I wear the uniform of a University of California police officer, but I am no cop. Below the shield-shaped patch, a much smaller piece of fabric identifies me for what I really am: *aide.*

"You worked in *law enforcement*?" Janice looks at me like she's never seen me before. Janice is one of the best criminal defense lawyers in the city, a woman radiating softness and warmth but with combat-like trial skills. She once shredded a seasoned, hardass FBI agent on the witness stand with such finesse she made the agent cry. Another attorney witnessed this scene outside the courtroom during a recess, overhearing the agent sniffling to Janice, saying, "Why'd you have to be so mean?"

I take the photo from her hand and stare at it myself. "It was a long time ago," I say. "College."

I remember posing for this picture. I stood in the Putnam Hall dorm room of Kim Baldonado, my roommate from freshman year, the friend who would be my roommate again the following year when we abandoned the chaos of the UC Berkeley dorms for an off-campus apartment. I had insisted that Kim take a second shot, an action shot of me bursting through the door yelling *"Freeze!"* although my superiors at the University of California Police Department had made it clear that under no circumstances would I be speaking such words. Ever. As a UC Police Department aide, I would act in a "nonconfrontational capacity," serving as another set of eyes and ears for the real police officers of UCPD, patrolling campus and surrounding neighborhoods, calling in suspicious activity on my police radio. I would be certified in CPR and first aid in order to assist in medical emergencies, and from 6:00 p.m. to 11:30 p.m. I would be dispatched to serve as a uniformed police escort, walking female students home safely from the library when they called the campus police line at 642-WALK. I would work the department's Lost and Found room and staff the Bike Bureau, selling bicycle locks and issuing licenses. I would do this twenty-five hours each week, calendared around my class schedule.

It's funny what we remember and what we don't. I remember posing for this photo. I remember sitting in the kitchen with my mother listening to fragmented stories as she handed me her childhood photos. But what I've forgotten is the name of the man who changed my view of the world, the man who taught me the most shattering lesson, the man who would teach me that lesson a mere three months after this photo was taken. That man's name, no matter how hard I try to reclaim it, has vanished.

SUMMER
1984

CHAPTER 4

Berkeley, California—July 19, 1984

I HAVE NO PARTICULAR skills or qualities that make me a good police aide. I'm five two, one hundred and ten pounds, and afraid of guns. I'm not especially graceful under pressure and am ill-equipped to handle any kind of emergency, a fact I've demonstrated more than once. Two months out of training, I witnessed a small grass fire next to Sather Gate in Sproul Plaza. I ran toward it, screaming the code for *Fire!* into my radio, clueless as to what I might do when I reached it. A crowd was gathered, people standing, arms folded across their chests like they were watching a show. Only after I pushed my way through did I finally see the Berkeley Fire Department's fire prevention officer. It was Earthquake Awareness Month and he was making a safety presentation, demonstrating the proper way to use a fire extinguisher: shoot from the base of the fire and move up. The crowd laughed as I called in "10-22," cop code equivalent for *Never Mind*. Within the hour, the head of the UCPD aide program radioed me with instructions to come to her office. She politely reminded me of the directive to use a calm, steady voice at all times. My screeches over the radio had caused everyone in the department to jump out of their skin.

My working-class parents always made it clear that if I wanted money I had to earn it, so I have held jobs since I was twelve: cleaning houses, babysitting, then graduating in my teens to work retail at the mall, hostess at a fish restaurant, answering phones at a law firm. Working for the University of California Police Department is my first post carrying any real responsibility. Located in the basement of Sproul Hall, UCPD has primary law enforcement jurisdiction for the university. It's a full-service state police agency and officers receive the same training as city and county peace officers throughout the state, plus additional training to meet the needs of a campus environment. It's an agency I joined with pride. I wanted this position because making friends at Berkeley had proven difficult, and I needed to connect with something bigger than myself.

As an incoming freshman, I had endured rush to join a sorority, chattering with hundreds of young women, tolerating skits and songs, a smile plastered on my face to prove how worthy I was, how much I belonged. It had been explained that during rush, would-be pledges gradually cut sororities from their list of choices, while sororities simultaneously cut prospects from their own lists. On the final day, this process would leave each girl with the names of two sororities who sought them as a pledge, then the applicant would choose which of those two sororities she wished to join.

On the final day of rush, I tore open the envelope containing my computer-generated form, the all-important piece of paper that would reveal the Greek letters of the sorority where I would join a house full of new sisters. Around me, girls jumped up and down, hands covering their faces, some of them screaming with joy. But as my eyes scanned the page, my mind steeped with confusion. My form was blank.

I walked across the creaking floors of Hearst Gymnasium, showed the empty page to one of the young women administering rush, and told her I didn't understand.

"Oh," she said with a flash of embarrassment. "Wait here."

She moved quickly for help while I stood alone, shifting my weight from side to side. The head of rush walked toward me, her face serious. She took my paper, then ushered me to a pair of brown metal folding chairs at the side of the room and suggested we sit down.

"This almost never happens," she said, voice sympathetic, "but you didn't get in."

When I didn't say anything, she added, "No one picked you."

The look on her face said she was prepared for tears, for sobbing histrionics over this devastating event. And it's true I was stunned, that I felt waves of humiliation coursing through my body. But I was raised to keep quiet, and I wanted to play the good sport, the easygoing woman who wasn't flustered by minor events like wholesale rejection. "Oh," is all I said, "okay." I was too dumbfounded to say anything else.

I slipped away, returning to my Stern Hall dorm, the rooms still deserted because I had arrived early for rush and the semester hadn't yet begun. I didn't know it yet, but that event would mark the beginning of my separateness, my sense of isolation. It reinforced my belief that I didn't belong on this campus, that I wasn't smart enough, wasn't pretty enough, that I was inherently flawed and unlikable. But becoming a UCPD aide had changed that. By joining the police department, in putting on that police uniform, I was seeking to reinvent myself: lonely young woman lost in sea of thirty thousand students converted into member of a powerful tribe. Weakness morphed into strength. Powerless transformed into powerful. Sure, the badge might belong in some cheap dress-up costume purchased at a drugstore for a kid who wants to play cops and robbers, but for me it was an emblem of coolness, of belonging, and I needed to belong somewhere.

I studied hard for my written police department test because the lexicon in a police department is different. We say "vehicle" instead of "car," "affirmative" instead of "yes," "negative" rather than "no." And speaking in code feels good. It means we are special, different. There is *Us* and there is *Them*, and it feels so much better to be part of *Us*. I prioritized the test over my midterms, made flash cards, tested myself until I knew them all, the 10-codes, the 11-codes: 10-23, stand by; 10-97, arrived at scene; 11-99, officer needs help; Code 3, expedite cover. I learned military time, police alphabet: Adam, Boy, Charlie. David, Edward, Frank. King, Lincoln, Mary. Then the California Penal Code, Vehicle Code, Health & Safety Code, Welfare & Institutions Code: Battery, 242; Assault with a Deadly Weapon, 245; Armed Robbery, 211; Kidnapping, 207; Torture, 206; Rape, 261. In Berkeley, the codes floating over the radio most often were Penal Code 148, resisting arrest, and Welfare & Institutions Code 5150, crazy. I studied so hard because I longed to be like the officers and sergeants and the more senior aides, all so capable and self-assured, ready for anything, itching for a good call to sound out over their radios, preferably something bloody.

◆◆◆

ALL NIGHT LONG I walk, on alert among the sly shadows, rescuing other women from the library, escorting them to the safety of dorm rooms, sororities, apartments. Elise at International House going to 2401 Bancroft Way; Caitlin at Alumni House going to Zellerbach Hall; Gina at Haviland Hall going to Oxford Street and University Avenue. I am savior only to women—no man has ever called for an escort home. My police uniform is a superpower and wearing it allows me to do what other women cannot: walk alone down a city street, roam the darkest corners of campus, tromp through the dirt alongside pitch-black Strawberry Creek leaving only boot prints behind me.

When I appear in uniform in public, I adopt the stance I have been told demonstrates authority, a pose that says I am to be obeyed, that I am not to be fucked with. Spine straight. Shoulders back. Head high. Feet apart. Face unsmiling. Eyes serious. If I am standing still and really want to make the message clear, I'll cross my arms over my chest. Male aides and officers don't need to think about "The Stance." Their bodies naturally transmit a message of authority. Mine does not.

I learned that The Stance holds impact even when out of the costume of my uniform. I have adopted it on and off campus while wearing my regular university student clothes of jeans, sweatshirt, backpack. The Stance makes me feel strong, in control, almost powerful.

Patrolling the dark shadows of campus and surrounding urban crime-ridden neighborhoods, I am not afraid. I've been born into a new world. I know I am suspect, that many people at UCPD expect me to fail, that some even want me to. Most of the officers and sergeants remain distant and cool. I am new and they eye me with suspicion, or worse, they ignore me. I am naïve but want desperately not to be. I am determined to prove myself.

Freshman year, dancing in the pit of the Greek Theatre I watched Annabella of Bow Wow Wow singing "I Want Candy," stalking the stage in her mohawk, her savage confidence palpable. God, I wanted to be her. So I tried to grow more bold. It was an act. But sometimes we have to pretend until we become the person we're pretending to be, right? I got a haircut. I kept my dirty blonde bob, but had my bangs cut into spikes I made stand straight up with hair gel. Part sorority girl, part punk rock chick. People weren't sure what to make of me and I liked that, liked keeping them off-kilter. That was another motivation for becoming a police aide: defiance. *You?* people would think: You can't do that job! You can't protect women! You can't walk home alone through the Berkeley streets after a shift!

Oh no? Just watch me, motherfuckers.

◆◆◆

10:45 P.M.

The shift is nearly over and I plant myself on one of the wooden benches in front of Dwinelle Hall, close to the station. If there are no more calls tonight, I will sneak inside, maybe get home early for once. Sitting while on patrol is strictly forbidden. Aides are not to contribute to the cliché of the lazy donut-eating cop. But I have easily walked nine miles tonight and my back is screaming, a blister is rising on the arch of my foot, and it is dark and no one is watching, and I can patrol just fine with my goddamn eyes.

My radio squawks and a voice speaks. "Dispatch to 155."

Shit.

My hand clicks the mic, and I lean into it to speak. "155," I say.

Since the fire incident, I have learned to lower my voice an octave, to suppress my natural Valley-girlish *OhMyGod!* tone, to emulate the cool unflappable tones of Channel 1, the police radio channel used by the real officers.

"What's your 10-20?"

"West side of Doe Library."

"Check. You have an escort waiting, main entrance to Moffitt Library. Wearing jeans, red backpack. Name is Cyndi. Headed to Chi Omega."

"10-4," I say. "En route."

It's after eleven when I finally trudge back to the station. The halls are empty, everyone from the 3:00 to 11:00 p.m. swing shift has gone home, and graveyard lineup has finished and moved out on patrol. I walk past Dispatch, a dark cave twinkling with red and amber lights, emitting sounds of voices, UCPD officers in the field. Softer in the background comes the radio traffic of Berkeley PD and Oakland PD, both monitored by UCPD dispatch to notify UC officers if something big leaks into our jurisdiction. Sitting inside is the UC Police dispatcher, Rachel, a short, wide-hipped redhead with a reputation for fucking anything with a badge. Perched next to her is John, my boyfriend of four months, Badge Number 159, another UCPD aide.

"Hey," he says when I stop outside the door of the booth.

"Hey," I echo, making sure to sound indifferent. I nod to Rachel, who gives me a smirk.

"I'm just hanging with Rachel for a while," John says.

"Cool," I say, voice still measured. Inside the station John and I maintain clipped, casual tones intended to minimize the risk of catching shit for sounding too lovey-dovey and not cop-like and hard. The razzing within a police department is unmerciful, even though it's public knowledge we are a couple. John wouldn't be caught dead calling me *Puppy* at the station, even though it's our pet name for each other, a name that started as a joke until one day it wasn't.

I'm not worried about Rachel. John sits nestled in the dark beside her tonight only because he wants to become a Certified Police Dispatcher and even though she's not supposed to, Rachel will turn over her headset to John and it will be his voice over the radio, firm, calm, in control, directing officers out in the field. John is mine, of this I am certain, because our favorite pastime involves alternating between kissing and gazing into each other's eyes, Phil Collins singing "Against All Odds" in the background.

John is one of the most senior aides, respected for his abilities, but equally admired and detested by the officers for his loud, cocky mouth. He lives in an apartment on Channing Way with two sarcastic chain-smoking seniors who divide their time evenly between studying and getting high.

I hated John when I first met him. And then I didn't. He was caustically funny and viewed law enforcement as the noblest of careers. He spoke of becoming a cop, then a prosecutor. On his bedroom wall, he had a black-and-white poster of Ronald Reagan, positioned so the fortieth President of the United States looked down onto John's narrow bed, observing whatever went on there. I met John within a week of becoming an aide. He caught my eye immediately, sauntering through the station, laughing with Gene King, another senior aide. He seemed wise, worldly, fearless. I wasn't just attracted to him, I admired him.

He was my first real lover. John was smart, relentlessly ambitious, and this drive had rubbed off on me. He made me want to be a better aide, made me want to know what was going on in the world, to get my grades up, to go to law school and also become a prosecutor. John and I shared the department and similar blue-collar home environments growing up. But mostly what we had in common was a desire to abandon the people we had been and become something great.

"We were just talking about the McDonald's thing," John says.

"Isn't it awful?" Rachel says.

I nod a wordless yes. The day before, in San Ysidro, California, a neighborhood in the southern portion of my hometown of San Diego, forty-one-year-old James Oliver Huberty entered a McDonalds carrying a 9mm Uzi semi-automatic, a Winchester pump-action 12-gauge shotgun, and a 9mm Browning HP pistol. He fired 257 rounds of ammunition, killing 21 people, 5 of them children, and injuring 19 others, a massacre lasting 77 minutes before he was shot dead by a police sniper. It was the deadliest shooting rampage ever in the United States. As he left home the afternoon of the attack, his wife asked where he was going. He replied, "Hunting humans."

I shuffle down the hall to the empty women's locker room. There are only two other female aides in the department and only a handful of female officers and sergeants. One is away at UCLA to help staff the crowds expected for the 1984 Summer Olympics, one is out on patrol, and the others have enough sense to maneuver day shift assignments.

I remove my badge, placing it in the corner of my locker. I ease myself down to the bench, unlace black combat boots that make my feet look enormous, peel back thick-padded socks, examine my blister. My frame is compact in my khaki uniform, the military creases still crisp. Removing the utility belt, putting away the radio, the heavy flashlight, my body becomes unburdened. I am light again, free. I am no longer police. With the simple act of putting on my street clothes, turquoise pencil-legged pants, white sleeveless blouse, scuffed white flats, I have transformed back into a young woman, a nineteen-year-old undergrad who has a problem set due in Econ, who is alarmingly behind in her Anthropology reading.

I grab my lavender backpack, pull out the keys to my apartment, and I'm ready for the walk home. I feel exhaustion setting in. I have gone to class, then to Doe Library to study, then straight into my shift. Once I leave my apartment in the mornings, I rarely return home until the day is finished. All I want to do is crawl into bed and sleep, awaken refreshed.

I leave the locker room and pass the dispatch booth again. Rachel is running license plates for an officer on patrol. "Comes back to Reginald Wallace, 1845 Dwight Street. No warrants."

Huddled next to Rachel in the darkness, John waves in my direction. "See you tomorrow."

I say goodnight and push open the station doors to step out into the cool summer night.

I don't know it yet, but this will be my last moment of calm, the last moments of *before*, the final moments of the first part of my life.

CHAPTER 5

July 19, 1984, 11:40 p.m.

WITH THE SUMMER EXODUS of students, the Berkeley streets are relatively deserted. The only people in sight at this edge of campus are a single cluster of students hunched beneath backpacks and the requisite assortment of Berkeley's colorful homeless population.

I know better than to walk down Telegraph Avenue alone this time of night. Most of the stores and restaurants are closed and the ratio of "normal" people versus crazy isn't favorable. So I take my settled route home, a path intended to keep me in reasonably well-lit areas for as long as possible. Past the edge of Sproul Plaza, down Bancroft Way, left on Dana Street, under the bright fluorescent lights of the Unit 3 dorms. I walk briskly, keys in hand, backpack slung over my shoulder. The night gets darker as I approach Blake Street, my street since the beginning of June. I've lived in my first off-campus apartment just seven weeks.

Finding a decent place to live in Berkeley, a place I could actually afford, hadn't been easy. It was April 1984 and all over campus people were talking about Marvin Gaye having been shot and killed by his own father. *How could such a thing happen?*

What kind of world was this? Kim and I paid no attention, too wrapped up in our own lives to worry about the suffering in the rest of the world. All we cared about were our grades and finding housing for the next school year.

Everything in our price range was a dump. We found a dilapidated one-bedroom in a converted hotel above Blondie's Pizza on Telegraph Avenue at the edge of campus. It was disgusting, but the rent and location made it bearable. Kim and I had looked at each other, shrugged in surrender, then pulled out our checkbooks and told the manager to get the lease. That's when a rat the size of a cat scrambled out of a cupboard, skidding across the kitchen floor in sheer panic, disappearing into the bedroom. Kim and I screamed and ran out the front door.

After another two weeks of searching, we found the Blake Street place. It was farther from campus than we wanted and as a half-basement unit situated in the bowels of the building, it felt like a dungeon. Shrubs out front covered dirty half-sized windows, leaving almost no avenue for sunlight. It had low ceilings, cinderblock walls, a hideous shade of burnt orange for a carpet. The coffee table was scarred, the plaid scratchy couch battered and lumpy. The kitchen had a sink, a stove, a wobbling table on a linoleum floor, and a pink refrigerator dating back to the 1960s, its freezer shrunken with frost. It wasn't a great neighborhood, but not as bad as some. And there were no rats.

"We'll take it," I said. If we didn't, it would be rented to someone else within the hour.

The lease started June 1. The thought of paying three months' rent for a place I wouldn't be living in started to chafe me. Plus, if I went home to San Diego for the summer, I would have to find a job, while I already had a perfectly good one here, plus a boyfriend, and I could go to summer school. It wasn't a glamorous summer, but one that made sense. Much to the disappointment of my mother, I opted to stay in Berkeley. Kim went home to Los Angeles.

◆◆◆

I PIVOT, TURN RIGHT onto Blake. The street is gloomy, overgrown bushes encroaching grimy sidewalks, a long expanse of darkness with only a few dim streetlights. There is no sound but my footsteps, my worn, white flats carrying me home. I reach my building and turn inside the concrete tunnel-like hallway leading from the sidewalk into the base of the building. The gold overhead light mutes the edges of color, turning everything in the hallway a bronzy gold. Inside, a row of metal mailboxes lines the right side of the wall. I don't bother checking mine. I just received a letter from my mother the day before so the most I could hope for was a phone bill.

Halfway through the hall, almost to my front door, I hear feet slapping concrete, the sound of someone jogging. I hesitate, turn to look and assess, see a man in blue jeans on the sidewalk running down Blake Street with his head down, about to pass the threshold of my open hallway. Just a man on his way, hurried yes, moving at a jog to get where he is going. Just a man. I catalogue him. Grad student. Squinty light eyes. Social prospects as thin as his pale hair. He has nothing to do with me. This is Berkeley. A man trotting down a dark empty street near midnight is nothing unusual. I discard him, turn back, satisfied, ready to finish my path through the hallway to my apartment.

But the footsteps change course.

I spin around again as his head rises, blue eyes locking on mine as he enters the hallway. They are wild eyes, blazing eyes that tell a story, the story of what will happen next. I feel them consume me, and I swallow their meaning. He has a plan. He has *intentions.* My stomach flips, sends electrical current straight up to my heart, and everything inside me goes still. *No,* I think. *Noooo.*

Then I see the knife.

It glints beneath the gold light from the bulb of the hallway, brass and wood in the palm of his hand. I feel myself leave my body, but just as quickly I return, registering. *This.* This is really happening.

With that thought my body knows this is over. My life. Over. And I had just started imagining I would have a future. We see only each other as I back away. His eyes are electric, focused, hard, intended only for me. The knife is shining, gleaming beneath the light, intended only for me. We are the only two people on earth. All at once I'm aware of everything. *This is real,* a voice inside me keeps repeating. *This. Is. Happening.*

A visible hunger rushes through his face and in the next instant he has me, pulled inside the trap of his arms in one fluid movement. Our dance is fast, a spin, as he catches my back to his chest and my fear turns savage as his fingers close on my mouth. Under his skin is muscle, bone. Under mine, rapid-fire heartbeat. I wiggle and writhe, but he holds tight. My mind registers powerful shoulders, the placement of each thick finger. It's only us now. No one else exists.

He holds me tight against him, my back pressed to his chest, his crotch to my ass, hand groping at my mouth while the other brings the knife to my throat. Both of us breathe, heaving breaths like dancers frozen in the final spotlight. No one says a word. Body pinned between his arms, random thoughts flash inside my brain. Psych 101. Kitty Genovese and the bystander effect. If I scream, will anyone come?

No more thoughts! Pay attention. He is serious. He is strong, powerful, and our dance turns clumsy. My white flats feel silly now, slippery soles sliding on the concrete, legs lifting off the ground turning me weightless. Face tilted upward, I see the gold-lit ceiling of a hallway, concrete and stucco. It is dusty, dirty, brushed with cobwebs. Terror strangles my throat, clogs it. Again, words slide through my mind. *Ineffectual. Helpless. Can't even stand on my own two feet.* Those feet keep flying into the air, running to get away while my body stays pressed in place against him. I am like some hapless cartoon character.

Facts. I weigh a hundred ten pounds and am five feet two inches tall. I am not athletic. I lack coordination. I am easy prey. Somewhere inside these facts tally. Somewhere inside I admit defeat.

His hand on my mouth hurts. Too tight, too close. I don't know this person. This person should not have his hand on my face. The salty taste of his humid skin, the heaving breath beneath my back, his chest rises and falls, rises and falls. The musky smell of his sweat, the scent of my fear. For a moment we are motionless in our awkward embrace. Every fraction of a second is a beat in time that seems to stretch out forever. Everything is amplified, every sense is pulsing, and I'm aware that I have never been so on the brink of losing myself. My soul shivers.

Together we breathe. We don't speak. There are no words. It's so direct. A different social code. No awkwardness, our roles are clear. *Who has ever held me so close?* I wonder. I feel precious somehow. I think I might be his first. There is a strange intimacy, as if we can read each other's minds, both of us debating our next move as the hallway light leaves us layered in color.

Is he pushing me down or am I falling down? Arms still pinned to my sides. I buck and thrash again, trying to break loose. He staggers behind my back but doesn't lose hold. He grips harder. My lavender backpack falls from my shoulder, slams to the ground. It sits there. It is not what he wants. Time stops.

His hand moves somehowm and I am struck with the simplicity of the decision before me: Scream, and he will cut my throat. Don't scream, and I am his. There is no debate. My mouth opens, a throat fills. There is a voice. It is mine.

I have had dreams, nightmares, where I open my mouth and no sound comes out. But what is flung from my body is an ugly primal sound, a noise that echoes and bounces off the walls, amplified into the apartments behind and above mine, flying up into the night. The debate is no debate at all. This sound that emerges is involuntary. Me, so used to controlling my voice, to lowering it an octave to exert my power, my control, my authority over those around me, so desirous of dictating how others hear me, perceive me. This sound knows nothing of control. I've unleashed a bloodcurdling sound, a sound that feels like it has come from someplace else. They are the screams of a woman fighting to stay alive. Terror, I realize, has a sound.

His muscles jump beneath my back. A shift in the atmosphere, in the dynamic of this dance, this clumsy embrace. A moment of indecision, the pulsing *what next?* firing off in unison in our brains. I feel a change, a hesitance now, the weight of the decision he has to make. It vibrates inside him. His own debate: slice my throat? drag me with him? dump me? run? His hand fights to cover my mouth, and I writhe out from under that hand and scream again. Bloody murder is the name of the sound. Someone needs to hear.

I have shattered the silence of the night, the screams hurtling through darkness. Doors fly open, swinging on hinges. Somewhere, stunned voices yelling, *Jesus fuck.* The spell is broken. He breaks away, pushing off me like a swimmer launching from a deck for speed, causing my body to scrape the wall. Gravity wins. I fall. From the ground I watch him, absorb his sound. Footsteps retreating into darkness.

CHAPTER 6

July 20, 1984, 12:05 a.m.

THE NEXT FIFTEEN SECONDS: Chaos. Keys dropped. Snatch them up, fumble into a lock. Fly through the hollow door. Lock it behind me. Flood the room with light. Neighbors I don't know emerge from doors, descend stairs in a frenzy. Shouts of "What happened?" I ignore them.

I have always been told: Rule number one in personal safety is to have your keys out and ready. Do not give a potential assailant the opportunity to snatch you as you stand fishing hopelessly in the pocket of your backpack for your goddamn keys. Keys can also serve as a weapon, perfect for gouging eyes. That had not turned out to be an option. We are told so much bullshit. How would I have ever gouged his eyes?

I lunge at the phone, punch in numbers, 9-1-1, see my hand shaking.

"Nine-one-one Operator, what's your emergency?"

I half scream into the receiver. "I just got attacked by a man with a knife!" My throat tightens. Strangling. Saying it out loud makes it real.

"Where are you?"

My voice disintegrates into jagged breaths, tears sting my eyes, my mouth lets loose an indiscernible gurgling. I can't get out the words. "Tweh-Twehnty Three—"

The operator interrupts, her voice curt, laced with disgust. "Calm down, Ma'am."

This woman has no time for my histrionics.

The directive to *calm down* has always enraged me. It's condescending. It says: your emotion is not valid. But in this moment these words snap me to attention. *Calm. Down.* It's as if she has slapped my face. I imagine this 911 operator sitting in her own dispatch booth at Berkeley PD, a hundred lights blinking on the equipment around her. She is not alone. Too many tragedies occur each night in the city of Berkeley to have only one dispatcher on duty.

Something shifts in my brain and again I leave my body, become an observer floating somewhere above my head, seeing everything from outside myself. Nineteen-year-old Karen, UC Berkeley sophomore, Psychology major, UC Police aide, daughter of Bonnie and Harold Thomas, girlfriend of John Bentivoglio, lavender backpack at her feet, holding a white phone. I hear her voice. I swim back inside myself, but I am different now. Cold, robotic. From somewhere inside, a place I didn't know existed, my training kicks into gear. Words spill off my tongue. Effortless. Machine-like.

"Two three three zero Blake Street. Penal Code 245. Direction of flight westbound on Blake Street, suspect on foot, less than a minute ago. Ready for a description?" My voice is now perfect steel. I know the answers to her questions before she asks.

"Go ahead."

"White male, blondish brown, thin hair, bluish eyes, mid-twenties."

"Clothing?"

"Jeans. Tennis shoes. Long-sleeved, rust-colored, velour-textured shirt with open collar."

"Stand by."

I am silent as she puts out the call. Her words repeating my words. They will sound over every radio of every police officer on duty in the city of Berkeley. They will sound within the dispatch room of Oakland PD. They will be heard by John and Rachel in the UCPD dispatch booth where I stood just twenty minutes ago.

The voice of the woman on the phone is cool now, all business. "All Units, Code three. Two three three zero Blake Street: 245, possible attempted 261. Description. White male, mid-twenties, jeans, tennis shoes. On foot. Direction of flight, westbound on Blake."

Seconds later, an explosion of sirens. A surge of patrol cars guns down Blake Street, blue-and-red lights flashing past my front window, speeding in pursuit of the twenty-something white male in jeans and tennis shoes. It's so fast. How could they get here so fast?

The dispatcher asks more questions, pausing to repeat my answers to her officers. My name, my own description. I describe the knife. A buck knife or jack knife, wooden and brass. Did I need an ambulance? I don't remember her asking, but I must have told her because the next thing I hear is her radio transmission to the entire Berkeley Police Department. "Victim is UCPD."

Three more seconds. A screeching of brakes, police cruisers lurching to a stop, shifting into park, doors slamming. A squawk of radios, boots stomping through the hallway where mere minutes ago I screamed. A thundering pounding at the door and a man's voice commanding, "Berkeley PD! Open the door!"

I fling it open and a rush of uniformed men push inside. I am struck by how awkward it feels, how impolite. Half a dozen

Berkeley cops are suddenly bustling inside the cinder block walls of my apartment and the room feels impossibly small, the ceiling dangerously low. They are so powerful, yet they look so strange, so out of place, tromping across my ugly orange carpet in their black combat boots, their leather utility belts squeaking from the weight of the real cop items they carry. Handcuffs and mace and guns. Things I'm not allowed to carry because I am not a real cop, just a pretender. They are so powerful, so capable, so ready to do the things I cannot.

A narrow-faced woman positions herself in front of me. She stands tall, anchors her legs in the stance of authority I try to imitate on patrol. She is the sergeant, I know this from the stripes beneath the patch of a shield on her black patrol jacket. She is in charge of the scene, which means she is in charge of me. She pulls out a notepad cradled inside a heavy black leather sheathe that matches the items on her belt.

She introduces herself. Sergeant Westinhoff. She tries to arrange her face to reflect sympathy but doesn't quite succeed. She shoots questions at me: What were you doing? Where were you coming from? Points to me: Is this what you were wearing? What happened? I answer her questions and those lobbed by the fat cop standing by her side, his belly pressing through the gaps between the buttons of his uniform. He keeps interrupting me, directing my narrative to the facts he cares about, the facts he wants to know.

The phone rings. On the other end of the line, a stricken voice. "Karen?"

John. I was right. He heard the call.

The ring of tension in his voice is so unfamiliar, so unlike him, and at the sound of it my own voice falters, turns wobbly again, and I unravel. "John, it was me. It was *me!*"

The interruption annoys the fat cop. "Hang up," he orders. He's a man used to being obeyed. I fight to win back my composure, tell John I have to go, the police are here.

Sergeant Westinhoff asks more questions, filling in details of what happened, how it happened, where, when. She listens to my description of the knife, jotting it all down into her notepad.

"How much time elapsed from the time you first saw him to the time he ran away?"

I can't honestly say how long it lasted. It happened so fast, yet each microsecond felt impossibly long, unimaginably drawn out. Time was no longer an objective measurement. Didn't they understand that?

I release a heavy sigh. "I don't know. Five minutes total?"

Sergeant Westinhoff scribbles on her pad.

Outside my door, a crowd of people hovers, eyes wide, bodies leaning in, eager for a peek at the horror show. Their faces are blurry, but I recognize Perry, the building manager. His face holds its typically irritated expression, the one he wears when he knocks on the door to remind me the rent is due. Our eyes meet and he looks away. I'm aware I have done something wrong, something that has inconvenienced him terribly. I'm surprised by the number of people who have gathered. The building had felt silent, deserted for summer. Being the subject of these strangers' morbid curiosity tells me something awful has happened, and somewhere inside it registers that I am a novice at this, that until tonight I had never known trauma.

I shift focus back to Sergeant Westinhoff. I know what information is pertinent. A description of the man who attacked me. Description of the incident. Facts only, no speculation, no embroidering the story with what had happened in my mind while the incident occurred. But I can't resist.

"In that moment I knew I had only two choices. Scream, and have him slit my throat. Or don't scream and take my chances." I stop, clear my throat. "I screamed."

I watch their faces grimace, bodies shifting in discomfort. I feel foolish now, childlike, a girl who has proven she is not one of their cop clan. Berkeley PD looks down on UCPD. UCPD doesn't see the kind of action Berkeley PD does. We are campus cops, one rung up from mall cops. And I'm not even a real campus cop.

Another officer moves in. "Did you scratch him at all?"

"I don't think so."

He has me hold out my hands, taking them loosely in his and giving them a once-over, like an impatient father checking to see if his child washed properly. But I have taken away nothing forensically useful, no trace of my assailant's DNA. Suddenly I feel dizzy, a heady sensation I feel when I am going to throw up.

But I don't. I step into the hallway and show the sergeant and officers where I had struggled with the man.

"245, attempted 261," Fat Cop pronounces.

Sergeant Westinhoff nods her head in agreement. A 245 is the California Penal Code section for assault with a deadly weapon. A 261 is the Penal Code section for rape. For some reason unknown to me, this officer's smug confidence pisses me off. He hadn't been there, I had. He is in no position to form a conclusion about what had happened, least of all the intentions of my attacker. Inside me a spark of defiance ignites. I want these cops to know I understand their language, that I can speak in code just like they do. I want them to treat me as one of their own, to sweep away what I perceive as subtle condescension.

"Or attempted 211," I interject, reciting the code for robbery.

I want this cop to know that he can't speak to me like I am a toddler, spelling out words so I won't understand. But I know the man with the knife did not want my wallet. This is clear to all of us, and by saying 211 I have made a fool of myself again.

It will be years before I can name what I felt as they questioned me. Shame in not living up to what they were. Shame from their subtle refusal to treat me as a member of their tribe. Shame in being both police and victim. Anger, frustration, and humiliation in not being embraced with one shred of validation or empathy. I was just another victim to them. But my anger at Fat Cop's pronouncement begs a question: What had the pale-haired man intended? What almost just happened?

John appears, running up to us. His face seems contorted, different from when I said goodnight at the station. Rachel will tell me later how she watched the blood drain from John's face as he heard the call, how his mind absorbed the location, the space of time that had passed since I'd left, realized that the victim Berkeley Dispatch described on the radio was me.

Sergeant Westinhoff pinches the microphone clipped to the strip of fabric on the shoulder of her uniform and leans her head to speak into it. "Go ahead 1 Lincoln 12." It's the same Motorola police radio I had worn earlier that evening on my shift. She steps out of the hallway, out of earshot.

John grips my shoulders, asks if I'm okay.

"Yeah," I say, fighting to hold my voice steady.

Before I can say anything else, Sergeant Westinhoff returns, stands with her arms crossed, assessing me like I am the perpetrator. Her face is serious and something sinks in my stomach.

"We've detained someone who meets the description you provided. Ready to go for a ride?"

CHAPTER 7

July 20, 1984 12:20 a.m.

I CLIMB INTO THE back of Sergeant Westinhoff's car, a plain white, beige-upholstered sedan, a sergeant's vehicle, a luxurious upgrade from the patrol cars driven by Berkeley PD patrol officers, their back seats sticky with filth.

We drive west on Blake to Fulton and Parker Streets, stopping where two patrol cars light up a sandy blonde-haired man in jeans. The man blinks in the brightness of the lights, blackness all around him. His eyes are wide, his breath rapid, like a bird trapped inside a house. I can't hear but see his mouth moving, speaking to the two officers who flank him on either side.

Sergeant Westinhoff shifts into park. "Can you identify this man?"

I know this is a "one-man show-up," that, in contrast to a properly conducted lineup, showing a single suspect to a witness carries a high risk of misidentification. A witness is naturally inclined to conclude that the person presented must be the offender because otherwise why would he be in police custody and on display? But I also know that in certain circumstances an on-the-scene one-man show-up of a suspect who has been detained for investigation does not violate due process: the flip side to the risk of misidentification is the increased reliability of identifications made promptly after an incident.

I want to be helpful, to do my job as a victim, but I am careful. This man in the lights looks like my attacker but I can't take any risks here, I couldn't bear the weight of identifying the wrong man. I would rather have the man who attacked me go free than identify the wrong person.

Gripping the seat of the car, I feel smooth luxurious leather beneath my fingers. My parents shunned leather, only ever allowed cloth interiors in their cars. "Sticks to your legs!" my mother complained. "Blisters you in the summer!"

Outside of me, a voice. "Karen?"

It's Sergeant Westinhoff.

"Yes," I say. *Focus.* "Yes, yes, sorry."

I scrutinize the man's hairline, his height, his jeans. I study the eyebrows, the angle of his forehead, the protrusion of his nose from his face. Something about him feels familiar, something indescribable, something in the movement of his body.

But he also looks different standing in the flood of headlamps, different than in the golden glow of my hallway. Still sweating, chest still heaving with each breath, his expression has changed. He is now the hunted. It's his turn to have wide eyes, to experience the adrenaline of fear.

I lean forward for a better look, head and shoulders hunched into the front seat. I remember doing this in my mother's car as a child, her telling me to get back, to sit in my seat. What I was doing was dangerous. What if she had to slam on the brakes?

Minutes pass. Everything feels surreal. Sealed inside the car, the scene outside is muted. The dark street is alive with headlights, squawking radios, patrol lamps. I hear radio traffic, other crimes happening to other people in other places. I feel myself losing focus again but force myself to stare, straining to see something that will make me certain. I need to be *certain*. I feel panicked with the weight of the decision I am being asked to make. I think it is him. I am 90-percent certain.

After what feels like a long time, I speak. "The pants are right, the shoes are right, the hair is right." I pause, silently listing what else matches. Same height. Same build. Same age. Same shape of face. He looks paler, but that is probably the light. The shirt is wrong. The collar drapes differently and isn't the rust velour or terry cloth texture I saw in the hallway. In the bright patrol lamps of the police cars, it looks almost white.

"It's hard to tell in this light," I say, voice trailing.

"Take your time," Sergeant Westinhoff says, but I sense impatience. She seems almost angry. Like she has gone to all this trouble and now I'm being difficult.

"I think it's him, but I'm not one hundred-percent sure."

"Take your time and *think*."

Think. Her command makes no sense to me.

She speaks into her radio. "S-19 to 45." A voice comes back, matching the movement of the officer next to the suspect. "Go ahead." The sergeant clicks her radio again. "Have him turn around." She pauses, clicks the mic again. "Slowly."

She is like a stage manager: She gives an order from inside the car. Outside, the order is carried out. I watch the man turn, studying his movement.

Sergeant Westinhoff steps out of the car and slams the door. Again I feel like I've done something wrong. She walks over to one of the two officers and mouths words I can't hear. The officer who instructed the man to turn around looks in my direction, though I know he can't see me. I see his lips moving, his body language impossible to decipher. Then the pale-haired man gives a pained look, untucks his shirt, unbuttons the top buttons at the collar.

Sergeant Westinhoff hurls herself back into the driver's seat, the car bouncing with her weight. "This is how he looked when they first stopped him. Before you and I got here he'd buttoned his shirt, tucked it inside his jeans."

So he'd tried to alter his appearance.

I study him harder, frustration swelling inside me.

"I can't be sure," I tell Sergeant Westinhoff. "I think it's him. I'm pretty sure it's him. But I can't be absolutely certain and I want to be certain." I feel ashamed, incompetent.

Suddenly I feel impossibly tired. My head hurts. I want to go home. The sergeant's radio says "S nineteen," and she steps out of the car once again to confer with the other cops.

When she comes back, she turns in the front seat to face me. "Listen," she says, voice softer now. "You know what you're doing. You've been trained. Sometimes you have to trust yourself." She turns back around and I can no longer see her face as she speaks toward the windshield of the car. "And sometimes it's all on you. We can't arrest him until we hear it from *you*."

Trust yourself. Trust yourself? What does that even mean? We sit in silence for another full minute while my mind rages.

Finally I heave out a sigh that empties my lungs. "Okay," I say. Her eyes in the rearview mirror tell me this isn't enough.

"Okay. Yes, it's him."

She gets out again, slams the car door without a word, walks through the beams of light to the other officers, leans in and speaks. There's no warning when they bend the pale-haired man over the patrol car hood, snapping on handcuffs. I know this sound. I know the satisfying *click*. They search through his pockets, pull something out, show it to Sergeant Westinhoff.

Sergeant Westinhoff gets back in the car and shifts into reverse. "The man you just identified?" she says, "He was carrying a knife exactly like the one you described." She pauses for effect, eyes connecting with mine once again from the rearview mirror. "Exactly."

CHAPTER 8

AFTER, THERE IS NO doctor, no ER. There is no need. There is no blood, no bones that need mending—just a bruise, a puffy soreness at my lips where his hand gripped my mouth.

And a ravaged, rattled mind.

CHAPTER 9

July 20, 1984, 2:05 a.m.

WHEN THE COPS LEAVE, it's just John and me in a repugnant little apartment, huddled on a scratchy, plaid couch. Adrenaline still pumps, filling my body with electricity, currents bouncing through my blood. The rest of the world sleeps and I'm exhausted, wrung out, but I cannot close my eyes. Nerves jump, my mind races. Suddenly I hate the sound of silence.

I turn to John. "Can we do something?" I hear the pleading in my voice. "Anything?"

We pile into John's rusted Audi, a hand-me-down relic of the 1970s bestowed by his older brother. John has a six-pack of Coors and we drive the dark streets in search of a secluded place where two underage students employed by a police department can drink illegally. We head to the north side of campus, toward the one quiet neighborhood of this city, a stark blissful contrast to the ugly urban south side where I live. John stops at the Berkeley Rose Garden, a place to get drunk without fear of getting busted and losing our jobs. We climb out of the car, plunge ourselves into shadows, walk deep into a wide, flat lawn. I plot a position in the center of the grass where we will be safe, where I will have time to react to a potential intruder.

A breeze bends thorned branches and blooms sway beside us, colorless in the night. The air chills my arms and face, and I lean into John, needing to feel his weight against me, the solidness of him. I don't stare at the moon as I usually do from this garden. I don't see the sky with its stars. I watch only the corners of the lawn.

John's voice. "You cold? You're shivering."

I look down, see my arms hugging my chest. I have not yet come fully back inside my body.

John squeezes me against the warmth of his chest. I want John's arms around me, am desperate for their comfort, yet some piece of me rages violently, some piece wants to scream *don't touch me!* An embrace is no longer comfort. An embrace is a violation, too much like that other man's arms wrapped around me, enveloping me in terror. I still feel his touch on my back, neck, shoulders. He's still here with me.

What he was thinking, I have no idea. To cut? Rape? Kidnap? The weird thing was he didn't seem crazy. He seemed like a regular guy. I make up stories about him. I imagine him as a man who likes to stay informed, a man who pays attention, who reads the newspaper, gleaning what lessons he can about this world. He knows a lot about science, physics, engineering, but he is not good with words. I imagine him a thoughtful person, a smart person, disciplined and wild at the same time. I think he has a good eye for other people's weaknesses. Like me, he doesn't have many friends. I imagine him in an interrogation room, bright lights probing. He gets one phone call. Whose number does he dial? Who is the person who answers, who listens, silent, on the other end of the line? Who would I call if I were arrested? Where would I fling myself in my desperation? Other than John, who has the qualities to be of any real help?

Sitting on the hard, damp ground, I try to feel lucky. My assailant had failed his mission. A predator with more conviction could have kept me quiet and still, could have stuffed me into a van, driven me home to hide me in his basement. Every cell of me is aware of the choices I had made in my brief time with this man, the indecision, how it so easily could have turned out worse. My leaving that hallway with only a bruised lip is nothing but sheer dumb luck, luck that wouldn't always be there, luck that couldn't be counted on.

John leans in, presses his lips to my ear, whispers, "I'm so glad you're okay."

Confusion bubbles beneath my skin as I struggle to steady all the mismatched emotions, to regulate the thoughts darting through my mind of their own will. My fragile sense of safety in the center of the lawn flits away. I search the darkness. Trees at the edge of the grass move. A man hides there.

"Shhhh," I tell John, "I hear something."

John looks at me, follows my eyes. "There's nothing there."

I sit absolutely still, straining to hear. Adrenaline surges again, eyes focus. Just a shadow. The beer sliding down my throat seems to hold no alcohol at all. I drain the bottle, then another, but I am jittery, amped, out of control. Fear crackles through me and I know, am absolutely certain that someone lurks in those bushes, someone who intends us harm. Something moves in the shrubs on the other side of the lawn. I can't take it, I start to stand. "Let's go."

"What?" A flash of confusion crosses John's face, or maybe it's irritation. He is not the type to tolerate flightiness, a woman who arrives, then wants to leave, a woman who can't make up her brittle mind.

"Can we just go? I don't feel safe here." I walk toward the car, leaving John no choice but to follow.

Standing at the garden's edge looking back at the lawn, I see it now for what it is: a scene from a Jamie Lee Curtis flick where the stupid hapless couple is making out, the boy sweet-talking the girl out of her Calvin Kleins, sensuous innocent bliss until the killer makes himself known. Then struggle. A hacking to pieces.

I am vaguely aware I have never thought this way before. From some small ugly pit inside, I acknowledge I may never think any other way ever again.

CHAPTER 10

July 20, 1984, 8:20 a.m.

THE MAN IN BED beside me is twenty years old, a Life Sciences major, a UC Police Department aide intoxicated by the fun of dressing up and playing cop, who craves the thrill of police life, but who ultimately believes there must be something more for him in a career. This man beside me is smart, capable, brimming with self-confidence. Sometimes I think he loves me. This man beside me asks if I'm okay.

I tell my first lie to him, and this is fitting because he is my person, the only soul in this city who really knows me. I speak the words I wish were true, the words I know should be true because nothing happened really, I'm not even hurt. I speak the words that mark my own self-betrayal. "I'm fine," I say. "Go to work."

He kisses me, rushed, relieved, and I see a tuft of dark chest hair curling from the neck of his white crew neck T-shirt. I realize he is already dressed for a shift, that he has been lying next to me in his narrow twin bed fully clothed. While I have finally slept, he has already showered, made a sandwich for lunch. As the door closes behind him, the apartment loses its life. I am alone. It is time to walk home.

◆◆◆

OUTSIDE IT IS MORNING and the whole world looks wrong. My mind still darts all over and I think about the week before, during the Grateful Dead concert at the Greek Theatre on Gayley Road. Amy Bryant, head of the UCPD aide division, had taught me and another aide to direct traffic. I didn't think I could do it, didn't believe I could make a line of cars obey just because I stood in the middle of the street with a whistle and an upheld palm in the air signaling *stop*. But it turned out I could. Not just cars, but hundreds of stoned Deadheads in Jerry Garcia tie-dye. They had all stood on the sidewalk waiting for me to give them permission to use their own two feet and walk. It fascinated me how these crowds obeyed me, how I could make all these people stop in their tracks. The secret to directing traffic, I learned, was the secret to life: Stand your ground. Don't let anyone ignore you. If you do, everything falls apart.

Now I feel the need for someone to direct me, to tell me when to stop and start, to tell me which way to go. Walking on my own legs feels strange, like something I am trying for the first time. The soles of my scuffed white flats feel slippery, dangerous. I need something sturdier, something to grip me to the ground.

The sky is different too. More shut down, more finite, worming its way to dingy haze. Its steely edges taunt me, and I realize how groggy I am, neck aching from sleeping squeezed between John's body and a wall in a bed meant to hold one body, not two. I'm still wearing what I had on last night, the white button-down blouse more crumpled now, the turquoise peg-legged pants looser from wear. My clothing is something Berkeley PD had made note of. As the female victim of an assault, it mattered what I had been wearing.

◆◆◆

It's when I reach Blake Street that my body feels stricken, hit with the urge to spin around, to run back to John's, to lock the door behind me and never leave, not ever. But my mind knows that isn't an option and it forces my legs to keep moving.

I reach my building and step across the threshold into the hallway just as I had entered it the night before. That's when a dissonance swells. Blood beats inside my ears and my mind begins a loop I can't control. *This hallway is an entrance. This hallway is a wound. This hallway is a pulsing red throat.*

I pause at the spot where I first turned, first saw the man and his knife. I see eyes, primal ferocity. These walls seethe with memory, so loaded with sensation they might detonate, and yet also look the same as they always have. There is not one shred of evidence of what happened here, and this sameness is an affront, a truth that feels unspeakably lonely, grossly unfair. The space between how I felt standing here *before* and how I feel *after* is a vast chasm, and I have no idea how to cross it.

I see myself. I'm inside my own life, but I'm barely here at all. My mind spins faster and faster.

This threshold. This man. This glance. This knife.

How often have I been touched? How often have I been held? Two bodies.

This chance. This fate. This choice. This end. Fight. Surrender. Rabid unfurling. The scream that rings in my ears.

How many beginnings have I had? How many endings?

The loop makes me dizzy. My mind has never done this before and I can't quiet it. *Stop it*, I tell myself. *Just. Stop.*

◆◆◆

INSIDE. THE APARTMENT IS freezing cold and dead quiet, a silence so deep I feel it at my core. This silence guts me, leaves me empty.

Like the hallway, the apartment looks exactly the same. Itchy plaid couch, scarred coffee table, big, ugly lamp. Wobbly kitchen table, two chairs. Grout-tiled bathroom. Burnt rusty-orange carpet, the same color as his shirt.

The thin Berkeley sun strains through the bushes, through the filthy windows, and still it is dungeon dark. Staring at the empty walls with my new pair of eyes, I realize how little I have. Clothes, bedding, books, a few hand-me-down dishes from my mother. I don't even own a TV and my only radio is part of a digital alarm clock. This space doesn't feel like it could accommodate the half-dozen cops who had trampled through it in their heavy black boots. And what about him? Is he still in jail? Out on bond? Has he had his homecoming yet? Did he turn his key in its lock, oh so grateful to be home? Maybe he snapped on his radio because, like my apartment, it just felt too quiet inside.

I look around at the flimsy windows, the hollow doors. How could I have ever felt safe here? Safety is an illusion, a lie. My ears fill with the sound of my own screams.

The phone rings and I feel myself jump.

It's Amy Bryant, my boss. Amy is twenty-two, a Cal grad who worked as an aide, who loved the department so much she stayed on to manage the entire aide program. Amy has never called me at home before.

"Hey!" she says brightly, "Let's meet for coffee!"

I'm not prepared for Amy's perkiness. Her voice sounds false. It hurts my ears. We exchange some words, each of us awkwardly trying to pretend we hang out together all the time, that Amy calling me for coffee is an everyday thing.

My instinct is to say no, to go about the business of my day. I have class in two hours, I still have studying to do. But the thought of being with another person, even a person I don't know too well, sounds like salvation. Other than John and a handful of acquaintances at the department, I don't have a single friend. I force my voice to feign cool indifference and tell Amy, yes. Yes, I can meet for coffee.

I feel like looking nice today. If I see my reflection in a window or bathroom mirror, I want to feel good about the face looking back at me. It's a trick I pull on exam days to arm myself with confidence. I wash and curl my hair, shave my legs, put on a decent outfit. Maybe it's a silly ritual, but I always feel it makes a difference, a self-worth makeover for no one's benefit but my own.

But looking pretty takes too long. And if I stay inside this cold lonesome place any longer, I know I will come undone. I shower and rush out the door in jeans and a T-shirt. I don't bother to dry my hair, don't even put on makeup.

Outside again, the hallway still holds no trace of what happened. I stare at the spot where he held me. In the daylight, without the golden bulb, the walls are washed white again.

CHAPTER 11

July 20, 1984, 9:30 a.m.

A MY AND I MEET at a cafe on Durant Street one block from campus next to Yogurt Park. *The Official Preppy Handbook* has been in circulation for a while now, and Amy obliges in her ensemble, wearing a pink Izod shirt, plaid Bermuda shorts, and penny loafers. In my present state, I can't be mistaken for a preppy or a yuppie or anything other than a slob. We order cappuccinos and croissants. Amy refuses to let me pay.

Settling in at a table, every sound stirs too loud inside my ears. Milk steamers whoosh, cups slam saucers, spoons clink glass, voices overlap in a dozen conversations. When I first arrived in Berkeley, I had never tasted espresso before, had barely experienced coffee. Now I'm an addict. When I'd first arrived here, the sheer number of coffeehouses amazed me. Every day, each of them had lines out the door—professors slogging briefcases, students bearing the weight of backpacks, all waiting to fork over two hard-earned dollars for a latte.

I sip my coffee, feel the foam cover my lip, dab it away with my hand. Amy is silent and in this muteness it dawns on me. Every single person in the department knows. My assault occurred at the beginning of graveyard shift. Rachel would have announced the news over the radio and it would have spread the moment day shift set foot in the station at 7:00 a.m. It was the type of incident to have been announced at morning lineup. That was how Amy had heard.

Amy stares at me. "Why don't you take a couple days off?" she asks, twitching a smile.

I pick at my croissant, tearing off layers, stuffing them into my face in pieces. Inside my mouth each shred is tasteless, the texture of drywall.

I explain I would rather be working, that I want to feel normal, want to put this behind me as quickly as possible, that I just want to forget about it. I explain that I'm fine. I wasn't even hurt. What is the point of dwelling on it?

We lapse back into silence.

"Any vacation plans this summer?" Amy asks, smiling again, using that too-bright voice.

I shake my head. "I have summer school."

"Oh! What classes are you taking?"

I am heavy with dread, exhausted by this effort at small talk. Amy is a nice person, a competent manager, but she is my boss, not my friend, and although I appreciate her kindness, the conversation feels painfully forced. "Economics 101 and Cultural Anthropology."

"Well you should at least take a few days off then—go somewhere with John!"

Amy chatters away, asking if I'd seen Bill Murray in *Ghostbusters* yet. Shifting gears, she tells me what I already know: that she had been the first female police aide in the history of the UC Berkeley Police Department. Then she shares something I didn't know. One night while on uniformed patrol, she was grabbed on campus by three men. One held her arms behind her back while another snapped a Polaroid of the third man smooching her dramatically on her mortified face. The men then disappeared into the darkness, their whooping laughter echoing into the night. It was a fraternity prank, the task to photograph one of their own assaulting someone in uniform. Amy tells me she has never shared this story with anyone, and I understand why. It would be too humiliating. It would affirm what so many of the male officers in the department already suspect: that women aren't cut out to wear a uniform.

I know Amy means well, that she intends for this to comfort me, to assure me that, well, shit happens. But this is what terrifies me. This is the lesson I had learned less than twelve hours ago, a fact I had previously been blissfully unaware of. In nineteen years, I had never experienced anything ugly. No accidents, no violence, the only death that of a childhood friend's eighty-year-old grandmother. But now I knew: shit did happen. It happened all the time, to everyone, everywhere, and now it had happened to me, and it could easily happen again and worse. If Amy had been assaulted—a five-foot-nine, 160-pound woman with a load more smarts and guts than me—what the fuck was I doing walking around in uniform, clothing that now seemed more like a Halloween costume, its magical power to ward off harm having evaporated like a fallen superhero's? And if a police uniform couldn't serve as protection, how was I supposed to feel roaming campus in my jeans and sweatshirt? I had heard it said many times: life changes in an instant. It was something my mother said, automatically rendering it an anxiety-induced musing to ignore. But now I vaguely understood its truth.

I keep picking at my croissant while Amy pretends to ignore the fact that I am not holding up my end of the conversation.

She continues in her falsely chipper voice, sharing more tidbits, pieces of information she has never before incorporated into our conversations: another movie she saw with Sergeant Banks, a new restaurant that opened on Shattuck Avenue. Banks is Amy's fiancé, a quiet, hopelessly nerdy man with thinning hair and a desperate comb-over.

She asks me for a second time if I have vacation plans for the summer. The question stumps me. Didn't I answer that one? I feel myself stumbling, brain scrambling for an answer to this simple inquiry. It's summer. People take vacations in summer. I am supposed to take a vacation.

After what feels like a long time, I say, "No. Summer school."

"Oh, right," she says.

It occurs to me that Amy is nervous, that what has happened to me makes her uncomfortable, that she is in uncharted territory herself, but she's determined to find her way through. Amy continues her monologue. She and Banks have a camping trip planned for August.

"I might go see my parents," I blurt out, halting Amy midsentence.

"Oh!" she says, visibly pleased to have engaged me finally. "That sounds nice!"

She asks about my parents, where they live. It's the first time I have thought of my parents since my attack, and it makes my throat tighten to the point I think I might cry. My mother would be horrified. She worries so much anyway, she doesn't need news like mine to fuel her fears. I think of her, sitting in her chair every evening, watching TV with my father and crocheting one of her afghans, the ball of yarn falling when she stands at the commercial to go fill her glass with Coke and ice cubes, the yarn a trajectory of unraveling.

My mother has a great deal of respect for all that can go wrong in life. It's her religion, her core belief system, and it makes sense. Her own mother, a woman who today would be diagnosed at a glance with Borderline Personality Disorder, abandoned her repeatedly. Since her birth in 1925, my mother lived intermittently with whichever random relative agreed to take her in, or with whatever new stepfather happened to be around for that year.

At age nine, my mother caught the chicken pox. In spite of her fever, in spite of the pink bumps that made her skin feel like armies of ants were marching across it, my grandmother put her on a bus, alone, traveling from Dustbowl Oklahoma to Denver where she would be collected by the sister of an ex-stepfather. For the three-day ride she was provided only a single peanut butter sandwich to sustain her. Her formative years were peppered with dozens of such instances, and those events left their mark. In 1945, she married at age nineteen and became pregnant immediately. Her husband deposited her with his mother and stepfather, then disappeared, never to be heard from again.

For years I obsessed over my mother's childhood, carving out hours to sit with her at our dining room table, scribbling notes, pressing for details, desperate to cobble together a chronology that made sense. I pulled out photo albums: pages and pages of my grandmother with different men.

Who's that? I asked again and again.

My mother responded with shrugs. *I have no idea.*

When I pressed her with my hardest stare, my mother relented, parsing out one more sliver of fact. *Aunt Dot had so many boyfriends I couldn't possibly keep track.*

Aunt Dot was what I called my grandmother. Since my mother was nine, her mother had insisted on the ruse of being sisters. She didn't want people knowing she was old enough to have a daughter my mother's age.

Where did she go after the ex-stepfather's sister picked her up from the bus terminal and wiped down her pox with calamine? My mother couldn't remember. Why did she quit school in the ninth grade? She didn't know. The missing pieces in her story had always left me suspicious, certain there were other secrets I was not being looped in on, camouflaged mysteries that explained my mother's lifelong case of nerves. After a point, I stopped asking questions. It seemed cruel to make my mother dredge up these memories, to force a messy life onto a page as filtered by the daughter who would never truly understand what her mother had experienced no matter how many questions she asked.

My mother had learned to expect the worst, and her anxiety was infectious. She smoked nonstop, hands often shaking as she brought the cigarette to her lips again and again. Nerves caused her to break out in thick pink painful welts no doctor could diagnose. Growing up, my mother taught me not to get my hopes up. Her lessons came in the form of words. She said things like: "Don't count your chickens before they're hatched." "Life doesn't come with a guarantee." "People are rotten." She warned me about men, some of them relatives, who "touched little girls where they're not supposed to." Her lessons came in the shape of actions: avoiding the freeway, driving under the speed limit on surface streets, eyes darting, ready to slam on the brakes, staying inside after dark. I learned to appreciate her good intentions. If you don't get your hopes up, you won't be disappointed. If you don't try, you'll never fail. If you internalize the opinion that people are rotten, you'll be more guarded, less of a chump. As a child, I knew things other kids didn't. I knew risk rarely brought reward. Risk guaranteed disaster.

Even after meeting my father and living out thirty-six years of stability (dinner on the table at six, bed by eleven, out to eat on payday), she is still a nervous wreck, always bracing for the next tragedy. I have always believed there are many bad habits a person can have, and that pessimism and fear might be the most dangerous. Now I'm not so sure about that.

◆◆◆

SOMETHING IN MY FACE has changed because Amy's has taken on a grave look. After what feels like a long time, she asks, "Are you okay?"

Amy is offering herself to me. Offering to listen, offering to help. I shrug her off. I tell her again I am *fine*. I remind her again, I wasn't even *hurt*. I am fidgety now, uncomfortable. I don't want this forced intimacy.

I have Anthro in twenty minutes but feel like blowing it off. The caffeine is not kicking in. I'm painfully aware of how little sleep I got.

Outside the café, the world is entirely the same, the world is entirely different. Everything is imbued with the hue of *after*. There was before, and now there is after. *It's over*, I tell myself. I'm determined to push this thing down. If I let myself feel it, let it seep in even a little bit, it will take everything. This I know for sure.

◆◆◆

I SKIP ANTHRO. IT feels good to be with someone, so I shuffle alongside Amy in a daze, following her into the station. Immediately I am aware of eyes on me. I was right—everyone knows.

I like attention. But this isn't the kind I want. What I sense is worse than pity. It's judgment. Frail little baby girl got herself attacked. Little baby girl fucked up. Frail little baby girl doesn't belong in this department, this brotherhood of police. The effect on my being, on my sense of self, is that the essence of who I am, of who I am trying so desperately to become, has been scraped away.

Officer Tai, a new guy, stops me. "You all right?" he asks.

He is genuine. A nice guy in a sea of machismo. I am grateful for a straightforward question, a query that seeks truth, yet I am unable to provide it. "I'm fine. It was nothing," I lie.

He squeezes my shoulder, continues out the door, and that's the end of it. No one else speaks to me about my incident. I imagine no one knows what to say. It's awkward.

I glance around the station hoping to see John. Instead I hear his voice echo over the radios holstered to the waists of the men scattered throughout the halls and holding cells. He is on Hill Patrol, in a real UCPD patrol vehicle complete with a portable red flashing light slapped on the roof like the plainclothes detectives of TV. He's securing the acres of university-owned property in the Berkeley Hills, a special duty reserved only for the most senior aides, the aides who know what they're doing.

Exhaustion digs into me. I wander back home again, pass the threshold into that unchanged hallway, unlock my door, step into the silence, crawl into the bed tucked against the cinder block wall. But the moment I close my eyes, my nerves scream. I open my eyes again, then close them tight. So many sounds. Imagined or real? The breeze scraping shrubs against fragile glass windows. A man coughing somewhere. All I want is to sleep but I am wide awake. I get up, make myself a sandwich, but can't make myself eat it. Anxiety grips me, firing electric tremors through my body, depleting me further. It wants to swallow me whole and I fear I might let it.

I don't know what to do with myself, so I grab my backpack, head back to campus to Moffitt Library. The study carrels are nearly empty. I have my choice of seats. Out of habit, I search the faces of the handful of students for someone I know, but there is no one. I sit, open my Econ textbook.

The page blurs. The effort to focus is too much. Words make no sense. I slam the book closed.

Outside again, the day has turned sunny and people are out celebrating it. In Sproul Plaza, students move purposefully in all directions, going to class, returning from class, stopping for a quick lunch with friends. Inside the station, everyone knows. But out on campus I am anonymous again, invisible.

Berkeley is an uncanny mix, a hub of infamous history and brilliant minds, mingled among urban decay, a stately world-renowned campus surrounded by a city with a reputation for crazies roaming the streets. It's surrounded by neighborhoods known as Southside, Westside, Northside, and Downtown Berkeley. On the south side of campus, it's difficult to find beauty. No granite hallways or high ceilings, no crickets humming at sunset, just the engines of cars and motorcycles, punctuated with psychotic shouts of homeless people to the empty space beside them. *"MOTHERFUCKER! I SAID YOU A MOTHERFUCKER!"* Famous for People's Park, the antiwar protests of the sixties, and a left-leaning population, it's often called the People's Republic of Berkeley, or *Berzerkeley*. When I moved here in August 1982, I knew nothing about the campus or city other than what I'd read in an orientation booklet mailed with the registration materials to my parents' home, the only house I'd ever lived in. I hadn't visited colleges. I didn't even know people did such a thing. I just assumed people applied blindly like I had, then showed up on the appointed day to the highest-ranking school that had sent an acceptance letter.

The UC Berkeley campus occupies 1,200 acres on the eastern side of the San Francisco Bay with the central campus alone sprawling 200 acres. Berkeley is the flagship institution of the ten-campus University of California system, offering 350 undergraduate and graduate degree programs in multitudes of academic disciplines. Founded in 1868, UC Berkeley is home to over one hundred buildings, gardens, museums, and works of sculpture. It's a montage of granite and concrete, bronze and marble, greenery and brick, all associated with generations of students, faculty, and traditions I know nothing about. The physical drama of the campus comes from the trees, the architecture, the history, the rich smell of moss growing on buildings more than a hundred years old. All of this forms the heart of one of the world's greatest teaching and research universities, a campus boasting thirty-two libraries, collections holding more than eight million books.

Marble foyers, buildings inscribed with Latin, long white staircases, the Campanile clock tower—with all that beautiful stateliness and awe came a sense of inferiority, of being below average, of knowing I was someone who had yet to have an original thought in her head. During my first days on campus, I had been struck by the notion that I didn't belong here, that I was surrounded by thirty thousand people and every single one of them was smarter than me. I had no sense whatsoever of how I would survive.

The first time I walked through this plaza, my eyes glazed from the sea of people swirling in all directions around me. They had all seemed to strut: confident frat boys in polo shirts with collars turned up, prissy sorority girls traversing campus in smiling packs, bearing the shiny white teeth that matched the pearls around their necks. They moved in stark contrast to the pear-shaped women with green short-cropped hair, the men in dreadlocks, the steely-eyed intellectuals discussing Sartre.

Plus there was the exotic assortment of human oddities who populated the entrance to campus: Orange Man, who handed out a seemingly endless supply of orange plant saplings to passersby; Polka Dot Man, who stood in the plaza daily, dressed head to toe in polka dots; the man who growled like a dog at people as they passed, "*RAWWWRR!*"

I had somehow found the entrance to the ASUC bookstore and bought my textbooks for Freshman English, Beginning French, Modern European History. I got myself a UC Berkeley sweatshirt and a book of stamps, so I could write weekly letters to my mother and to the high school friends scattered at colleges and universities across the country. To pay for these things, I wrote a check, the first check I had ever written. I felt terribly grown up. I felt terribly scared. But I reminded myself I was there to have fun. In the year that followed, I had gone to frat parties, guzzled beer, stumbled into Blondie's for a slice before crawling home to the dorm drunker than I had ever been at any high school party. I had gained the freshman ten and then some but walking ten miles over campus on patrol four nights a week had slimmed me back down again.

◆◆◆

I AM DEEPLY REMORSEFUL for having skipped Anthro and feel myself flinch at every voice, every sound. Heart racing, my breath is shallow. I know there is nothing to fear, that the person with the thudding footsteps behind me means no harm. No one would assault a woman in this crowded plaza in broad daylight, would they? *Of course not.* But my body won't listen. *Why won't it listen?* An understanding clicks somewhere deep within, a perception seeping like a stain. I am separate now, different from everyone else. I know something they don't.

I move beneath the bronze archway of Sather Gate. As a freshman, I'd been told this gate was designed as the Telegraph Avenue entrance to campus, a symbolic passageway to the "City of Learning," a portal to the architectural heritage of campus. Crossing through that portal, the stately bells of the Campanile ring across campus, signaling the passage of one more hour, and inside that sound I think I hear my name. I know it's my imagination. No one here knows me, no one would be calling for me. I walk faster.

There they are again. Footsteps. Louder now. Behind me. They quicken to a run, shoes slapping concrete, and with each rhythmic beat I feel myself losing control. At the base of my spine is a tingling, the shiver of a tambourine, then it's harder, as visceral as nails scraping a chalkboard. The prickling rattles all the way to the base of my neck, and I can't will it to stop. I spin around to confront my attacker.

A skinny boy with a buzz cut pulls his body backward with a jerk, hands held up in surrender. "Whoa, whoa, sorry! It's just me."

The boy stares into my face, unmoving, his eyes wide. Then he drops his hands to his sides.

"Karen, it's me," he says, "Beckman?"

My mind churns, finally renders recognition. "Sorry," I say.

Tommy Beckman is a funny-looking guy, skinny, gawky, only a couple inches taller than I am with ears sticking out from the sides of his head, a curse exacerbated by his shaved ROTC hair. Beckman is another aide, someone I've partnered with at events. He and I worked the Grateful Dead show together the week before. Patrolling the university buildings across the street from the Greek Theatre, we nearly walked right into a gorgeous Adonis-like man, his shiny blonde hair moving in the breeze. He was bronzed, beautiful, wearing nothing but soft-worn Levi's, and his hands and naked arms were soaked in blood. He stood still, bright electric eyes staring down at his limbs, perplexed, like he couldn't figure out what had happened. On the concrete path, shards of glass glinted in the sun. As blood dripped, spattering the cement, we radioed for officers and an ambulance. The beautiful man became a rabid dog, limping and placid one minute, howling and biting the next. He was high as hell and wouldn't let us near him. Officers arrived and handled him while Beckman and I watched. He had dropped acid, then something in one of the campus windows caught his eye. As he reached out to touch it, his hand broke through the glass. That day I had learned how much blood a cut to the hand could cause. For days I couldn't shake the image of that man, how beautiful he was, how bloodied and befuddled.

Beckman takes my arm, leads me to a bench, and sits me down. "Jesus fucking Christ, I heard what happened. Are you okay?"

"Yeah," I say. "I'm not hurt at all. It was nothing, really."

For the second time that day, I attempt to have a conversation with a well-meaning person I don't really know. Beckman's voice is soft, cadenced with loping vowels that identify him as Southern, though I've never bothered to ask where exactly he comes from. I know he owes a piece of hide to the Army after he graduates. I know he orders the German frankfurter link at Top Dog and prefers ice cream to Yogurt Park. I know that, like me, his paychecks are already earmarked down to the penny before Amy hands them out every other Friday. But of all the important things, all the little pieces that make a person a human being, of these I know nothing.

Beckman and I fall silent. Sitting in the middle of Sproul Plaza, we're surrounded by the bustle of students, professors, staff, people going about the business of their lives seemingly without pain. I watch the young women from the all-female Mills College step out of the van that transports them from their Oakland campus to UC Berkeley's famous libraries. A high school friend goes there, so I know in truth this van is just a free ride to parties and sex. Frat boys call it The Fuck Truck.

Beckman's knee touches mine, and I jerk my leg away. "Sorry," he says.

"No," I say. "*I'm* sorry. It's not you."

I shiver in the breeze, and we are quiet again. I watch the wind stirring leaves and notice it is late afternoon because the shadows have started to sift through the trees and somewhere inside I know something. Nothing else in the world has changed. Only me. The nineteen-year-old girl-child, she had been consumed in those minutes in that hallway. She has been spat back out in a different form. Her strength has been stripped, and like the Adonis man she is bewildered. What does the world mean when you no longer trust it?

As Beckman and I sit in the fading Berkeley sunlight, two miles away in Alameda County Municipal Court my assailant is arraigned. He enters a plea of Not Guilty to charges of false imprisonment and assault with a deadly weapon. Bail is set at $5,000. He is released.

CHAPTER 12

July 22, 1984, Berkeley, California

SUNDAY COMES. MY DAY to call home. Since leaving for school I have called every Sunday afternoon, a weekly connection both my parents and I count on. Now that bond feels faulty, tenuous. I can't tell my mother what happened. I want to, but haven't the foggiest idea how and know I won't be able to endure the strain in her voice or how her anxiety-laden words would impress upon me that what happened was as awful as it seemed.

Halfway underground, bushes covering the windows and seizing all the light, I sit down on the scratchy couch, put my face in my hands, and bawl. When I finish, I blow my nose and at the appointed time dial, let the phone ring once, hang up. This is my mother's clever scheme to avoid the expense of me calling collect.

When the phone rings in response to my signal, it's just Mom on the line. My father is at the store picking up fresh corn on the cob for supper. I put on the most chipper voice I can muster.

"Do you have a cold?" my mother asks, alarm in her voice. This is the great tragedy that has befallen her daughter. She has caught a cold.

"No. Might just be allergies?"

"Well, doctor up just in case." This is my mother's admonition any time I get sick. Doctor up!

♦♦♦

I'M THE FIRST PERSON in my family to go to college. My father joined the Army as an airplane mechanic, then worked as a mailman. My mother's scrapbook holds a newspaper clipping from the late 1940s where he is interviewed about the job and explains that he took it for the security. This sums up my father pretty well. Steady, cautious, reliable, steely work ethic. A kind man but also shy, socially awkward, sometimes taciturn to the point of rudeness. I love my father deeply and know he loves me, but as a traditional male, his primary role as father is provider, not confidante.

While I grew up, my mother stayed home, served as the PTA mom, the Camp Fire Girl leader. When I started at Berkeley, she went back to work at a menial clerical job at the Naval Supply Center in downtown San Diego. She is too nervous to drive, so she takes the bus to work, rising at five thirty each morning to make it on time. Her boss treats her like she is stupid, and most of the time she believes him. She takes as many smoke breaks as she can, in a futile effort to calm her nerves. Then she comes home, cooks dinner, takes a shower, and falls into bed, exhausted. She does this for me. Her paychecks pay for my tuition each semester and my wildly expensive textbooks. They count for half my rent. I give her my love, I think we have a good relationship, but it never once occurs to me to say thank you.

I don't remember what I hoped for in coming to Berkeley. I recall writing college admissions essays at my bedroom desk in my parents' house, giving vague answers to open-ended questions about what I wanted from college. I wrote that I wanted to experience *everything*. If I had been more thoughtful, if I had focused on the truth rather than pandering to some faceless admissions board, I wouldn't have written that. Because in truth, we don't want to experience everything. In truth, there are some things we work very hard to avoid.

My mother and father drove me in their Allegro RV up the long expanse of Highway 5 to reach Berkeley. I was seventeen. I chose Psychology as a major because of my fascination with how the mind works, how it can betray us. At family gatherings I enjoyed mortifying my parents by reporting that I planned to become a sex therapist, delighting in watching my parents blush to hear me speak the word "sex" out loud.

◆◆◆

I FEEL MYSELF WAVER. I want to tell my mother about this thing that has happened because I am desperate for comfort. But when I try to form the words, I can't. I don't trust her to know what I need to hear, to say the right things, to be capable of soothing me, of not making this worse. Most of all, I'm afraid she will convince me this place is too dangerous, that I need to leave, that I need to come home. Though my mother radiated anxiety while I was growing up, she also beamed love for me. A good part of that love was making sure I was safe, protected, close by. As a child, I sometimes presented her with some new version of myself, floating the idea, "This is who I think I could be." Often she shot it down. Not out of cruelty, but out of desire to protect me. When I said I wanted to be a writer, she warned that writers were poor. I didn't want to be poor, did I? No, I did not. Accurate caution, again well-meaning. When I told her I planned to go to law school, she groaned, warned against it. She had seen the movie *The Paper Chase*, saw how grueling it was, how fierce and competitive, how it drove one character to attempt suicide.

Instead of sharing my pain, all I tell my mother is that Econ is really hard. Much harder than I'd expected.

She doesn't know how to respond to this other than with a startled, "Oh?"

I hear her take a drag, listen to the sound of the slow hiss of air as she exhales the smoke from her Pall Mall. I imagine her face, forehead crinkling with worry. Guilt seeps in immediately at having troubled her. So I shift gears into more generalization. "But school is good. It's tough but it's good."

"Oh, that's wonderful!" There is relief in her voice. I have made it better. I have removed the burden I sought to place on her. I shift the conversation further, ask her questions. Did she and Dad have any camping trips planned? How's the weather down there? On the ledge next to the phone is the new issue of *Time* magazine. Geraldine Ferraro is on the cover. A week earlier, Walter Mondale had named the Representative from Queens as his running mate, making her the first woman ever to be selected as Vice President on a major party ticket. I ask my mother what she thinks of this woman, but she doesn't have much to say.

The conversation turns to the McDonald's massacre. "People are rotten," she says.

I say, "Goodbye, I love you." Then I hang up. In the dim silence of the apartment, a pain rumbles inside me. It starts as a low howl, somewhere deep inside my chest.

CHAPTER 13

July 26, 1984

I AM TOUGH. I am a wannabe cop baby girl. This shit doesn't bother me. I shrug a lot. A dozen times a day people ask me questions. I answer these questions with two words: I'm. *Fine.*

I set about the job of pretending it never happened, of reassuring those around me, of proving I am unbreakable, that a little thing like a man charging out of the darkness, grabbing me, holding his glinting knife to my neck is not the type of thing to rattle me. This is my chance to show how resilient, how competent, how graceful I am under what to a lesser woman might feel like pressure. I refuse to be the self-pitying victim, to let this event define me, so I wear the guise of my uniform, grit my teeth, and fake it.

The uniform is armor. In it, I feel different, special. I watch the sorority girls walking in their packs, collars of their Izod T's flipped up at the neck, and I feel something like power. They call me when they are alone and vulnerable. I protect them. In uniform I can still almost beam the illusion of strength, shift my persona, disappear inside the sheath of my role as police. The way I inhabit my own body changes, the real me eradicated.

In a police department one cannot show weakness, one cannot admit fear. It is not an atmosphere where people talk about their feelings. I want to feel normal, and confiding in colleagues I barely know does not feel normal. But what is normal, anyway? Somewhere inside, in a place I cannot name, something is dawning on me. That this state, this feeling of shattered angst, this could be the new normal.

The moment my eyes rested on his knife, then moved back to his face, questioning, disbelief pulsing until his expression told me yes, yes this is happening, I'd left my body. Because I'd watched from somewhere outside my body, that is the moment I can't shake, and with that moment my mind still runs its loops, obsessing.

For how long had he planned this? Did he know it would happen for sure this time? Certainly he knew as he lunged, as his arms grabbed me. Perhaps he'd waited in the darkness before, willing himself to make that lunge. But something held him back. What? Fear? What told him this was the night, that I was his? Coincidence? Fate? Why did he choose me? Did he choose me? Where was he waiting? How long did he wait?

How did it feel to dress that night, to tie those shoelaces, to slip the knife inside his pants pocket? What was he thinking as he left his house? Was the night air on his face a tonic? A caress? What about that knife? Did he hold it in his hands and know the power it gave him? Did he think about what he would do with it? Hold it to a throat. Then what?

Gloom seeps in, roots itself inside me, takes hold. This unraveling is an affront to my ego, telling me something I don't want to know. It whispers in my ear, *You aren't tough.*

The strangling feeling I suffer through each day is the fear-laced knowledge that life as I had known it is gone. I had, in a way, lost my life that night. I had learned a horrible lesson and that lesson was: I am vulnerable. I had come very close to death. If a random person appears out of darkness to take my life, how powerful am I really? And if it had happened once, it could happen again. And if I now know that this thing could happen anytime, how can I possibly feel confident ever again? And how can I possibly feel confident when all along I had been pretending about my power in the first place?

And so I sway back and forth, playing my role as the tough law enforcement woman unphased by this trifle of an attack, then lapsing into the silent lonely girl who is coming unhinged. I wake up every morning unsure which of these two people I might be.

CHAPTER 14

July 27, 1984

NO ONE SAYS ANYTHING to me directly, but in the days following my assault I hear through John and Beckman that certain members of the UC Police Department view my "incident" as another excuse to shut down the aide program. Politics have developed around aides. More of the officers and administration have grumbled recently that aides have no business wearing real police uniforms. They complain that people on campus and surrounding neighborhoods are often confused by the virtually identical uniforms, and that most Berkeley residents believe officers and aides are one and the same.

Some of this I understand. Our misjudgments and fuck-ups reflect poorly on the real UCPD officers, and they have enough of a chip on their shoulders already from being "campus cops." But in addition to my internal fear, the talk around the station triggers a further conflict of emotions:

1. I don't understand how my *incident* has anything to do with this discussion about aides and our place in the department, and it feels ludicrously unfair.

2. I know these cops' issues, insecurities, and systemic problems are being projected onto me because of my assault, but their dialogue has occurred without me. I have no voice, and this too feels unfair.

3. I feel judgment register in the eyes of some male officers, and I feel frail, at fault, like I fucked up somehow. I'm ashamed about what I let happen, and if I'm honest with myself, I have to acknowledge I am the weak. I am now among the class of people I have always loathed: victims. They'll never admit it, but some people like being the victim. They find satisfaction in knowing they are the wronged party, they enjoy the significance victim status provides, they revel in the certainty and self-righteousness. They get to be angry.

I am not one of those people. John and I had contact with crime victims. After our shifts, we talked about them, deciding everyone held responsibility for their own actions, including being involved in an accident or falling prey to a crime. Our subtext was that victims were the weak, while we were the strong. Perhaps we adopted this heartless point of view as a defense mechanism, to steel ourselves against the things we saw up close. But I think that would be too generous, that these feelings stemmed purely from arrogance and ignorance, from children who thought they were tough and street-smart, but who in reality had simply never had anything really bad happen to them yet.

Who is to say I was innocent? Who is to say I was not at fault?

There are many who would say a woman walking home in the dead dark of night grants tacit approval of her assault. How did it come to be this way? How in holy hell can a woman be at fault when she is assaulted?

◆◆◆

AMY IS MY ALLY; she tells me it's nothing personal, that some officers at UCPD are always looking for any excuse to shut down the aide program. She tells me it's policy now: any female aide or employee whose shift ends after 10:00 p.m. must be driven home by an officer on duty—all she has to do is ask and dispatch will call a car to the station. Given that I am one of only three female aides, this "policy" is meant mostly for me.

The talk around the department gets me thinking: A young woman earns her money walking other women home because it's unsafe to walk the Berkeley streets alone in darkness. All night long she rescues women, escorting them home through that perilous darkness. Then she walks home alone without the armor of her uniform, near midnight, into the shadows of her own sketchy neighborhood. Why?

I knew I wasn't invincible. I knew the only thing protecting me and the women I escorted home was a police uniform, a uniform I wasn't wearing the night I was attacked. As a superhero without her powers, a knight without her armor, danger on the streets of Berkeley was everywhere. I understood this, lived this, yet I flaunted it. Was I scared? Oblivious? Feeling invulnerable? Why did I do it?

Amy offers her feminist interpretations of why I walked home alone that night and all the other nights after a shift: by risking what I must have known was a genuine chance of assault, I was asserting my power, flipping the bird to men and their threat, denying them their control over me. It was a desire to claim the Berkeley streets as my own. A courageous, determined, feminist refusal to capitulate to fear. It was an act of defiance, of saying *fuck you, Berkeley, I've got this*. By walking home alone, I was "taking back the night," I was transcending.

Beckman opines it was the delusion I'd acquired by virtue of roaming campus in the shield of a police uniform: the fantasy of invulnerability, of omnipotence, of being untouchable.

If Amy is right and my walk home alone in darkness was a refusal to capitulate to fear, that refusal was viciously punished.

If Beckman is right and my walk home alone in darkness was self-delusion, that delusion was viciously punished.

What I come to know is that the truth is less weighty, less heroic than reasons offered to me. The truth is more practical: I simply needed to get home. I'd walked out the basement door of Sproul Hall without any thought of whether I should walk home or not. Of course I would walk home. What were the alternatives? I walked home alone because I was tired and wanted to crawl into bed as soon as possible so I could sleep and be ready for a full day of studying ahead. I would be cautious, take the safest possible route, be conscious of my surroundings, but I would walk home alone. I could have asked an officer for a ride, but doing so would have diminished my authority at the department. I believed I could take care of myself. It was a calculated risk. But Amy is at least partially right: I also did it because I should have the right to walk home when and where I goddamn please without fear of a man chasing me down and holding a knife to my throat. All things considered, I did it out of equal parts foolishness, rebellion, pride, laziness, impatience, and practicality.

When I ask myself, was I at fault for my incident? Do I accept responsibility for what happened? The answer is no. No, I do not accept one ounce of responsibility for being attacked because I chose to walk home alone after dark in what is supposedly the world's greatest society.

A woman should be able to walk home alone in darkness without fear. But she can't. A woman who walks home at night after a full day of classes, a full night of work—that woman takes her chances.

The talk around the station tells me: All of this has happened to someone else before. All of this is happening to someone else right now. This thing will always happen. This thing will never stop.

Unless we make it stop.

CHAPTER 15

July 31, 1984

I STILL HAVE CLASSES to attend, papers to write, exams to take. I have rent to pay, still need to eat. I want this feeling to be over. I want to focus on me, on building my life. I want to get my shit together, to get good grades so I can get into law school, to become a prosecutor, to be the best aide I can be, to save some money, to be independent. And I want to do all of this while feeling pretty.

I also want, someday, to marry John. He is my only break, the only solid thing in my life, the only thing keeping me tethered to earth. Without him, I will float away, fading until I'm a mere dot in the sky, before I disappear altogether. But with John by my side, I can relax, laugh, be a normal nineteen-year-old college student. We drink beer and eat pizza, joke about the officers in the department, speculate that the cops who carry the biggest guns are compensating for tiny cocks. We go see *Purple Rain*. We fuck all the time. The weight of John on top of me feels divine, safe. Him filling up my empty insides is what I need. Afterward we lie tangled in each others' limbs, falling asleep with our sweet sticky bodies pressed together. In the mornings we kiss goodbye and exchange I love yous, but within a block of parting, the splitting inside me starts aching, growing larger, until it becomes a black, gaping hole.

Around me, life moves forward, cold and distant. Long minutes pass. Hours feel like days; everywhere I internalize the threat in the *slap slap slap slap* of feet hitting concrete. The fear is always there, taunting me. What am I sure of? I no longer know. I know the boy with the long lashes keeping step next to me toward Wheeler Auditorium never tried to hurt me. I know the scraggly bearded man in Birkenstocks walking behind me never held a knife to my throat. Rationally I know none of these men around me plan me any harm. But they terrify me nonetheless. I had been educated that the jump-out-of-the-bushes assailant was a rarity, that most sexual assaults are committed by someone the victim knows, maybe even trusts. This was one more fact that had proven untrue, upending my worldview.

People buy Mace and guns, knives and brass knuckles. They take self-defense classes, karate. They move to safer neighborhoods. They see doctors and have sleep meds prescribed. They call and ask their mothers for help.

I do none of these things. I can't move because I don't have the money and there is no place else to go. My mother is giving everything she can. I can't ask for more. I have to figure this out. I think about finding another job. But this one works around my class schedule and pays two dollars more than minimum wage. Also, I don't want to be a quitter. I need to face this, work through it somehow. I don't want the bastard in the hallway to win. I don't want these cops to look at each other knowingly, shaking their heads, muttering, *Yep. Girls like her aren't cut out for this kinda work.*

The line between waking and sleeping blurs. Days a relentless cycle. Each too fast, too slow. Wash the dishes, work a shift, go to class. Grad students pace around lecterns, droning out questions as they scratch words on a chalkboard, not even trying to hide their boredom, their disgust for our undergraduate ignorance. We are only a paycheck to them, something they must endure. Econ lectures, when I can force myself to go, are in a room seating three hundred people. Waiting for the professor to step to the podium, three hundred voices all talk at once, laughing and chattering, the sound of people sharing their lives with one another. Among these voices I feel as lonely as I do in my apartment. This alienation knows no bounds. Berkeley is a thriving campus with thousands of people. I have lived here for two years and I know almost no one. If I'm honest, I know I have chosen to self-isolate. Now I don't want solitude, but it's too late and I can't find my way out. When the room quiets and the professor speaks, it is a language I no longer understand. I sit scribbling notes, trying with all my might to listen, to comprehend, to not let my mind drift.

I have become acutely aware of lighting, the pixels of every image charged, and compulsively I make comparisons: the morgue light of the police station in the Sproul Hall basement, fluorescent lights of a classroom, contrasting with the floodlights of squad cars illuminating a man, contrasting with the yellow-gold bulb of a hallway.

I'm impatient with the fear, want it gone already. I have to *get over it*. But I can't seem to do that. Instead I seem to be getting worse. Something is wrong with me, but I don't know what. Leaves scatter in the wind and I jump at the sound. Every person, every place is a threat, and if I'm not careful, if I'm not alert and prepared to react, I will fall prey. It turns out my mother had been right all along: the world is a dangerous place. I want to be the person I had been: blissfully unaware of this fact. When you're a nineteen-year-old college student, your identity as an "adult" is just beginning to take shape. You're learning who you are. You're learning who you want to be. You're examining the expanse between those two places and how to construct the bridge between them. But my bridge has crumbled.

I keep asking myself, what can I do? What can I do to feel normal again? How do I get back to where I was? But these are questions with no answers.

CHAPTER 16

August 1, 1984

I WATCH SHADOWS ACCUMULATE, signaling inevitable dusk, followed by the blackness slipping across Blake Street. With a sliver of hope for a ride to the station, I call John, but there is no answer. I hang up, resign myself to walk alone in darkness to campus, to my first graveyard shift since my attack.

Each aide is required to work a minimum of six graveyard shifts per semester. Roll call is at 9:00 p.m. with the officers, though aides sit in the back of the room where we are expected to be seen but not heard. The shift lasts until 7:00 a.m. Ten hours of eternity that destroys a body's clock for days.

Leaving the apartment, I am skittish, racing through the hallway straight into the center of Blake Street, head darting in every direction to ensure the road is empty. I walk up the middle of the street, a plan designed to give myself more warning, more time to react, more of a chance to fend off attack should I hear footsteps coming at me from the shadows. When I reach the intersection of Haste and Dana streets, approaching the Unit 3 dorms, I know I am safe again. It's still early, only 8:45, and scattered groups of students linger about. But as I insert my key into the basement door of Sproul Hall, slipping inside the safety of the florescent light of the station, I notice with a quiver of shame that my heart pounds inside my chest.

An aide who is afraid of darkness is no longer really police.

◆◆◆

AFTER LINEUP, WE HEAD out. I am uniformed, booted, and supposedly brave. In a few hours campus will be deserted, a different universe, empty of the students, staff, professors, and homeless who cross through it every day. And if someone is out in the middle of a summer night, it's likely someone to steer clear of, someone dangerous, a criminal, the category of persons whom I, as a UC Police aide, am supposed to simultaneously avoid and protect others against.

Before my attack, graveyards were an adventure if I could partner up with the right person. Because we were on patrol, we were loosely supervised, left with more freedom than any minimally trained nineteen-year-old in a cop uniform should be given, just enough rope with which to hang ourselves. Most of us were inept, bumbling around under the color of law enforcement authority in remote areas of a sprawling campus. On graveyard, we did things aides weren't supposed to do: pretended we were real cops, stopped pedestrians for the hell of it, ordering them to break out some ID. We did it because it was three o'clock in the morning; we did it because we were bored; we did it because we could.

The handful of times I'd paired with John on a graveyard shift, he made me feel bold, like nothing could go wrong. John's belief in his own invincibility inspired me. Partnered with him, I felt wild, fearless, unlimited, intoxicated with power. A month before my assault, John and I met up with another aide, Ty Kanes, at the forbidden zone of Dwight Derby. These were buildings originally part of the California School for the Deaf, a kindergarten through twelfth grade boarding school on the Berkeley campus from the 1870s through the 1970s. For part of that period, the school was conjoined with the California School for the Blind, and together they were referred to as the State Asylum for the Deaf, Dumb, and Blind. By the early 1970s, the schools had relocated to Fremont, and in 1980 the property was conveyed to UC Berkeley. Plans were underway to tear down the buildings and build new dorms, but in 1984 construction had not yet begun and the bleak empty rooms had the feel of a haunted house. The boarded-up buildings were completely black inside, petrifying in their darkness, terrifying in their promise of trouble. Any aide who ventured within was there to find it.

I, of course, wanted to prove myself a badass, someone up for adventure anytime, anywhere, anyhow, so I was willing to break the rules for the sake of it. Aides were expressly forbidden from going inside Dwight Derby, and if caught we would be fired on the spot.

I had shivered with giddy excitement as I crossed the threshold into pure pitch blackness. I couldn't see my hand in front of my face and there was absolute silence beyond the creaking of our leather belts. John clicked on his flashlight, let the beam of light crawl up walls straight out of a horror film: creepy faded murals of blonde braided girls and their flocks of sheep set against a dark forest. From the looks of them, the murals had been painted in the early 1900s, scenes no doubt set to soothe the sighted children of the asylum, but which made the hair rise across my arms.

Ty signaled John to snap off the flashlight. We couldn't risk revealing our presence. I inched forward through the blackness, Ty to my right, John so close behind me I could hear him breathe.

We moved through the building, practicing our low-visibility patrol skills, sneaking around every corner not knowing what we'd encounter, certain it could be anything, positive that whoever it was, we needed to see them before they saw us.

In one sharp, sudden swing, Ty threw his arm out in front of me, hitting my chest, stopping my movement cold. I looked at him in alarm. *What?* I mouthed, not even sure he could see my face.

Kanes cupped his hand over the bulb of his flashlight, clicked it on, pointed to the floor. At the tips of my boots was a body: a homeless man asleep at my feet. One step farther and I would have tripped over him, triggering chaos: the disorientation of my body falling in darkness, landing on the body beneath mine, that other body waking to my weight pounding down on him, each of us screaming in befuddled terror. Ty put a finger over his lips and the three of us tiptoed out of there as fast as we could. Back outside in the coolness of the night, in the relative safety of the 3:00 a.m. Berkeley streets, we howled like hyenas.

"Holy shit!" Kanes laughed.

John slapped my back, convulsing in laughter. "Can you even imagine?"

No. No, I couldn't.

As the adrenaline passed and my heart returned to normal, I felt changed. I felt a deep connection, a newly formed bond with Kanes and John that I had never felt with another person ever before.

◆◆◆

TONIGHT, I HAVE NO partner, but to pass the time, I meet up with Alfred Ling for a while. Alfred is tall and thin, sweetly shy, his rimless glasses giving him a nerdy air. He has somehow obtained a master key, a prize only officers are supposed to possess because the master unlocks every single door to every single building, lecture hall, and office on campus. We go exploring, searching out places most Cal students will never see. The private hallways of the Essig Museum of Entomology, hundreds of species of insects stretched and pinned behind glass, labs and empty lecture halls, eerie in their silence. We peer over the edge of the flat black roof of Barrows Hall, clouds hovering above as if contemplating our presence on that expanse of asphalt, knowing we don't belong there. I stand so close to the edge of the flat roof I feel dizzy, like some magnetic force in the sky wants to pull me off.

◆◆◆

MIDNIGHT. ALONE AGAIN IN the moonless night. I roam the campus, calling in to dispatch every hour on the hour to confirm I'm alive and accounted for, "Control, 155—10-97." Rachel responds with a chipper "10-4, 155," and the long black night goes silent again.

I patrol California Memorial Stadium, home to the Bears, slumping through the stadium halls to find the coaches' offices, letting myself in with the special keys provided. The office walls are covered with memorabilia, most of which is lost on me. I stop to linger on a photo of Oski the Bear, the California Golden Bears mascot who debuted in 1941. Live bear cubs had been used as mascots at Memorial Stadium until some genius decided in 1940 that a costumed mascot would be a more practical alternative.

I walk the cement halls of the stadium, my footsteps echoing in their emptiness. I stop to peer into the sea of empty seats that will be packed full on fall Saturdays. Students, staff, alums, all dressed in blue and gold, cheering on their Golden Bears.

Then I hear voices. Male voices. I stop, try to sense where they are. My heart pounds its panic. I don't have it in me to confront them, to fool them into believing I possess any authority, that I am stronger because of my uniform and police radio. I could call for a 10-98, but Alfred's shift ended, we are light-staffed, and I know from the radio traffic that anyone I can come close to calling a friend is nowhere in the vicinity. I could call dispatch, call the voices in as a trespass. But if an officer comes and it's nothing, that officer will be pissed, and my reputation will sour further than it already has. I hurry back to the coaches' office and lock myself inside. The sheer insanity of my being out on patrol roots itself deeper inside me.

◆◆◆

1:00 A.M.

I shine my flashlight into corners, peering into shadows, eyes alert for movement, fearing I'll see a face. Anyone observing would see an aide serious about patrol, but I am focused only on my own safety. I do my job, barely, staying on the wide main paths, steering clear of the high-danger places. As freshmen, Kim and I joked and giggled to mask our unease, calling these byways "Rapers' Row" and, even while walking in the "safety of two," avoiding them whenever we could. Even before my assault I avoided the footbridge over Strawberry Creek flowing into campus near Tolman Hall. The light there is so dim it's almost nonexistent, one of so many unnerving paths on campus. One of the other female police aides is said to have been raped at the foot of this bridge amid a pile of leaves, the creek trickling beside her as it happened. After he finished, her rapist kissed her, shoving his tongue deep inside her mouth, where she is rumored to have bitten it off. Whether or not this story is true, it has stayed in my mind, worrying me he might still prowl among the trees shivering alongside the bridge.

On patrol, alone, like in my apartment, I have too much time to think. The Summer Olympics have begun and I try to pretend I care, reading about sixteen-year-old Mary Lou Retton, Mary Decker, Zola Budd. O. J. Simpson is slated to conclude the Olympic torch relay and Lionel Richie will perform "All Night Long," lyrics to taunt my sweat-soaked insomnia.

But in spite of my efforts, I've become obsessed with all that can go wrong. I read about Lawrence Singleton. On September 29, 1978, he picked up fifteen-year-old Mary Vincent while she was hitchhiking in Berkeley, raped her, then severed both her forearms with a hatchet, throwing her naked and nearly dead off a thirty-foot cliff outside of Modesto. Somehow she managed to pull herself back up the cliff and alert a passerby, who took her to a hospital. Singleton was arrested, and at his trial six months later, Vincent, fitted with new prosthetic arms, faced her assailant and relived the ordeal in court. As she left the witness stand, he swore he would kill her. But her testimony convicted him. Singleton was sentenced to fourteen years, the maximum allowed by California law.

Someone the newspapers are calling the Night Stalker is terrorizing Southern California, breaking into homes, murdering victims at random. And then there is nineteen-year-old Patty Hearst, kidnapped in 1974 from her Berkeley apartment on Benvenue Avenue, just blocks from where I live. Single events. Some random, some not. Changing the trajectory of lives.

I think back to my first days as an aide, when Sergeant Bertini trained us in the art of collecting fingerprints, rolling the dusting brush on the surface of glass, peeling back the tape, studying print patterns and friction ridges. She showed us how to take prints from a light bulb. Why would we ever need to take prints from a light bulb? we asked. She described a case where a man had hidden in women's restrooms around campus. He removed the light bulbs from the ceiling fixtures, tossed them in the trash, then waited. When a woman entered and snapped the light switch, he probably felt her hesitation, her discomfort in proceeding into the dark bathroom, sensed her checking her watch, weighing the fullness of her bladder against the fact that class started in two minutes. Some of these women had made the wrong choice, had told themselves to not be such a ninny and just use the damned toilet. Multiple women were sexually assaulted before the man was finally caught and prosecuted.

Maybe my fixation is a way of comforting myself, of proving that compared to these tragedies, my experience seems trivial. But the more I tell myself that my own pain has no right to feel so devastating, the riptides of terror tug at me harder, pulling me under, threatening to drown me.

If someone had asked me if I understood there are things I cannot control, I would have answered quickly, blithely, "Yes, of course." But no one had ever asked me, and I had never stopped to ponder this. There were too many other things to consider: How would I squeeze in twenty-five hours of work on top of classes and studying? How would I ever be able to make enough money to have a decent wardrobe? Would John call and want to go out for beers?

The lesson my attacker taught me is that there are things I cannot control. But as I process this lesson, I only try harder to contain and direct everything around me, a figurative grasping, until my knuckles turn white.

◆◆◆

2:00 A.M.

Wind sweeps the campus, coming in waves, throttling me, pushing my body from behind, sending my hair flying in all directions. I walk beneath the black treetops, stop, stand, listen.

Leaves skitter on gusts of air, bringing me to my knees. *Mother fuck.* I move to stand on a steam grate for warmth, its gasping garbage-scented mist rising to my calves.

It starts to rain. The department has slickers, but I can't wear one. The black water-resistant ponchos hide the uniform, erasing my shield. In a slicker I'm just another vulnerable young woman. In a slicker I am prey, more so than I already am. So I let the rain soak through me.

Aides have been lectured repeatedly that interior patrol during graveyards is permitted only sparingly, this edict having come down after two aides were caught spending most of their graveyard shifts "patrolling" certain faculty lounges with their plush couches, free coffee, and remote-control TV. One aide was fired after a duty sergeant snapped a Polaroid of him on one of those couches, sleeping in uniform. The sergeant had found him by the volume of his snoring, and it had taken several tries before the aide could be prodded awake.

But with the shivering wet branches creaking in the silence of the night, I decide certain interiors need patrolling as much as exteriors. Unlike Alfred, I don't have a master key so I'm in the same position as the homeless people occupying this city, checking for open doors until I find one. I slip inside the lobby of Wheeler Hall, checking the doors to the eight-hundred-seat auditorium, making a show of ensuring they are locked. My radio is turned down low, yet I recognize the sound of my badge number as one recognizes the sound of her own name.

"S-59 to 155, what's your 10-20?"

I pause, consider lying, but know I may have been spotted by Chris Galan, the graveyard duty sergeant. The timing of his call is too coincidental. I click the mic of my radio. "South side of Wheeler Auditorium." This is more or less the truth.

"Check. Stand by for a 10-98."

I hightail it to the door, make my way outside, and immediately there comes the unmistakable sound of a police cruiser humming in the darkness. Light emerges, the headlamps of Chris's patrol car. Through the passenger-side window I see him lean over the center console, across the shotgun in its rack, opening the door like he is picking me up for a date.

John and I see Chris as success and failure wrapped in one. Chris was a Cal undergrad who became an aide, then after graduating went to the police academy and came back to work as an officer for UCPD before being promoted to sergeant. John and I can't understand why anyone would throw away a degree from UC Berkeley just to become a campus cop.

I climb inside the warmth of Chris's patrol car, grateful for the company as much as the escape from the wet, miserable cold. The only sound is the soft chatter of KALX, the student station that plays nothing but extremes, either violent punk rock or whispering voices discussing the Farabundo Marti National Liberation Front, the group whose initials are spray-painted all over campus. Chris says nothing about my interior patrol.

The heater roars as Chris drives, left hand on the wheel, right hand freed up for the radio. Waves of wind knock the car and campus buildings slide past the window. We ride in silence, waiting for something to happen.

"Where's your rain slicker?" Chris asks, peering straight ahead through the windshield.

"Oh," I say, trying to sound casual. "I don't need one. It's not that bad."

"That's ridiculous, you're soaked." Chris turns in his seat to face me. "I'll swing you by the station so you can grab one."

"No!" I say, too fast. I catch myself, even out my voice. "I'm fine like this."

Chris shakes his head. "Suit yourself."

I know he doesn't have a clue, doesn't have an inkling of what significance the rain slicker has, because he's never had to worry about the threats that trouble me. He just thinks I'm dumb, a dog who doesn't have enough sense to stay dry.

We ride in silence again.

"Wanna get something to eat?" Chris asks.

"Sure," I shrug.

Chris reaches for the radio. "S-59 and 155 out 10-7."

Rachel's voice comes back, "10-4, S-59." I hear her snark, her knowing tone, and I'm wary now, afraid what John will think, worried of winning a reputation like Rachel's even if it's unfounded. To be female in a police department is tricky. Spend too much time with a male officer and the gossip starts: "Did you hear about Chris? He's fucking 155." But spend time with the handful of female officers and it's worse. The men in the department snicker, say you're out having tea and knitting, or they call you dykes. Catty sniping and gossip among cops are unparalleled.

We drive to the only place open at 3:00 a.m., the hospital cafeteria at Alta-Bates Hospital on Ashby Avenue, where we eat scrambled eggs and limp bacon. We talk about Polka Dot Man, the handful of officers in the department who are able to talk with him in Sproul Plaza. I tell Chris how I once stood in line behind Polka Dot Man at the Bank of America on Telegraph Avenue, how he had stood silently, staring down at his checkbook waiting his turn, then stepped up to the teller and transacted his business like anyone else. It had stunned me to realize someone as exotic as Polka Dot Man engaged in the tedium of everyday life.

We climb back in the car and head back to campus. Chris says nothing about dropping me off to continue my foot patrol and neither do I. Driving past Strawberry Creek, it seems to sing in the silence of the night, trees dripping from the rain. Then Chris spots a Sus Per, radio parlance for "suspicious person," who roughly fits the description of the man spotted lingering earlier outside Evans Hall before the burglary of a professor's office. I step out of the car and follow because I want to be cool. I want the Sus Per to think I'm a real cop and I want to impress Chris with my boldness. Reputation is everything in a police department and mine can use any help it can get. But since I'm armed with nothing more than a flashlight, I keep a safe distance.

Berkeley is a diverse city. There are 5150s, frat boys with Roman numerals after their names, Nobel laureates, undergrads, graduate students, professors, protesters. If you see a weird-looking man with long scraggly hair and an intense gleam to his eye like he is one word away from snapping, he might be a murderer, a terrorist, a victim of a bad acid trip, or a prize-winning physicist. We all size people up, sort them, categorize them. It's a mechanism, a means of processing information. Everyone does it, though some pretend they don't. There is outer appearance. There is inner imagination. Only sometimes do the two converge. We all constantly assess our surroundings. Some of it's conscious, most of it's not. We make up stories to make sense of what is happening around us, what is happening to ourselves. It's an internal information-management system. We judge by job, clothes, car, haircut, makeup, speech, race, sex. We make assessments and often we are wrong. We work so hard to make sense of things, but we only know a small fraction of what holds true in this universe.

The Sus Per turns out to be a student with no priors. Chris fills out a Field Interview Card, a shorthand report to document a conversation had in the field that didn't result in a reportable incident, but which relates to crime prevention or investigation efforts. It's also a way for lieutenants and the chief to measure who actually gets their ass out of their patrol car and works as opposed to driving around all night doing nothing.

Back in the car. Breathy squawks on the radio. As duty sergeant, Chris monitors Berkeley PD calls. It's a quiet night, nothing but mundane codes, the low voice of the Berkeley PD dispatcher reporting suspicious-person sightings. I listen to the voice, trying to see if I recognize it as the woman who dispatched my call.

To be alone in the car this long with Chris begins to feel unsettling. There is an undercurrent. A hope of something. I want his protection, but I don't want the quid pro quo of it. So I start weaving John's name into the conversation as much as I can. It feels awkward but I'm not sure what to do.

"Well," I say, sounding as casual as I can, "I guess I'd better get back out there on patrol."

"We are patrolling," Chris says.

I pause, trying to figure out how to navigate the situation, trying to determine whether there even *is* a situation. "Yeah, but I feel bad..." My voice trails off.

"Okay," Chris says, and hits the brake.

I step out of the car, say an uncomfortable thanks, slam the door closed, and I am alone again. I roam campus for another few hours until finally the pale pink sky that is morning starts to appear. Inside the ruddy sunrise, a city is waking. I've survived another patrol shift and my reward will be sleep. Sleep during the dusty, hazy safety of day.

CHAPTER 17

August 16, 1984

MULTIPLY THAT GRAVEYARD SHIFT by ten? Twenty? Each shift I survive feels like I've dodged a bullet and the pretending becomes too much to bear. Patrol becomes endless hours of waiting, holding my breath, positioning my body to cover my back. This city is loaded with crime. The best I can hope is that it doesn't happen around me.

Cringing beneath the weight of my shame and without admitting it to anyone but John, I ask to be assigned to the department's Bike Bureau, a program consisting of sitting at a folding table in front of Moffitt Library selling bicycle licenses and Kryptonite locks to undergrads. This is an assignment I had loathed before my incident.

◆◆◆

I STOP AT THE metal mailboxes to find a new letter from my mother. I tear it open, smiling at her familiar stationery, a note card crawling with vines of pink flowers. Inside is the recipe for beef stew that I'd asked for, something simple that I might actually be able to make. I miss my mother's cooking, her elaborate Sunday dinners of chicken fried steak, corn, biscuits, and gravy. Her message begins with a perky *Hi Love!* and proceeds with news of the latest camping trip, how our dog, Salty, had gone to the vet for a back problem, but he was *fine* now, absolutely *fine*. Salty, our beloved black mutt with his white-tipped tail and muzzle, a puppy saved by pure chance—the woman who needed to dispose of him had to stop at the post office on her way to the pound and my father intervened, saving this doomed dog, changing its fate.

My mother's note goes on to explain that she hadn't told me about Salty before because she didn't want me to worry, didn't want to distract me from my studies. Her naïveté of what might flood my mind with angst is at once touching and sad. My mother no longer knows me, no longer knows my thoughts. It's not she who has changed, but me.

It's four in the afternoon and the fog rolls in, eclipsing the hills, refusing to budge, erasing the whole season of summer. I walk to the station in the gray.

Two hours later, I'm not taking any chances. It's not even dark but I situate myself close to the entrance where my table and I are covered in fluorescent light streaming from the Moffitt lobby. It is this light and the steady succession of harmless-looking undergrads that make me feel something resembling safe.

It's after the heavier inflow of traffic abates that I start to feel spooked. The night's too quiet, and sitting at my post I feel like a target. My eyes dart, taking in my surroundings. Ugly Moffitt, a rectangular concrete beast, the bulletin board to my right with its swarm of notices: Statistics Tutor Wanted, Romeo Void at the Mab Saturday night, doors open at 8:00 p.m. A breeze rustling the bushes is a warning, panic crawls across my skin, and I feel myself losing control until a pimply-faced freshman approaches to buy a bicycle license. The task of collecting money and filling out the form focuses me, redirects my mind. The freshman thanks me, disappears inside the doors, and I pull out my Econ textbook, hoping to keep my mind in check. From the corner of my eye, I notice Sergeant Kistner driving by, eyeballing me, incorporating me into his patrol.

Kistner had scared the living shit out of me my first months at the department. Gene King, the aide who had served as my training officer, warned me to steer clear of him. "He's not a fan of aides," was all King had said. That was enough. I know nothing about Kistner other than he is a leather-like son of a bitch known to speak in a growl, and after serving in Vietnam he had returned home to the Oakland Police Department, a jurisdiction that is not for the faint of heart with its gangs and staggering violent crime rates.

My first night shift after completing training and being unleashed to patrol the university campus alone, I was dispatched to a crime scene, to make sure no one wandered through a deserted portion of the blacktop path bordering Hilgard Hall. More specifically, I learned upon arrival on location, my assignment was to stand on the path and make sure no one walked through a puddle of blood until the crime scene techs could come do whatever it was crime scene techs did.

Sergeant Kistner and Officer Ocello sauntered by, lingering to ensure I didn't fuck up this simple task. I sensed their disdain had more to do with my gender than my status as an aide, but I tried to swallow my paranoia, telling myself I would show them. They would learn just how capable I was.

I stood there for hours. The end of my shift came and went. No one came to relieve me, so I stayed put. Kistner and Ocello chain-smoked and shot the shit, swapping stories from their days together as Oakland homicide detectives.

"And remember that one time?" Ocello's voice sparked with hilarity.

"Yeah!" Kistner cut in, starting to laugh.

They were like an old married couple, finishing each other's sentences.

"Fucking looked like someone'd thrown a plate of spaghetti against the wall."

"I know, right?" Kistner bent over then, laughing so hard he lapsed into a coughing fit.

From the remaining pieces of conversation, I understood they were reminiscing about a murder-suicide they had responded to together. I had smiled, awkwardly trying to share in their joke. They had shot me looks of disgust, then continued to ignore me. I'd stood there another two hours before they finally acknowledged me directly, finally giving me permission to leave.

◆◆◆

ON HIS THIRD TIME cruising past Moffitt, Kistner parks his patrol car and ambles toward my table gripping two Styrofoam cups. Amy is rumored to be more than just friends with Kistner, notwithstanding her engagement to Sergeant Banks, and I know she has asked Kistner to check up on me, to make nice even though I'm a chickenshit aide.

Kistner is in his early fifties and wears a full-drooping handlebar moustache. Sharp blue eyes peer out from behind round glasses in thin metal frames, and his thick graying hair and moustache make him look like a threatening walrus. He hands me one of the cups and stands next to my table, hiking his boot on the rung of my chair, leaning in as he eyes the students coming and going beneath their oversized backpacks loaded down with textbooks. He taps a cigarette from his pack and lights it.

"How you doing?" he asks, exhaling a cloud of smoke.

"I'm fine," I say, providing my standard answer to everyone's favorite question.

Kistner squints through the smoke and gives me a look that says we both know I'm a liar.

We are silent, sipping our coffee. I'm flattered he is taking the time to talk to me, but I know he's not a man for small talk and I'm not sure what to say. I don't know Kistner well—don't know him at all really. I know I admire him, look up to him even if he intimidates me. I know he is revered at the department as "the real deal," a cop who has seen it all. As the silence stretches out, I have the sense he has an agenda for this meeting, a checklist of wisdom he wants to share. For the first time, I feel ready to listen and I sit poised for the strength of his words, feeling fairly certain that if anyone has the answer, the solution to my hellish fear, it has to be Kistner. Not my mother, not Amy, not Beckman or John, but this tough Marlboro man with his solid foot pushing on my metal chair.

"You know," he says. Casual pause. Long sip of coffee.

I hold my breath.

"After something like this happens to a person, the likelihood of it ever happening again is pretty goddamn low." He stops, raising his bushy eyebrows at me.

I look at him and nod, not sure I understand what he is saying.

He puffs on his cigarette, exhales another cloud of smoke, and stares into me again. "Statistically, you know? It's just not likely to happen again."

I sit perfectly still, holding his stare with my own, trying to absorb his words. Did I understand correctly? Tough, rugged Kistner is offering statistics for comfort? That's his best reassurance? That being assaulted once meant you probably

(*probably??!*) would not be assaulted again? Where are these statistics? Who keeps them? How is this data gathered, regulated, controlled? Really? Is this some kind of joke? But Kistner's face is unsmiling. This is all he's got. Maybe my face betrays me, reveals my shock, my disbelief, because then he speaks again.

"And he'll probably plead out." Kistner says, dragging from his cigarette. "You'll never even have to testify, so don't worry about that."

Jesus. I hadn't even considered this. I would have to testify. The thought sparks a new wave of fear. When? What was I supposed to do? I work for a police department but am woefully ignorant of the criminal justice system, of the court part. I know there will be a trial, and I know something happens in between arrest and trial, but I don't know what. My ignorance panics me. Fuck! I don't want this thing, this multilayered burden. I want it to go away. But instead it keeps getting bigger.

Kistner gives me a look of concern. "You talk to anybody yet?"

"Just the police that night," I say.

"No, I mean a professional."

My face flushes as I realize what Kistner means. "A shrink?" I say, scoffing.

No way, I think. No fucking way. Crazy people see shrinks. I'm not crazy. And what would my mother think of such a thing? Mine was not a family who sought such help. In any case, a shrink is unheard of in police culture. It's an admission of weakness, a loss of control, and in a police department, even if you're only a wannabe like me, the perception of control is everything. What even happened with shrinks? I'm a newly declared Psychology major, but that doesn't mean I have the vaguest understanding of an actual therapy session. I can only picture myself sitting stiffly on a chair, my alienation and self-consciousness presenting itself through monosyllabic answers to probing questions.

"Why not? Sometimes it helps." Kistner drops what's left of his cigarette, squashes it with a boot. "My wife and I saw one for a while."

Like the day of coffee with Amy, I'm being let in on little secrets. Kistner is opening up, revealing a softer side of himself, an alter ego. *Kisty*. He lingers a few more moments, soft beats of radio traffic floating up from our belts into the silence. Then he takes a long final gulp, crumples the Styrofoam, and tosses it into a trash can. "I better get going," he says.

He tells me to radio him anytime if I want to meet up for coffee, anything. I thank him, feeling flattered again. Even though I know he is doing this as a favor to Amy, it feels good to have another almost-friend, even if that almost-friend doesn't have any kind of an offering to actually help me. Apparently no one does.

Kistner climbs into his patrol car and glides away, disappearing into the darkness.

CHAPTER 18

August 17, 1984 12:15 a.m.

BACK AT MY APARTMENT, it's the same as every other night: I'm too afraid to sleep. I worry that if I shut my eyes a man will crawl out from under the bed or the corners of the closet and carve me into pieces.

I turn on every light, willing them to burn brighter, to protect me, to insulate me from the darkness and all it holds. I stare at the thin windows, fragile and brittle and as ineffectual as my own mind. Outside, every sound is a threat and I brace myself. It was my vigilance that saved me that night in the hall, so I know I can't let my guard down, not even for a second. Something percolates deep inside, a blistering start of unraveling, and it terrifies me how infirm I feel, like I will lose myself at any moment. I dig for the only self-help advice ever given to me by my mother: "Talk to yourself. You have to talk to yourself is all." She has never explained what this means, but I understand. It means, tell yourself good things. But that's where I get lost. I don't know what those good things might be anymore.

Kistner's voice rings inside my ears. *Statistically. Unlikely. Probably.* I'm still reeling from these meager words, stunned that a man of such strength and power had so little to offer. This was why I couldn't ask for help: no one had any real help to give. This knowledge, this realization that I am totally alone in this, that no one can make this better but me, has left me a little more shattered. Everything I thought was true in the world had been a lie. I'm not safe. No one is. Safety is a fairy tale, an illusion; safety is relative at best.

This weight. This burden. It is with me always and I am so tired. The simple act of inhaling and exhaling becomes difficult. I forget to do one or the other and the silence won't stop. The apartment is dead quiet. The silence grows bigger until I fear it will swallow me whole.

This mindset makes me so lonely my skin might fall off. The sound of silence overcomes me, opening up inside me like a wound. I am stretched over the edge, losing my grip, losing myself, and I want—no, need—to scream, a primal wail. I feel it rise up inside, consuming me, even as I fight to press it down. Hours pass and I float away, vanishing, drifting to that place where I have lost all control. I have read stories with the words, "Her body went numb." "Her chest hollowed." "She was weightless." A cliché or not, hollow is how it feels when it gets this bad. There is a coldness, an emptiness that is physical. Panic sets in. I have lost control of my mind. *Shhhh*, I tell myself. I stroke my face to try and calm myself down, plus there is no one here to see how weird this looks.

I lower myself down to the middle of the orange living room floor, pull the white phone onto my thighs, feel its weight like a cat in my lap comforting me. I pick up the receiver, stretch the cord taut, listen to the dial tone beckoning. I place it back in its cradle. It's far too late to call my mother, and it's John I need anyway. With every ounce of reserve in my body, I will myself not to call him. But unless John is near, I can't quiet my mind. I am desperate. I need him to fill my emptiness.

Maybe this is what it feels like to lapse into insanity. Maybe I do need to see someone. No one will know and it can't hurt, right? What have I got to lose?

Another hour. I can't take it anymore. I call John, beg him to come get me. He responds with silence then consents with a sigh. Moments later he arrives in his beat-up Audi, honks the horn. I step outside, cautious, even though John sits slumped behind the wheel twenty steps away. I open the passenger door, thrilled and grateful to be rescued. The moment I slam it closed behind me, John jerks the car into gear. He doesn't say a word.

CHAPTER 19

August 23, 1984

A S A STUDENT ENROLLED in the University of California, Berkeley, I'm entitled to certain health-care benefits, including mental health services. Attempting to take Kistner's advice, attempting to regain control of myself, I've made an appointment on campus with a UC-sponsored therapist.

Passing South Hall, tangled ivy clinging to its stately brick walls, I remember how proud I was standing next to it last spring. I'd served as part of the security detail for President François Mitterand's visit to campus, backing up the officers and Secret Service entourage as the French president walked through Sather Esplanade, past the Campanile, down the wide paved path to Wheeler Auditorium where he spoke to students and faculty. Before that day, I hadn't even known who François Mitterand was.

A woman ushers me into an office, points to a couch, tells me to make myself comfortable. I still haven't a clue of what goes down in this thing called therapy. I know I'm supposed to talk about my feelings, that the therapist listens, maybe says something in response to my words, and then I'm supposed to leave, feeling somehow better than when I walked in. It's this hope of feeling better somehow that I am forfeiting this hour, a precious slice of daylight time that should be spent studying Econ.

A man walks in. Tall, thin, with an already receding hairline though he can't be more than twenty-five years old, wearing a corduroy jacket with patches on the elbows and a kind, bland expression. I suddenly realize this man isn't an actual therapist, but a graduate student, and I can almost hear my mother's voice, *You get what you pay for.* I can tell from the uncertainty in his eyes that he doesn't have a much better understanding of this whole business than I do.

"So," he says, after an awkward length of silence, "What brings you here today?"

I'm skeptical. But I'm here. I've carved out this time and know I must go through with this session, lower my shield of swearing I'm *fine.* I am desperate for a solution to this mess that is my life, and to get it I have to be honest for once.

So I gasp out my story. All of it. Walking home. The footsteps. The attack. The do-I-scream-or-not-scream dilemma. The constant terror, the sleeplessness, the lack of friends. I explain how my fear of the dark is particularly difficult given my job, a job I need not only to stay in school but to keep one last thread of self-respect. I explain that my boyfriend is now my babysitter. I blurt out all of this through racking sobs, bawling so hard I can barely catch my breath, tears splashing hot and wet all over my face.

The man blinks rapidly, alarm flushing his broad face as he hands me tissues, his expression rearranging into what can only be described as pure helpless horror. I'm aware that I have never cried so hard in my life and as I continue to sob-speak, choking out words, I notice this man has physically pulled back in his chair, his discomfort rising, transforming into quiet panic as it slowly becomes apparent to each of us that he does not possess a single word that will make anything better for me.

Spent, I finally shut up. Still whimpering, I stare at him. Waiting. Waiting for him to say something to make this telling, this raw nakedness, this admission of utter helplessness worthwhile. I wait for him to fill my black gaping hole of need.

He doesn't.

He is well-meaning, but he and I both know that he is not equipped to help me. He chooses words, carefully, with difficulty. He speaks them, mouthfuls of small useless syllables. A promise I'll be okay, that this will get better. He is visibly worried and so I set about the task of reassuring him. I tell him, yes, he is correct, yes, of course I'll be okay. I thank him. I do this because I am a good girl, a polite girl, raised by my parents to put others' feelings ahead of my own.

I leave wrung out, exhausted, feeling foolish for even trying this thing called therapy, angry for wasting the hour, zapping my energy, rendering myself even more hopeless than before. How could I have thought talking about my terror could help? Talking about it, saying it aloud, only made it more real, gave it more power. All I wanted was to maintain a reasonable amount of order in my life, a modicum of control, and that possibility has been blasted. It isn't cathartic to tell someone my truth. It is terrifying, an affirmation of my deepest fear: that if I don't push this thing down it will overwhelm me. Destroy me.

Outside, I pause on a patch of grass. The Campanile tells me it's almost six. I pull a mirror from my backpack, attempt to repair my tear-mottled face. I take a deep breath, try to pull it together. I head toward the basement floor of Sproul Hall. I have a shift starting in ten minutes.

CHAPTER 20

August 27, 1984

I SENSE THE ATTITUDE inside the station: *We're cops, for fuck's sake, not chauffeurs! And if a person can't get her own self home safely after a shift, well then that person has no goddamn business wearing a uniform.*

Amy's directive that all females of UCPD are entitled to a ride home after a late-night shift has generated pushback from the officers. No one says this to me directly, but I hear sanitized versions of passive-aggressive complaints via Gene King.

"Well," he says, looking down at his scuffed black boots, an uncharacteristically sheepish tone to his voice, "Some of the guys are a little conflicted..."

Shit like that. Roger that, I think, 10-4. Message fucking received.

◆◆◆

IN THE LOCKER ROOM at the end of my shift, Sergeant McClaughlin is coming on for graveyard. She is my height, with thick bleached-blonde hair and an absurd amount of makeup. She's a well-meaning woman, relates well with students as she roams the campus on patrol, but with the makeup and the Carol Channing voice she has, she catches a fair amount of shit. In an interview, she was once described by one of the *Daily Californian*'s cop-despising student reporters as "wearing mace, a revolver, and a face full of Revlon as she sat across from me, politely not answering my questions." Part of me thinks McClaughlin asks for this abuse by flaunting her forty-something femininity in the testosterone-soaked environment of a police department. Part of me thinks, why the fuck not? Why not both? My own makeup choices had been criticized from time to time too, leaving me uncertain of what balance to strike, of how to simply *be*. But the fact remains that the more one asserts one's femininity, the more one risks not being taken seriously.

McClaughlin lowers herself beside me on the bench, concentrating on rolling thick wool socks over her feet to mid-calf, then lacing up her black combat boots. The boots are identical to mine, right down to their size-six shape.

"How you doing these days?" she says, eyes still focused on her laces.

I stop, stare inside my locker, then surprise myself with a rare moment of honesty. "Not so great."

I hadn't planned to share any kind of truth, but the moment the words escape I realize what a relief it is to admit this to someone other than John and that bewildered excuse for a therapist.

McClaughlin stands, latches up her utility belt, holsters her radio, night stick, flashlight, gun. She snaps on the radio, speaks into it. "Dispatch, S-16, Test."

The radio squawks back, Rachel's voice. "10-4, S-16. You're loud and clear."

Sergeant McClaughlin looks at me. "Hang tight for a minute while I run lineup? Then I'll give you a ride home."

I nod, exhaling a sigh of relief. I'm grateful not to have to beg a resentful officer for a ride. Most nights I am left waiting a minimum of thirty minutes, sometimes as long as an hour, for a ride home. This after an eight-hour shift of walking ten miles, of feeling the weight of having an exam the next day. Sometimes I gave up and walked home. Sure I was terrified—but what choice did I have? For someone to offer this up freely is a gift.

◆◆◆

THE PATROL CAR IS warm, the soft sounds of the radio and blinking lights on the console comforting. McClaughlin wastes no time. "Tell me anything. No shame. Doesn't go beyond us," she promises in her Carol Channing voice.

Staring out the window, unable to look at McClaughlin, I blurt the words out. "I'm afraid of the dark."

"No shame there." Her voice is matter of fact. "What else?"

Outside the car window, a homeless man presses his crotch into some bushes, taking a piss.

"I can't sleep. I'm afraid to close my eyes."

"Okay, good. What else?"

We're already on Blake Street, idling in front of my building.

"I'm scared to be alone in my apartment."

"Not a surprise. Very common. Want me to come inside?"

I turn away from the window then, search her face for sincerity. She really does wear a lot of makeup, I think. But this offer is just what I need and so I nod, feeling a surge of solace.

McClaughlin walks inside, all brisk business as she moves through the rooms of my apartment, snapping on every light. In a rush of words, I tell her everything: How I see the world through a new set of eyes; how my bedroom windows sit four feet from the ground facing a narrow alley where someone can stand for hours and not be seen; how those windows are cheap, thin, easy to pry open; how the living room windows are even lower, surrounded by bushes; how anyone can slide behind those bushes and break a window in seconds; how what happened before can happen again. I tell her I have learned the critical lesson that I am not safe and never have been; how I can't believe how stupid I had been; how I now see my vulnerability everywhere; how it isn't so much that I worry my attacker will come back to finish what he started, it's that I now understand *anyone* can break in *any* time, that I am filled with the certainty that if they can, they will.

McClaughlin holds my gaze, not speaking until I've finished unloading.

"Mind if I look around?" Without waiting for an answer, she opens every closet door, hands gripping the hanging clothes like she's frisking them. Then she gets down on hands and knees, whipping up the bedspread that hangs over the side of my bed, shining her flashlight beneath it.

She checks every side closet, behind every door, all without an ounce of mocking. "All clear!" she announces.

She looks ridiculous and I love her for this absurd indulgence, for knowing this is exactly what I need though I could never have asked for it. I know none of the men in the department would ever do something so silly, so necessary, so kind, and I think about all the missed opportunities for showing humanity, tenderness, empathy in this world. I think about how we as women need to take better care of each other.

With McClaughlin here I feel safe, whole even. But the feeling flutters away. I know she can't stay. I know that the terror and helplessness will return, surging back through my veins the second the door closes behind her, that while so selflessly well-intended, what McClaughlin has done for me is also futile.

I don't know it that night, but as she leaves me this is the first dawning, the first flicker of understanding that the worst part of being afraid is the shame that comes with it, how the shame fuels the fear further, stoking its power. It's the first flash of understanding that trauma is a singularly solitary experience, that even with help, the path to healing is a long, lonely journey, a road that can ultimately only be taken alone.

CHAPTER 21

I HAVE FOUR MORE distinct memories of that summer:
John leaves Berkeley to go to his parents' home in Novato for a few days. He says he wants to visit family before fall semester begins, but while this may be true he is equally motivated to escape me.

"I can't take care of you all the time," he had said more than once lately, exasperation bubbling to the surface.

In his absence, summer school finally ends, leaving me with a C in Econ, B minus in Anthropology. Nothing to celebrate except that it's over.

It's a Tuesday afternoon and I'm a little startled to realize I have nothing to do. No problem sets. No classes. No work. No boyfriend.

Because one of my many unrealized summer goals had been to **Get Tan!!** and since the Berkeley haze has for once dissolved and it feels like an honest-to-God summer day, I pack a towel and a novel and walk to the campus swimming pool, where simply by displaying my student ID I will get in free.

I lie on the sloping grass reading, glancing at the people around me. Next to me is a young woman with honey-colored hair and a huge melon-shaped belly. She hops in the pool and swims laps, the muscles of her arms flexing as she pulls herself through the water. She gets out smiling and sits down on her towel. She points to my book. "Are you an English major? My husband teaches in the English department."

"No," I say, returning her smile. "Psychology."

As she rubs her belly with oil, our conversation turns to her pregnancy. How far along? Hoping for a boy or a girl? Talking to this woman feels soothing. She laughs easily, and I think she is a person with whom I could be friends. The ease of connection is like a tonic, so simple and beautiful I want to cry. It's only in this moment that I realize how lonely I am, how my separateness has strangled me. Why can't I feel this connection more often? Why is it so hard to talk to people?

Here we are, both at a public swimming pool all alone, each of our lives in different phases. I find myself envying this woman, imagining how much better her life must be compared to mine. At the end of a day, she can look forward to her husband coming home, to sharing time together at the same table every night, his presence an unspoken promise. I imagine her cooking dinner tonight, how she'll use only organic vegetables. I imagine her sense of safety, the unquestioned belief in her own security.

Our encounter is brief. The woman leaves, waving goodbye, and I am alone again. I jump into the pool and on my back I float, weightless, staring up at the clear blue sky. I close my eyes, listening to the water lap against concrete edges, hear the percussion of liquid moving in and out of the filter as a melody. When you don't have music, everything sounds like music. Someone told me that once. But I can't remember who.

◆◆◆

THURSDAY NIGHT. STANDING BEFORE the bathroom mirror wrapped in a cocoon of white towel, getting ready to meet John for pizza, beers, and *Hill Street Blues*. Leaning over the sink, face to the mirror, stroking layers of mascara onto my lashes, the apartment goes pitch black and soundless. A single stunned second passes before I realize the power is out.

It's dark as Dwight Derby; I can't even see my hand in front of my face. I grope the walls of the bathroom to reach the bedroom, searching for light switches, flipping them hollowly back and forth. When they don't work, when they fail to do what I expect them to do, that's all it takes for the fright to unfurl. My mind fires its barrage of questions. Was this intentional? Will a man now crash through the pathetic excuse of a window to carve me up? It feels like someone is sitting on my chest, and I hear myself gasping for air. I realize I'm having some kind of panic attack but knowing this doesn't permit me to reclaim my own body.

I make it to the front door, pause for one dreadful moment, open it. The rest of the building is black. I hear another tenant clunking clumsily upstairs, so I slam my door shut again. Relief washes over me knowing this is not about me, that I'm not alone in this. It's just a power outage, I tell myself. It's okay, it's just something that happens, it's no big deal. I start to breathe more normally.

I stun myself by discovering I have two small candles in the kitchen cupboard, amaze myself further to learn I also have matches. I light the candles, set them on the bathroom sink, try to finish my makeup. The contrast of dead quiet to the voice of Boy George floating from the clock radio moments ago is striking, and the silence makes me brittle as the flicker of flames cast eerie shadows in the darkness. With every move I make the light bounces, reflecting the lunge of a body in the shower curtain behind me. My breath turns jagged again. As the tears come, streaking my cheeks with the mascara I applied so carefully, it's not lost on me that I have become a woman who is literally afraid of her own shadow.

◆◆◆

SATURDAY MORNING. I HAVE John's rust-dappled Audi and it feels like a prize. I can go to the grocery store without the limitation of purchasing only so much as I can carry the eight blocks back to Blake Street. If I want, I can buy a ten-pound sack of potatoes, a giant box of laundry detergent, a twelve-pack of Coke, infinite cans of Campbell's tomato soup. The simple luxury of this makes me giddy as I drive to the Park N Shop at the corner of Telegraph Avenue and Derby Street.

Pushing my cart up and down the aisles, I take my time, loading items that delight me: a gallon of milk, a thirty-two-roll pack of toilet paper, four different boxes of cereal.

As I steer toward check out, I notice a man walking among the other shoppers. He grips a loaf of Wonder Bread and a carton of orange juice.

I know this person, know I should say hello, but I can't quite place him. I pause, stare, trying to recall who he is. A former teaching assistant? But which class?

Then his eyes meet mine.

Those eyes.

Those blue, blue eyes. Holding mine.

Just as they had in the hallway.

A swift chain of explosions go off in my brain and a jolt passes between us as we freeze, each set of eyes widening as our minds register recognition, a moment that interrupts the beats of my heart. All of the oxygen has left the store. For a few stunned moments we stand there, motionless in the bright fluorescent aisle of Park N Shop, other shoppers pushing past, oblivious to us, of all that we are to one another.

He snaps out of it first, averting his eyes, pivoting, fleeing to the checkout lane at the farthest edge of the store. His flight feels familiar, like the escape triggered by my screams. I turn then also, forcing my body to make its way to a check-out stand on the opposite end of the store. My hands shake as I remove the items from my cart, placing them on the conveyer belt.

Focusing my mind on this simple task takes tremendous effort. It feels surreal, so strange to think of him engaging in a task as mundane as grocery shopping. But why the surprise? We are both human, both animals, both moved by the need to feed ourselves. Attackers have to eat too. But Wonder Bread and orange juice? *I* eat Wonder Bread. *I* drink orange juice. And what's the proper social protocol for such an encounter? Did we handle that well?

I take deep breaths through my nose, releasing them through my mouth. *Inhale. Exhale. Inhale. Exhale.* Spots flicker across my eyes, and I hold the counter to steady myself. I manage to pay, then make my way back out into the cool morning air. I climb into the safety of John's car, pushing down the locks on the doors. My eyes dart around the parking lot, searching for my assailant. But he is gone.

◆◆◆

JOHN AND I GO to the movies. I'd wanted to see *The Hotel New Hampshire*. But on the screen is the scene of Frannie's rape. It hadn't been this vivid in the book, had it? It goes on too long—longer than I can take. I can't watch anymore. I hit John on the shoulder.

"I can't do this," I say. I stand, stumble over the legs of perturbed moviegoers, march up the aisle in a sweat, once again leaving my boyfriend with no choice but to follow.

FALL SEMESTER
1984

CHAPTER 22

September 7, 1984

I OPEN THE *DAILY CALIFORNIAN* and there is the article.

"Females Encouraged to Join Police Aide Program"
By Modesto Fernandez, Staff Writer

It's late, on the kind of night when you'd rather not walk home alone. You're kicking yourself for not leaving with the others. What do you do?

If you're on campus you can call 642-WALK and request an escort. Among the UC police aides who could come to the rescue is Karen Thomas. The 105-pound, 5-foot-2 junior is one of three female student aides working for the UC police.

She is dressed like a cop: khaki uniform, black leather utility belt with a mag flashlight and a radio, which is her electronic link to the university police. Aides don't carry guns or clubs.

"Aides have a nonconfrontational job," Thomas says. "Their primary concerns are service and safety."

The university police are looking for a few more good students like Thomas, but today is the last day to apply to be a police aide.

Aides are also responsible for the bicycle bureau, crime prevention programs, and 'high visibility' patrols. The thirty-member unit is the eyes and ears of the police.

"We're a liaison between the police and the campus community," Thomas said.

An aide gets sixty hours of training in general first aid and CPR, radio procedures, and report writing.

Thomas said she got into the job because she likes to help people and it provides flexible hours to work around her class schedule. Like many aides, Thomas doesn't plan for a career in law enforcement, but the experience can be very helpful for those who do…

Thomas said women are still often surprised and uncomfortable when she comes to "rescue" them.

The UC police strongly encourage women to join the program.

◆◆◆

WHAT A CROCK OF *shit*, I think. But I cut out the article anyway, knowing it will impress my mother to see my name in a newspaper, even just a campus rag. The *Daily Californian* occasionally ran a piece on the aide program and this time I had been the subject. Because the *Daily Cal* loathed all things law enforcement, I had entered the interview with trepidation. During the interview, I'd felt exposed watching the student reporter scribble hard on his long rectangle of a notepad, waiting on edge for the questions about my fear of the dark, my own assault as evidence of my inability to protect others. But his questions hinted only at motivations rooted in feminism. I was one of only three female aides. Did I feel oppressed working in a male-dominated profession? Yes, I had answered. It's always a challenge to be female in a male-dominated profession. But with that I had shrugged. I had nothing more to add. The reporter's face registered disappointment. Did I derive satisfaction in stymieing male aggressors whose mere existence steals women's freedom to move about? Yes, I had answered, pandering further. I enjoyed the women-helping-women aspect of the job. Again I failed to elaborate. What else was there to say?

In truth, I had never given it much thought. Working at the department satisfied my need to feel I belonged somewhere. But the reporter hadn't asked about my desire to belong, and even if he had I wouldn't have admitted that need.

Sometimes there just isn't enough room for the truth.

CHAPTER 23

October 10, 1984

CYNDI LAUPER WAKES ME at 7:00 a.m. *"Girls just wanna have fu-hun! Girls just wanna have fun. They just wanna! They just wanna!"* I snap the clock radio off before it can wake my roommate, Kim, then sit in silence. My shift last night stretched nearly to midnight and I am bone weary. I shower, silently search Kim's side of the closet for something respectable to wear. I am due at the district attorney's office at eight thirty.

Stepping out into the gray morning, I learn the chill of fall has set in and hug my coat tight against my body. I trudge alone down the sidewalk toward Shattuck Avenue. The streets are quiet, the sun struggling to find its way through the fog. I pause at Fulton & Parker Streets, where I identified my attacker, absorbing how different it looks in the ashen light of morning.

A subpoena had arrived in my mailbox alongside a letter from my mother two weeks earlier. I showed it to John. Piece of cake, he told me. It's part of the process, you'll do great. No one knows about this hearing but John. I wanted him to come with me but didn't dare ask. I haven't told anyone at work because my assault has finally disappeared from the landscape of conversation and

I'm not about to remind them. I am sick of being known as *The One Who Got Herself Attacked*. So I am going to the hearing alone.

It's farther to the courthouse than I thought. It takes me nearly forty minutes to get there and blisters rise on the backs of my heels from the black low-heeled pumps I borrowed from Kim. I arrive at the Berkeley branch of the Alameda County District Attorney's Office barely on time.

The county building is outdated, and the halls smell dusty, old, like somebody's grandmother. On a bench outside a courtroom, I speak with a frazzled deputy DA for less than five minutes. She is young, not even thirty. She explains that I have been subpoenaed to testify at the preliminary hearing in the case of the People of the State of California versus Peter David Kostenka. My assailant has been charged with Penal Code sections 236 and 245, false imprisonment and assault with a deadly weapon. The theme of the defense will be misidentification, that Mr. Kostenka is an innocent man who had simply been in the wrong place at the wrong time. The knife he carried, though identical to the one I described to Berkeley PD, was like a million other knives, available for purchase at any sporting goods store in the country.

I can't make sense of the false imprisonment charge, but I understand assault with a deadly weapon. I like it. It sounds serious. The words of this crime validate me; they mean I am not weak. This charge says there's a reason I'm afraid of the dark, a reason I can't sleep unless John agrees to tuck his body beside mine.

The DA disappears inside the courtroom and I remain on the bench and wait. Down the hall I see Sergeant Westinhoff. She looks straight through me without a hint of recognition. The bailiff calls her name, and she too enters the courtroom.

Fifteen minutes later, another bailiff opens the door and calls my name as Sergeant Westinhoff leaves. He pushes open the swiveling gate to the well of the courtroom and motions for me to enter. The young DA stands at the table next to the empty jury box, looking down at the notes on her yellow legal pad. My attacker sits at the opposite table with a mustached dark-haired man, each of them wearing suits the color of charcoal. A clerk busies herself with paperwork, seemingly unaware of my existence. The judge is a forty-something woman with frizzy red hair. She wears fat dangling peacock feather earrings that brush the shoulders of her black robe. The bailiff points to the witness stand. "Please be seated."

That's when my heart starts to pound.

The feathers hanging from her ear lobes make it difficult to take her seriously, but the judge offers me a kind smile as I settle into the witness chair. A smile, such a simple gesture, a small act of human kindness probably taken for granted in other circumstances, but which in this moment fortifies me. I raise my right hand and swear to tell the truth, the whole truth, so help me God.

The questions from the DA are simple, open-ended. What was I doing on July 19, 1984 at approximately 11:40 p.m.? From where was I coming? What happened next? She cuts me off from time to time to flesh out details. What did the man look like? How far away was he when I first saw him? And then what happened? Is the man who attacked you sitting here in the courtroom today?

The hearing feels mechanical. There is no talk of intent, no speculation concerning why this man at the defense table committed acts satisfying the elements of Penal Code sections 236 and 245, no concern that these acts were a prelude to a more shattering violence. That is not what these proceedings are about. It dawns on me that this is just another day in court for these people, concerning a minor incident. No blood. No rape. No death. Just a little knife attack. A felony, sure, but no big deal in the grand scheme of things.

In twenty minutes it's over. With my testimony, this preliminary hearing has apparently concluded. I start to step down but the judge stops me. "You can stay put."

The judge directs herself to the DA. "Madam Prosecutor, I don't see the false imprisonment charge here. But there is sufficient evidence to hold the defendant to answer on the assault with a deadly weapon. Readiness conference April fifth. Jury trial May first." She slaps a file closed, stands up, and steps down from the bench. She leaves this pale-haired, orange-juice drinking man in his gray suit wedged inside my life.

No one smoothes my hair or coos, *Good job, baby. Let's go home.* My mother would do that if she were here, brushing my temples with her long dry fingers, wouldn't she?

Outside the courtroom, the DA tells me her office will be in touch. Then she too disappears, leaving me in the empty hallway. She doesn't thank me for coming, doesn't acknowledge that I missed class to be here. She doesn't say she's sorry, doesn't tell me I'm brave, doesn't tell me everything will be okay. I am not special. I am just the victim. One among hundreds of thousands.

I walk back home, blisters now the size of quarters on my heels, and try to shift focus back to school. I have reading to do. I can't get behind. Midterms are coming. But I am suddenly so, so tired.

I sleepwalk through another day until it finally tapers off into darkness. That night, John and I sleep together in his twin bed. It's crowded but I don't mind. Ronald Reagan stares down at us from the wall like a voyeur, but under his gaze, pressed between the wall and the warmth of John's body, I know that at least for now I am safe.

CHAPTER 24

November 1, 1984

I AM TRYING (AGAIN) to develop the habit of caring about what's happening in the world, to get outside of my own head, to identify with events far from my little Berzerkley universe. I've learned it's fashionable to understand international affairs, unattractive to say, "The *what's*?" when someone refers to the Contras in Nicaragua, so instead of merely glancing at headlines I start reading articles. I sit at Café Roma across from Boalt Hall, the law school I dream of attending, though unless I get my grades up it's a fantasy likely to go unfulfilled. I'm drinking a latte, nibbling a blueberry muffin, reading the details of Indira Gandhi's assassination, how she was gunned down by members of her own security team.

I am an ignorant baby, a self-absorbed little girl-child who knows virtually nothing about this woman, yet the news feels unspeakably sad. I feel the tragic injustice at my core. As the first bullet hit, I wonder if she had the sick sensation of realization, of stunned bewilderment, followed by the same understanding I'd had. *This is happening.* Somewhere deep within my body a somber certainty imbeds itself, a certainty that I will never understand this world and the beings who inhabit it.

Days later, Ronald Reagan sweeps almost every state, beating Walter Mondale by a landslide, and the chance for a female vice president, a woman as second-in-command of the most powerful country in the free world, has vanished. But there is something else in the news. Something closer to home.

On November 4, 1984, UC Berkeley sophomore Roberta "Bibi" Lee goes missing. Her disappearance is all over the *Daily Californian*, the *San Francisco Chronicle*, and every other Bay Area newspaper. Bibi Lee, her boyfriend, Bradley Page, and their friend Robin Shaw went jogging together in the Redwood Regional Park in the Oakland hills. During the run, Bibi got separated from Bradley and Robin and disappeared. Her friends assumed she had returned home to the Northside Co-op where they all lived, but when she failed to turn up hours later, her roommate called the Berkeley police.

In the days to follow, the Contra Costa Search and Rescue Unit scours the area where Bibi was last seen. Thirty-seven people and five bloodhounds search until midnight but find nothing. Bradley Page and others form "The Friends of Bibi Lee," plastering posters of Bibi's face all over campus and the East Bay. They establish a headquarters in a donated apartment, organizing a phone bank to receive leads. I am hooked by the pointed intimacy of the fliers I see everywhere: "Imagine if she was your roommate, your classmate, your friend, your sister, your lover." Next to these words is an image of Bibi, a young, pretty, half-smiling Asian girl. There is a plea to contact the police with relevant information and Bibi's father, an MIT professor, has posted a $5,000 reward for information leading to her recovery.

Bibi Lee's disappearance is a grim, thrilling reminder of all that could go wrong in the world. But instead of shielding myself, I am riveted, a rubbernecker at a car accident, trying to piece together as much information as I can, just as I had been in the weeks following my attack. It isn't only the daily drama of an unfolding story, an entire campus, city, and region waiting, breath sucked in, for any piece of news. It's that I feel deep compassion for this woman, a kinship of sorts. Like the fliers implore, I do imagine. I wonder whether she's alive, whether she's been raped, tortured, held captive in some dark damp basement. I think of the family, friends, and boyfriend left behind. I imagine myself as her. Had I disappeared that July night, how would my flier have read?

Girl Missing. Nineteen years old. Dishwater blonde. 5'2." Ass pudgy from too much pizza and beer. Naïve as hell but great at pretending.

◆◆◆

No one would have even known I'd gone missing until I failed to show for a shift. If I disappeared, Amy and John would take action, a personal cops-have-each-others-backs outreach to Bay Area police departments. But eventually they would have no choice but to shrug their shoulders, give up, return to the vagaries of everyday life. What else could they do? And my family wouldn't post a $5,000 reward. It would never occur to them, even if they had that kind of money. My mother would break down, the mysterious pink welts arriving on her arms and chest, fueling helpless misery. My father would withdraw, go silent, shut down, incapable of finding words. My mother's mother would call, asking, "Any news?" stoking the fire of my parents' anxiety.

◆◆◆

I can hear the ring of the phone on the wall next to the stove, see my mother jumping with excitement when it stops after the single ring, moving to the sink to wash whatever she is cooking from her hands: flour from the beginnings of a cherry pie crust, shredded cheddar from the scalloped potatoes au gratin, maybe fat from the edge of a roast still lingering on her fingertips after she cut the strings. She will dial my number, which she knows by heart, even though it just changed two months ago. Then my own phone rings.

"Hi, Mom," I say.

I envision her settling into a chair at the kitchen counter, the place I had perched every Sunday, finishing homework, looking up intermittently to watch her as she moved about the kitchen, pausing to take long drags from the Pall Mall sitting in a glass ashtray next to the stove.

We engage in our usual small talk. I try to share as much as I can of my life, but the suitable topics are limited. I speak of John, venture to share that he's been irritated at my clinginess lately.

"Well, let him call you. You don't call him."

It's the same advice she'd given me in high school. Valid counsel if you think about it.

I know that soon she will boil green beans, place biscuits in the oven, conjure brown gravy from the grease drippings of a roast. I would kill for a home-cooked meal right now, not only for the thrill of watching butter melt on a biscuit or even the sensation of the fat of the roast in my mouth, but for the simple comfort of the ritual, of sitting down to a properly set table with napkins, flanked by my mother and father.

I ask my mom if the San Diego newspapers have reported on the Bibi Lee story.

"Who?" she says.

"Nothing, never mind. How's Salty?"

Our conversation feels unsatisfying. Maybe it's the phone. Maybe it's that the whole thing is a lie. Do we ever really know the people we love? Do mothers know their daughters? Do daughters know their mothers? I have extracted as many details as she is willing to give about herself and yet still there remains a chasm, a vast distance between us. I hear exhaustion in my voice. My mother hears it too.

"Don't overdo," she says, another one of her consistent directives.

I promise her I won't.

◆◆◆

I FIND MYSELF COMPARING Bibi's parents to my own. My assault underscored a suspicion that had begun to develop in the first months of trying so desperately to acclimate to my new life at UC Berkeley, a slow, seeping understanding that my parents were fallible, misinformed even, that we fell on a lower socioeconomic rung than I had believed while growing up. Such a notion was becoming harder to ignore and its lurking inside the phone line on our weekly calls unnerved me. I needed guidance, protection, assurance. I loved my mother and father deeply, but also knew I could not expect these things from them. I flinched with the guilt of my betrayal in wanting them to be different, in wanting them to give me the things they could never bestow.

A realization begins to settle over me like a layer of dust, an unspoken longing I'd had more than once before, a yearning I couldn't even admit to myself, a wish for different parents. I hungered for the take-charge, confident mother who would remove my burdens, make all of it go away. I yearned for the powerful father who could afford to rescue me from my apartment, who could pick me up and put me someplace better, someplace with sunlight, who could shower me with cash so I could while away my hours at the San Francisco Esprit outlet like the sorority girls I loathed for everything they had and I didn't.

But I brush these thoughts away like so many others. It shames me too much to take these thoughts out and examine them, to allow myself to acknowledge their existence, even for an instant.

◆◆◆

TWO WEEKS PASS AND no one hears from Bibi. A witness claims to have seen a white man and Asian woman struggling near the Warren Freeway shortly after her disappearance. The woman wore jogging shorts and a long-sleeved T-shirt—precisely what Page and Shaw described Lee as wearing when she was last seen. The witness described the man as in his mid-forties, six feet tall, 250 pounds with a big beer belly, and unkempt curly hair. He had been pulling the woman up a slope toward a van parked on the street.

The eyewitness account is reenacted in a video distributed to law enforcement and media outlets. The hope is that it will generate more witnesses, more clues. I watch it at the station, feel the clench in my stomach as the man grabs the girl playing Bibi, wrapping his big arms around her petite body. I watch her struggle, watch the defeat register on her face as he stuffs her into the van. The bond I feel with Bibi grows stronger. She stays with me as I walk the campus, a reminder that anything can happen at any time, that the threat of danger is always present, a cruel reminder that I had been lucky, that luck sometimes runs out.

◆◆◆

THEN, ON DECEMBER 11, 1984, another photo of Roberta "Bibi" Lee appears on the front page of the *San Francisco Chronicle*. But what sends a current through my body is the headline: Bibi's boyfriend has been arrested:

Bradley Page, twenty-four, Berkeley, was arrested Monday night for the slaying of Roberta "Bibi" Lee, twenty-one. On

December 9, 1984, Bibi Lee's body was found in the Oakland hills approximately seven hundred feet from where she was last seen November 4. The back of her skull had been fractured. The decomposed body, covered with brush and dirt, was discovered by a searcher with a specially trained dog.

The next day Page was questioned by Berkeley police and confessed he had struck Bibi and left her unconscious in the woods. He admitted he had gone back to the scene that night, where he had sex with Bibi's dead body, then buried her using a hubcap from his car. But immediately Page recanted, claiming his confession was the product of police coercion and his own guilt and confusion.

Reading, I am breathless. This world. This *world*. How it never ceases to astonish. Just when we think we have an inkling of understanding, that we have it sort of figured out, at least enough to maybe get by, this world pulls a fast one, turns us upside down, shows us how wrong we are about everything, how badly we have misjudged.

CHAPTER 25

December 19, 1984

I FLY HOME FOR Christmas. I haven't been home since spring break, since *before*.

It's the longest stretch of time I've ever been away from home and I see the neighborhood with new eyes. It's shabbier than I remember. Gangs have infiltrated the apartment buildings down the hill from our house on Hugh Street and all the houses, my parents' included, look worn down, tired. I see with starkness what has changed inside as well: my father's weight gain, my mother's graying hair, the thin layer of dust infiltrating the home my mother has always kept devotedly clean. My fresh point of view reminds me that my mother and father haven't seen or felt any of the things I have seen and felt in these last months. They haven't read the books I've read, haven't endured the sleepless vigilance, haven't sworn in court to tell the truth. It makes us different, feels like the beginning of us becoming separate.

I kiss my mother hello, feeling the bones beneath her skin as I hold her shoulders. I hug my father, bury my hand in the fur of Salty's neck as he thumps his tail on the entryway carpet. Growing up in this house, I had been the small, wispy, white-haired object of protection. I loved my mother fiercely, worriedly. It had been my job to make her happy, but somewhere inside I understood I was failing miserably. I left this house to live, to see new things, to have new experiences, to escape my mother's watchful anxiety. Security wasn't a desire when I left. But coming home now, I realize safety is all I want. I don't want new experiences anymore. I long to know what's going to happen next. I crave only certainty.

Night comes and I find myself contemplating honesty, something that had always been used sparingly in our household—most notably the revelation that the woman I had been raised to believe was my mother's sister, the woman I had grown up calling Aunt Dot, was in fact my mother's mother, a truth shared only days before I left to begin my freshman year at Berkeley.

I'm thinking about honesty because now I have a secret, a secret I am doing a lousy job of keeping. It's dark out and even in the safety of my parents' home, my fear is back. It makes no sense. This isn't Blake Street. The windows are thick, high off the ground. No one will hurt us here. No one will hurt me. Still, I'm afraid, and the fact that I'm afraid here rattles me all over again, tells me I am losing my mind. I try to think of what lie I can tell my mother, what innocuous story can explain why her now twenty-year-old daughter can't go to sleep without the light on. My mother remains hypervigilant in her observations of me and my fear of the dark has not gone unnoticed. She leaves the light on in the room we called the sewing room, the small spare bedroom across the hall from mine. My mother had done the same thing when I was a child, leaving the light on so it seemed she was there or had only stepped away and would be right back. It calmed me as a child. Now it isn't enough.

◆◆◆

On December 21, 1984, Prince Harry is christened at Buckingham Palace and, like his brother and other royal children before him, he wears Queen Victoria's Honiton silk-and-lace christening robe. I know this because I can't sleep and have nothing to do but read the newspaper.

The next day, I move through the house like a gray-faced zombie. A high school friend calls. A group is going out to see Arnold Schwarzenegger's new movie *The Terminator*. Do I want to go?

I do not. I hang up, return to my room, and spend the remainder of the day listening to Madonna, singing along under my breath, wishing John would call. *Gonna give you all my love, boy. My fear is fading fast.*

◆◆◆

Night returns. I thought that with my exhaustion sleep would come easily, but with the darkness comes the fear. Lying there, fighting panic, I recall the terror I felt as a child in this same bedroom, tucked inside these same butterfly sheets. I hadn't been afraid of the dark as a young child, but the hysteria kicked in when I was ten and *The Exorcist* came out. I didn't even see the movie. A black-and-white photo of Linda Blair in *TigerBeat* and an enthusiastic description of a few key plot points from an imaginative friend were enough. This friend emphasized the movie was based on a true story and that was what got me. If this lurid thing had happened to someone else, it could easily happen to me. I convinced myself that I too was possessed by Satan, a truth made painfully clear in the dark shadows of my bedroom. Night after night, I cried and crowded into my mother's twin bed while my father snored, oblivious, in his own bed three feet away. I couldn't tell my mother what was wrong, so I kept my secret to myself. I was simultaneously terrified and riddled with shame for being afraid of the dark. Finally I realized I could sleep, but only with a light on.

Maybe all of this is on my mother's mind as well because when I get up to guzzle a glass of wine, she is lingering in the kitchen.

She is smoking like always. She will pretend to quit a few years later, sneaking out to the backyard for furtive drags, assuming no one notices, that no one ever finds the crumpled gold Pall Mall package in her sweater pocket or smells it on her. I watch her take a long puff, exhaling smoke through both nostrils like a bull. I sense my mother knows I have bad news, she only doesn't know what magnitude of bad. She always had a sixth sense for sniffing out tragedy. Maybe it was because she searched for the worst until she found it. But I understood. She just wanted to prepare me. She knew what I did not yet know, that the world would dish out calamities in forms I couldn't even fathom. I wonder what catastrophe she imagines now. Pregnancy? Drugs? I've flunked out of school? I need a cash infusion she cannot possibly supply? Or maybe she has guessed spot-on.

I'm not certain why I don't want to tell her. Perhaps it's still the dread of what she will say. I don't want her to have been right all along, her worst imaginings proving true. In my first days at Berkeley, my parents accompanied me, awkward and uncomfortable among students, homeless people, kids with purple mohawks, one man shoving a half-crushed Styrofoam cup at my mother like a weapon. "Give me a quarter for a cup of coffee!" he yelled. Escaping inside the Bank of America on Telegraph Avenue where I opened my first checking account, cosigned by my mother since I was only seventeen, my mother gripped my hand so hard it hurt and leaned in to my ear, speaking through clenched teeth in her anxiety-laced whisper, "I don't want to leave you here!"

If I had squeezed back, said, "I don't want you to leave me here either!" I could have easily convinced my parents to leave, tires squealing, abandoning the promise of an education from a high-ranking school, a public university we could actually scrape by to afford.

We stand, silent, in the glow of the dimmed kitchen light, an orange-gold flush eerily similar to the gleam cast by the light fixture in the hallway to my Blake Street apartment. My father is in the next room, stretched out in his faux-leather recliner, watching *Johnny Carson* at full volume. My mother moves toward me but hesitates. She can't risk his hearing. My father does not hear bad news until it becomes absolutely necessary to include him.

My mother tries to whisper, but it comes out a hiss, an accusation. "*What's going on?*"

Now it's my turn to falter. I worry she won't be able to handle what I have to tell her, that she will say the wrong thing, something that will break me.

Finally, in hushed tones at the white-tile kitchen counter, I tell her. I strive to keep my voice level, my breath steady. She is quiet, sucking her cigarette down to a fiery nub. As I speak the words I have an almost surreal hyper-sense of my surroundings, like I had during the attack. We stand inches from the place where, thirteen and sick of drying the dinner dishes every night, I shoved her. I'm positioned exactly where I stood when my mother confessed that the woman I had been raised to believe was my aunt was in fact my grandmother.

I finish.

To her credit, my mother doesn't ask the question I have expected her to ask: *Why in the Sam holy hell were you walking home alone up there at eleven thirty at night?* If she had asked that question, if she had suggested all of this was my own goddamn fault, I would have crumbled.

What else she doesn't say: *Everything will be all right.* Because my mother is not a liar. Instead she simply asks if I am okay. I tell her, yes, I'm having trouble sleeping is all. This is untrue, but I can't bear to tell her any more. I don't even know how to describe the distress that I feel, the war raging inside the prison of my mind.

Afterward, though my burden remains, I feel better. I kiss my mother goodnight and return to bed. She pretends to busy herself in the sewing room across from my bedroom, though she hasn't sewn anything in years and has no possible need to be in there. It is just like when I was ten, too old to be so frightened of the darkness, and my mother came to my aid in the only way she knew how.

1985

CHAPTER 26

A FTER THAT NIGHT IN the kitchen, we never really discuss it
again. Occasionally my mother lobs an open-ended question
in my direction, something like, "You sleeping okay?" "You still
feeling scared?" "Whatever happened with that weirdo?" And
I will quickly shut her down, allowing only a mumbled response.
Yeah, yeah, I am. No, I'm doing okay. I don't know, haven't heard a
thing. And that will be it. The topic made both of us uncomfortable,
and in her I sense a fear of dredging up something painful for me,
a concern right on target. I remain fragile, knowing I can easily
brush up against something to trigger my complete unraveling,
a scrape as visceral and real as when the skin of my back rubbed
against the raw wall of that bronze-lit hallway.

◆◆◆

ON JANUARY 4, 1985, as I go about the business of settling in for
a new semester, the Alameda County Superior Court hears a
motion brought pursuant to California Penal Code Section 995
by my assailant's defense lawyer. The feather-earringed judge got
it wrong, he argues. There was insufficient evidence presented at

the preliminary hearing to hold the defendant to answer for the crime of assaulting Karen Thomas with a deadly weapon: the case must be dismissed.

The court denies the motion.

On February 22, 1985, the court hears another motion, a motion to suppress evidence. My attacker's lawyer argues that his client was illegally detained by Berkeley PD and because the detention was illegal, the subsequent identification of his client by Karen Thomas is tainted and the evidence of that witness identification must be suppressed, kept out of evidence. He also argues that Berkeley PD's failure to preserve the recording of my 911 call has prejudiced his client's ability to defend himself, that because of this failure to preserve the tape, all other evidence must be suppressed.

The court denies this motion as well. Trial is set for March 19, 1985. Later, at the request of the defense, trial is delayed to June 5, 1985. Then it's delayed yet again, to September 10, 1985.

I know nothing of any of this. I know nothing because no one in the district attorney's office bothers to tell me. I know nothing because I lack the sense to ask.

CHAPTER 27

FALL AGAIN, MY LAST semester of school. The yearlong Blake Street lease finally ends, and I find a new place to live at the corner of Haste and Dana Streets, a house I walked past on my route home the night of my attack. The house is run by religious fanatics who refuse to allow any male to cross its threshold. Not John, not my father. There is no kitchen. I share a microwave in the landing of the stairwell with eight other women. We wash our dishes in the sink of the bathroom we all share. It's perfect. My room is on the second floor where plenty of sunlight streams through the window, a space high up off the ground, and I finally feel safe. The carpet is another burnt-orange travesty, but in this light it looks different. In the beams of sunshine, it's the color of hope. The other women in this house stay tucked away inside their rooms, studying like I am so it's quiet, but not the eerie silence of Blake Street. I have a nineteen-inch TV now, a lavish gift from my parents, and sometimes on Friday nights I watch *Dallas* and *Miami Vice* while eating Häagen-Dazs, and this small simple pleasure feels like heaven.

I feel myself shaking off the trauma and start to resemble a normal college student again. My depression lifts. I'm finally able to sleep alone again and I do. Without the suffocating need, my relationship with John deepens. I have my eyes on the exit, focused on the Law School Admissions Test, on working my ass off to pull up my GPA. It's my last chance to boost my grades so I can have a chance of getting into a decent law school. I've surprised myself. I am genuinely interested in policy making and politics. I want to become a prosecutor, to put away bad guys, and then, who knows? Run for office? Become a judge? All of this will of course occur alongside John, who, I know with certainty now, I will marry. For the first time since my attack I feel like I'm doing something more than simply surviving my days.

CHAPTER 28

September 5, 1985

I'M SITTING AT THE IBM Selectric in Amy's office, typing my paper for Psych 153, an aptly titled course: Stress and Adjustment. John putters around the desk beside me. He's in uniform, about to start a shift, and his top button is open, allowing me a glimpse of the dark chest hair sprouting out at his neck. It's a tease to me, a peek of his body, and I feel something stir inside like a reflex.

Amy flips through a magazine, studying aerial photos from Madonna's wedding to Sean Penn. When the phone rings, she answers in her typically bright tone, then falls quiet, listening. Her gaze shifts to me.

"Put him through, she's right here." A pause. "Detective?" she asks. "Hold on." Amy stands, hands me the phone, tells me to take her chair. "It's for you."

The man on the phone is curt. "Karen Thomas?"

"Yes?"

"This is Detective Brisgaard. Alameda County DA's office." His voice is sharp, cocky, and rude. A typical law enforcement type. "You need to be at court next Tuesday, eight thirty a.m. for jury trial."

A jolt of panic lurches through me as I think of my schedule, my page-long to-do list. "I can't do that. I have class then."

He tells me in so many words that this is my tough shit.

"You need a ride?" he asks.

"No."

"You got a car?"

"No."

"No?" He chuckles. Derisive. "Then how you gonna get there?" Another little laugh. I am a silly little girl.

"I'll walk, like I did last time." I say this in my pissiest voice. This is the only way I know how to stand up to this man.

He laughs again, heavier this time. "You're gonna walk. From Berkeley? All the way to Lake Merritt?"

"What?"

"The trial's at the Oakland courthouse."

"Oh," I say, stupidly.

"I'll come get ya."

"No." My voice is as firm as I can muster. I don't want this asshole doing me any favors. I will figure this out for myself.

"Well," he hesitates, "you gotta be there on time."

"I will be!" I slam down the phone and scream at the wall. "Fuck!"

Amy and John shoot each other wary looks. John asks what's wrong, but I ignore him, like bothering to respond to his question will put me out as much as this surprise assignment to attend a trial, to be the star witness, the star victim. I pace back and forth and fume. I don't have time for this shit. I'm taking five classes so I can graduate early, working twenty-five hours a week. All I want is to focus on school, and now I'll have to miss at least a full day of class. I can't fathom the injustice in my schedule having no weight whatsoever. I have been randomly assigned to this investigator, this prosecutor, this trial date. I don't get to choose. No one cares what I want, no one cares what I need. What I need doesn't matter.

Amy and John stare at me, their expressions telling me I look crazed, that they're unsure what to say. I'm unsure too. So I do what I always do when I feel like I'm being bulldozed, pushed around, taken advantage of, yet don't know how to properly defend myself. I rush out of the station, move inside a slice of the cold Berkeley sun, and I cry.

CHAPTER 29

September 10, 1985, Oakland, California

DEPUTY DISTRICT ATTORNEY WILLA Esposito is small, compact, with olive-toned skin and dark bright eyes. Her chestnut hair is short, neat, professional. She is animated, confident, and tolerates no bullshit. She is precisely the woman I want to be but am not.

Willa spends a handful of minutes with me, asking questions, brushing over mine. I sit on a hard wooden bench in the lobby of her office, shifting my weight, trying to get comfortable and failing. I'm startled to learn that I won't see her again before trial begins. I am free to go for now but I'm to wait by the phone for Detective Brisgaard's call. He will advise what courtroom we are assigned to, and I will then need to wait outside that room until I'm told to enter. Willa reminds me that I am not to speak to anyone about the case. Then she is gone. For the preliminary hearing I'd received five minutes of prep time, and now, for the trial, I've received less than ten. It feels like this should take longer, that this should matter more, but maybe it only matters to me.

◆◆◆

LATER THAT DAY, THE case of the People vs. Peter David Kostenka is assigned to Judge Donald P. Masters, Department 22 for trial. Five women and seven men are seated for the jury.

On September 11, testimony begins. I'm told to arrive by 10:00 a.m. on September 12. I dress carefully that morning. I know my appearance matters and want to make a good impression, to prove to everyone in the courtroom I am worthy of their trust. John drives me to the Alameda County Courthouse in Downtown Oakland. Pursuant to Amy's instructions, his assignment for this shift is to take care of me. I'm grateful to Amy. Being on the clock will lessen any resentment that he too will miss classes for this event.

This courthouse is larger than the last one, set on a plaza next to Lake Merritt. The elevators are slow, crowded, stopping with a chime at each level. On our floor, John and I find a window where we stand gazing down at sunlight reflecting off water. The view is pleasant, though I'm vaguely conscious of not truly seeing it. I am tense, restless. But part of me is ready. Part of me can't wait to take the stand, to tell the jurors what this man on trial did to me that night, to let them know what he took away. I need to perform, need to get this right. I am at the center of this. All of this is because of me.

◆◆◆

HOURS PASS. TIRED OF shifting our weight on a brown wooden bench (not one comfortable seat in this whole damn courthouse!), John and I don't so much pace the courthouse halls as float through them, sipping lukewarm, overpriced coffee from the courthouse snack bar because I have been ordered not to stray too far. I am not allowed inside the courtroom except to testify. My assailant, on the other hand, by virtue of his constitutional rights, is permitted to be present for all of it.

◆◆◆

THERE ARE BREAKS IN the proceedings, and on these breaks we keep running into him. Turning a corner in search of another stretch of deserted bench where we can sit, wait for this thing to be over, there he is, emerging from the corner toward which we had been moving. This happens three different times, and on each occasion my assailant and I both startle like we did in Park N Shop, recoiling, jolting our bodies straight like we've been caught doing something wrong. I notice he wears his gray suit again, this time with a white shirt and solemn dark striped tie. He must have taken as much care in deciding what to wear as I had.

He is accompanied everywhere by an elderly man and two women, each with a full head of thick gray hair, each dressed in old-fashioned clothes like they have walked off the set of *The Andy Griffith Show*, and this makes them feel unreal somehow, fuzzy and black-and-white. They don't treat my attacker with the intimacy of parents and I surmise them to be aunts and uncle, suspecting the women will testify as character witnesses, placing their hands on the Bible and swearing their little nephew is a good boy, has never seen a lick of trouble in his life.

The woman I've nicknamed Aunt Bea is wide, plump, her face etched with lines, and I imagine she smells of mothballs and dust. She is the bold one of the group, eyes searching until she holds mine, beaming a hate-filled plea, a look I perceive as imploring me to stop this terrible lie. I look away. The old man, shoulders hunched inside a too-large suit, is more difficult to read. In his face I see something different. Shame, perhaps? Whatever it is, the look is mingled with resignation. He walks a step ahead of my attacker and the two women, and other than a fleeting second when his eyes meet mine, he stares straight down at the floor.

◆◆◆

FINALLY, AT 4:20 P.M., a pot-bellied bailiff swings open the courtroom door and calls out, "Karen Thomas!"

Obediently I stand, glancing at John, feeling a flash of panic as I walk toward the open door. My name seems to echo in the hallway. Stepping inside, my heart pounds inside my ears. *Thump, Thump, Thump, Thump, Thump.*

The courtroom is twice the size of the last one and the brightness of the fluorescent lights assaults my eyes. A judge sits on the bench; the jury in the box on the left side of the room. A dozen or so people sit in the audience: Aunt Bea and her cohorts, Detective Brisgaard, other faces I don't recognize. I hadn't expected so many bodies in the room and have the sense I've walked in late to an important meeting. Willa stands at the table closest to the jury. Defense counsel sits at a table on the other side of a podium, and with a nudge from this lawyer my attacker stands, smoothing his coat. Our eyes meet, the way they always seem to do, and he nods ever so slightly, an acknowledgment, like he is hosting a party and I am the guest of honor. The things I'd seen in his eyes the night of the assault—ferocity, wild violence—are quelled.

I walk toward Willa, who holds her arm stretched toward the witness stand, palm up like a maître d' guiding me toward a table. "Do I get to talk to you first?" I whisper.

Her face flickers with embarrassment. "Not now," she says and glances toward the jury, twitching an apologetic smile.

I may have only loose notions of what matters inside a courtroom, but Kistner and Amy have drilled down a few rules: Easy on the makeup. Don't dress like a slut. Be professional. Answer only the question being asked and offer nothing more. And, most importantly, keep cool.

I walk toward the stand, layered in dread. I have the distinct impression that every person in this room dislikes me, and this confuses me. What the fuck did I do? The judge is round, bald, grouchy. He seems pissed off. I miss the judge with the feather earrings, her quick kind smile. *Don't be paranoid*, I tell myself. *You're just nervous.* For a split second I think of my mother, her ambiguous self-help advice, *Talk to yourself.* The jury is blank-faced. I had expected a warmer welcome from them, looks of solemn sympathy, wordless communication from a female juror, an affirmation of our alliance, a nod that said, *Don't worry. We'll get him, sister.* I see none of this and I wonder, is this a jury of *my* peers?

I take my seat feeling like someone coming to the dark stage of a play, realizing as the floodlights hit that she doesn't know her lines. All eyes are on me. My assailant wears a blank, neutral expression. His attorney wears a look of disgust. This is going to be harder than I'd imagined.

As at the preliminary hearing, I swear to tell the truth, the whole truth, and nothing but the truth, so help me God. The second I do, Willa starts her questions. Easy ones. My name. Where did I go to school? Where did I live? I am hardly aware of what I'm saying, still taking in the courtroom, the defense attorney who never takes his eyes off me, the faces in the jury box. Willa quickly directs me to the night of July 19, 1984. Where was I at approximately 11:30 p.m.? With prompts from Willa (What happened next?), I begin to detail the events of that night.

Suddenly, the judge interjects. "Ms. Esposito, thank you. That's all we have time for today. This court will be in recess until Monday morning." He turns to me, voice still booming though I'm only four feet away. "Ms. Thomas, you are ordered back to this courtroom Monday, September sixteenth, at ten a.m. Do you understand?"

I nod, stumble out a single word: "Yes."

I have testified for only ten minutes. I was just getting started. I want this to be over with. It dawns on me that I will miss another day of classes, that John will miss another day of classes. We've sat around for hours, and for what? I feel frustrated, powerless. I have no say in scheduling, in what judge presides, in which jurors are selected. I barely even get to control what words come out of my own mouth.

CHAPTER 30

September 16, 1985, Oakland, California

THE FOLLOWING MONDAY, I retake the stand. It's my mother's sixtieth birthday. I cannot forget to call her today.

Wasting no time, Willa launches back in. "When we concluded last time, you were detailing the events of July nineteenth, 1984, correct?"

"Yes," I say.

Willa leads me through a series of photos: the hallway, the sidewalk lining the building on Blake Street, the spot I have come to call "the threshold." I have never seen these photos before. They were taken in daylight and the hallway looks nothing like it did the night of my attack. This feels hopelessly wrong, a factual inaccuracy that eats at me on a visceral level, and I'm agitated by the fact that no one in this courtroom is going to see the sidewalk and hallway as I saw it, no one will experience what I experienced. But immediately I sweep this away, realizing the absurdity of my expectations. How could I have been so foolish as to expect a true rendering? In presenting my assault to the jury, Willa and I are left with only what tools we have available, that principal tool being me, my voice, my telling.

In the photos, I mark the spot where my attacker stood when I first saw him, where he ran to me, where he grabbed me. I mark the spot where he held me in his arms with a knife to my throat.

Willa shows me an object and asks if I recognize it. The object has an evidence tag and I am seeing it through a plastic bag. I haven't seen it in fourteen months. It's bigger than I remember, its handle and blade as long as the width of a page of notebook paper. Still, I recognize it well. It's the knife he held in his hand, the knife that glistened under the gold light, the knife that touched my throat, the knife found in my assailant's pants pocket following his arrest four blocks from my apartment.

As instructed, I answer only the question I've been asked and indicate that, yes, I recognize it.

"*How* do you recognize it?"

"It's the knife that was held to my throat."

Without fanfare the judge states that the knife shall be admitted into evidence. His voice is loud and flat. He is either truly gifted in the art of the poker face or he does not give one shit about what I have described. Again, I feel something is missing. Everything about this telling feels too sanitized. None of the stark terror, none of the stupor, none of what my body suffered, none of what my brain fired in those minutes in that hallway is being conveyed.

Willa moves swiftly to my scream, the 911 call, the description I gave, my assailant's direction of flight, my identification of him from Sergeant Westinhoff's car. I feel the eyes of the jurors on me, watching me, their legs crossed, faces painfully empty.

"The man who assaulted you—is that man here in this courtroom today?"

I pause for a second, suddenly worried a trick is underway, that this defense attorney has seated a decoy beside him, that I will be duped and identify the wrong man. But I'm just on edge, I remind myself. I know that it is him.

"Yes," I say.

"Can you please identify him for the jury?"

I point. "He's sitting right there. In the gray suit and dark striped tie."

"Let the record reflect that the witness has identified the defendant."

"The record shall so reflect." The judge's boredom has a rushed quality now, like he wants to get this over with.

"Is there any doubt in your mind that the defendant is the man who attacked you?" Willa's voice is more dramatic now and I like it. It's the first hint of emotion in what I had hoped would be a vivid and powerful display.

"Absolutely none," I say. And there isn't.

"No further questions, Your Honor."

With that, Willa is finished. It seems anemic, far too skeletal of a story, a mere outline, a thin sketch with none of the color filled in. But wait, I want to say, so much more needs to be told.

Bewildered, I start to step down.

"I'd like to ask a few questions too, if you don't mind." Defense counsel. Bert Machetti's voice is saturated with contempt.

I sit back down, feel myself blush. I'd assumed I would get a break between Willa's questions and cross-examination by the defense, a chance to regroup, to calm myself, to huddle with Willa and John. There isn't. Machetti moves right in.

From the way he jumps from his chair, begins speaking before he is even fully standing, it's clear to everyone in the room that he is on the offensive, that he has something urgent to convey.

He seems to vibrate with sheer energy. His voice has a passion, a certainty, a pulsating emotion lacking in Willa's questions.

"When you called nine-one-one, you gave a description of your attacker's shirt, correct?"

"Yes." I try my best to sound confident, but my voice feels thin inside my ears.

"And you described that shirt as a rust-colored velour or terry cloth-textured long-sleeved shirt, is that correct?"

"Yes."

"We'll come back to this shirt in a few minutes." He pauses, stares straight into me. "On direct examination, you testified that you struggled with the man who attacked you?"

His language makes me angry. I know what he is doing, phrasing his question to make it sound like some other man attacked me, not the one sitting in his gray suit and dark striped tie at the defense table. But there is nothing I can do to stop it. I feel helpless, out of control. "Yes."

"And for approximately how many minutes did that struggle take place?"

"I'm not sure. A few. Several." I feel wrung out, exhausted already, and this has only begun.

"Well, from the first moment you saw the man, to the moment he pushed you down as you say and ran away, how much time elapsed?"

I hesitate. "I'm not sure."

"More than ten minutes?"

"Less."

"Less than four minutes?"

His air is that of battle. He intends to crush me, to twist my words, to make me appear as a woman unsure of what happened, a woman willing to convict an innocent man who happened to be in the wrong place at the wrong time. I hate him, I fear him, and most of all, I want desperately to beat him. I need to win this fight. But already I feel myself unraveling.

"I don't know? About five minutes? I don't know exactly."

"You don't *know*?" He sounds incredulous. He's getting excited now. He is revving up to annihilate me. I feel myself starting to stumble.

"I'm not sure of the exact length of time. About five minutes maybe."

"But you'll agree it all happened very fast?"

"Yes, it did."

"And you were scared, right?"

"Yes."

"Terrified, even?"

"Yes."

He tees up his questions so he can argue *fear blinds*.

He is unapologetically aggressive, his questions tailored to discredit me, to manipulate my words, to limit and restrict how I tell the jury what happened. His words are their own form of assault. I couldn't know it at the time, but the sensation I felt—the physical nausea coursing through my stomach—was an intuitive understanding that this judicial process was almost as destructive as the assault itself. I have a new name for this lawyer. Not *Macketti*. Machete. His words are a hacking to pieces.

"And you saw the man for only a few moments before he grabbed you, correct?"

"Yes…" With every word my voice strains, trailing off. I am unable to speak without sounding, even to myself, uncertain.

"And after that night you never saw this man again, correct?"

"Um," I pause, careful. This too feels like a trick. Machetti wears an impatient look that says, *Well? I'm waiting.* In answer to this look, I rush forward to explain. "We ran into each other at the grocery store once, and I saw him in court at the preliminary hearing—"

"Objection! Move to strike, Your Honor!" Machetti is angry. Angry with me. I have done something very bad.

The judge speaks. "Motion granted. The jury will disregard the last answer." The judge swivels in his chair to face me. "You are to answer the question that is asked and only the question that is asked, do you understand?"

I swallow. Something inside my throat strangles me now. A paper cup filled with water sits next to me, but I know my hands are shaking so badly I won't be able to pick it up, to perform the simple act of bringing it to my dry white lips. "Um? Yes? I thought I was doing that?" I feel myself wilt beneath this judge's stony gaze.

He barks again, this time at Machetti. "Next question!"

Machetti stares at me with flat black eyes.

No one is fighting for me. I am totally and completely alone in this chair. Exposed. Only I am fighting, but I feel myself weakening and still I have to hit back or I will risk losing myself.

Then, something shifts inside my mind, something chemical. A fluttering panic, and I feel like I have slipped into the deep end of a pool. I am underwater, voices above me muddled. I speak but it sounds like a mumble. I can't hear my own voice.

"What was that again? Speak up, please."

Inside, I berate myself, *Focus. Speak up. Yes, speak up, goddamnit.*

I dig deep, pull myself back to the surface. "Yes, I was trained at the UC Police Department on giving descriptions."

I have learned to give a great description of hair (thinning, receding hairline), and to detail clothing (black high-top Converse sneakers). I have been trained to be sensitive to articles that could be discarded in flight, thereby throwing off a whole description. While the key article that stuck out in a viewer's mind, Red Sox baseball cap for example, a cap could easily be chucked on the run, throwing off the visual impact this person makes on anyone else. Equally important is the need to avoid details like "wearing navy blue Cal Bears sweatshirt" where any one of a thousand people on campus might be wearing such a shirt. But I have always been less comfortable estimating body weight, even less adept at estimating heights.

"Now. Back to the shirt the man was wearing. Let me make sure I got this right. You said it was a rust-colored velour or terry cloth-textured long-sleeved shirt, is that correct?"

"Yes, with an open collar that sort of draped." I make a lame movement at my own collar, trying to show what I mean.

At the defense table Machetti pulls out a plastic bag holding something I can't quite make out and strides back toward me. He stands close enough that I can smell his cologne. Something nice. Expensive smelling. Not the Old Spice that drenched my mother's uncles or cousins or whatever they were when they showed up once a year on Christmas for the sole purpose of gorging themselves on her cooking.

"Ms. Thomas, I'm showing you Defense Exhibit One." From the bag he pulls out a shirt and holds it up in front of me, moving his body to the side so the jury can see it too. "Is this a rust-colored velour or terry cloth-textured long-sleeved shirt?"

He hands the shirt to me and I hold it in my hands, feeling confused. It's wrinkled and stinks like the clothes at Aardvaark on Telegraph Avenue, the secondhand store where Kim and I go sometimes in hopes of finding some treasure we could afford. I don't want to touch it, but I don't have a choice. It's a shirt covered in tiny red-and-white checks.

"No," I say, hearing my voice trail off again.

"And it's a button-down collar—not a collar with lapels that drape across the shirt as you described, correct?"

I'm not going to let him get away with this. "No, if the top buttons are undone, the collar will drape just like I said." I hold the shirt up by the shoulders presenting it to Machetti to show what I mean.

He pulls the shirt from my hands. "Your Honor, the defense requests that Exhibit One be admitted into evidence."

"Motion granted."

Now, there is no sound beyond Machetti's voice. I am focused on the questions put to me, the work of my brain interpreting them, formulating how best to answer, how to avoid this man's traps. Nothing exists beyond his words. There is no world outside this courtroom. This is it. This is everything. And it all seems to have little to do with the truth. On that stand I feel helpless, condescended to. I have no voice. I am a hapless, stupid victim. And with this sense comes the heavy weight of shame.

"You've described an attack where a man grabbed you and held a knife to your throat. Were you injured?'"

"Not physically, no."

He slits his eyes at me in warning, like a parent to a kid who has mouthed off in front of company.

The judge interrupts. "Counsel, is this a convenient stopping place to adjourn for our noon recess?"

"Certainly, Your Honor." Machetti flashes the judge a sycophant's smile.

The judge's voice booms. "Ladies and Gentlemen of the jury, we will now break for lunch. You are ordered to return at one thirty p.m." He bangs a gavel and I feel myself jump.

◆◆◆

There's not enough time to go anywhere for food, so John and I share a turkey sandwich from the snack bar, eating it on the rock-hard bench outside Willa's office. The meat is processed and gray. Inside my mouth it turns to the texture of sand.

I whisper to John. "Why didn't she warn me about the shirt?"

"Shhhhhh," he whispers back, head shooting side to side to see if anyone is within earshot. "You're not supposed to talk about the case."

A flicker of anger passes through me, irritation that my bold boyfriend is being such a straight-laced prude. But I also know he is right. I have to follow the rules. Even if those rules seem stacked against me.

Five minutes before we're due back in court, Willa glides through her office door, face flushed, glowing with perspiration. She sees me staring at her.

"Sorry," she says, "I showered but I'm still sweating. I went for a run on Lake Merritt over the lunch recess."

I'm struck with disbelief. If she gave a shit about this case she would have spent the noon hour preparing, finessing her examination, strategizing with me, coaching me. That's what I would have done as a prosecutor. The fact that she has squeezed in a run proves she doesn't care. Not about me. Not about winning this case.

◆◆◆

I retake the stand at 1:56 p.m. feeling exhausted and betrayed. The concept of a jury trial is absurd. Placing your life in the hands of twelve strangers, rolling the dice, then standing back and hoping they get it right. The prosecution has to prove their case beyond a reasonable doubt. The strategy of any good defense is to create that doubt, I know this. But what does reasonable doubt even mean? What is doubt? What's reasonable and what isn't?

I feel hard, adversarial. But I can't let that show because this process is like a job interview. Present myself in precisely the right way by answering questions over which I have no control.

And those questions come way too fast now, making my face feel hot. Listening to them, *What had you been doing that night? How old are you? Why did you have a set route home? And what were you wearing? So you must have been tired, right?* I realize it's me who is on trial. I hadn't known I would be subjected to such painful scrutiny, that I would feel so degraded, so at fault. I feel violated, helpless. Again. What I want to tell is the story of what he took from me that night. But that is not what this is about. No one here cares about that.

And just as I feel it all coming apart, something happens.

Machetti shows me a photo, another that I have never seen before this trial: a photo of my attacker taken at the Berkeley Police Department following his arrest. The lighting in the photo is poor, dark. But in its dim light: a magic trick. The red-and-white checked shirt is transformed into exactly the shirt I had detailed, the shirt I had *seen*: a shirt that is textured, almost velour-like, the color of rust, even draping at the neck as I had described. In the light of the photo, the red-and-white checks have blurred to rust just as they had under the golden bulb in the ceiling fixture of my hallway.

But I don't get to say this. I'm only allowed to answer the questions I am asked. I try to answer Machetti's relentless questions calmly, knowing that being argumentative will make me look bad to the jury—Willa has warned me about this. But this man is still twisting everything. He's not asking the questions that could permit me to tell the jury *that the shirt is exactly as I had described it.* That I was RIGHT, goddamnit. My stomach cramps, and for a fleeting second I fear I'm going to be sick.

How do I fix this? How do I prove I am right? But allowing myself the luxury of my own thoughts makes it even harder to focus on the questions thrown at me, questions designed for one purpose: to invalidate me.

"We're almost done here, Ms. Thomas." Machetti licks his lips, walks back to the defense table. More drama, I think. But as I allow myself to feel a sliver of relief, sheer joy even, that this goddamn ordeal is almost *over*, Machetti comes in for the kill.

"A young man has accompanied you to court these last two days, correct?"

"Yes."

"And if I may ask, who is this young man?"

"My boyfriend." More stupid fucking questions, I think.

"And how tall is your boyfriend?"

This stumps me. Like my age, how could this possibly matter? I don't understand, and I also have no idea how tall John is and this realization fills me with embarrassment. I don't even know how tall my own boyfriend is! What an idiot! I feel myself fluster. I am terrible at estimating height. Hadn't I told everyone that? I look to Willa for help, waiting for her to object, but she only looks at me, eyes expressionless. "I'm not sure, exactly."

"Fair enough. How tall would you estimate?"

The room is impossibly quiet. Everyone is waiting. Waiting for me to answer this one simple question.

My face burns. "Uh, five feet eight?" It is a wild ass guess.

John makes a face like someone has struck him.

Machetti strides across the courtroom, directing his words to John now. "Sir, can you please stand up?"

What's happening is difficult to comprehend. What's happening seems ludicrously unfair. I look again to Willa to do something, to put a stop to this, but she is turned around in her chair looking toward John like everyone else in the courtroom.

John obliges, shoulders hunched forward, hands grasped together in front of him, a fake flat line of cooperation glued across his lips. He looks at me, eyes so big and brown, brimming with apology. "Sir, can you please tell the Ladies and Gentlemen of the jury how tall you are?

John swallows, pauses, then speaks. "Six feet."

"Thank you, sir. You can be seated." Machetti is giddy.

It's that moment in the movies, where a murmur of shock floats through the packed courtroom and the grandfatherly white-haired judge with the gravelly voice pounds his gavel shouting, "This court will come to order!"

But this courtroom is perfectly silent. And it's in that silence that I feel myself crumble. Do *not* do that, I want to yell. Do not smear me with the words of my only friend in this world right now. But I do not say this. I cannot. I am not allowed. I do not have a voice of my own. I have only the voice they give me in the tight walls of their questions. This attack feels so low, so colossally unfair, like every moment of this entire trial. This asshole has used my own boyfriend against me, he's elicited testimony from my own lover's mouth *against* me.

Finally, Machetti stops. "Your Honor, I have nothing further." His voice carries the air of victory. He is done with me. He has left me battered and bleeding and every person in this courtroom knows it. I'd messed up the shirt, I was a woman who couldn't even describe a man's height accurately, not even her own boyfriend's height, let alone the height of a man she struggled with in a hallway for mere minutes. How could I possibly be believed?

The judge barks, "Redirect."

Willa stands. I see dismay in her face, resignation in her posture. I remind myself to breathe, tell myself to have faith, to trust Willa knows what she's doing, that this is where she will clean things up, guide me with gently crafted questions allowing me to fill in the craters Machetti has left in my story. Together we will make the jury understand the significance of the Berkeley PD photo, how it proves I got it right. She will make sure the jury knows that even if I didn't know my own boyfriend's height, I nailed my assailant's height spot-on when I called 911.

But Willa doesn't ask the questions to permit me to say any of this. She covers only minor points, repeating some of the queries she posed on direct examination. Panic spikes again as I sense her wrapping up, coming to a close, realizing I won't get to tell her what I've seen in the photo, that the jury won't know what I said to the 911 operator.

Willa concludes. "Thank you, Your Honor, I have no further questions."

Machetti calls from the defense table, not bothering to stand. "I have nothing else with this witness."

"Can I say something?" I ask.

Willa frowns, revealing her frustration with me, and this friction transmits to everyone in the courtroom. Before Machetti even objects, the judge snaps, "No."

I start to stand, body leaded with disbelief. It can't be over. I haven't had a chance to explain. No one has even really heard what happened. I haven't been allowed to explain how I'm *right* about the shirt. Will the jury notice? Will the jury see what I saw in the photo?

Now that redirect examination has finished, now that it's too late, the judge calls a ten-minute recess. I slump down from the stand, cross the courtroom drained and destroyed. No one in the room looks me in the eye except John, and even his face holds a ray of disappointment. Outside the courtroom I tell Willa about the photo. How could she not have seen this? And what did John's height have to do with anything? I hear myself. My voice sounds desperate, crazy even, not the tone of a calm, credible witness at all. Willa tells me she'll take care of it. How? I demand. She shoots John a look that says, *Control her.* She tells me to go home, I should get some rest.

◆◆◆

IN THE CAR JOHN and I stare at a sea of blinking red taillights. Prince sings on the radio, *Oh no, let's go! Let's go crazy! Let's get nuts!* I am too wiped out to speak, too drained to listen to Prince tell me that we are gathered here together to get through this thing called life. I snap off the radio, fight back angry tears, cling to the shred of hope that the jury will see what I saw, that the shirt was precisely as I had described, that any height discrepancy was a small detail, something easily overlooked.

In the silence of the car, I struggle, fight to maintain control. Something has been taken from me, taken forcibly. That something is deeply personal, a something I did not want to give. I try to put a name on my jumbled feelings but they have no name. I turn the radio back on, try to focus on something outside my own head. Before I know it John is in front of the house, stopping to let me out. As I slam the door closed and turn to face my building, I know. This thing welling up inside me, this thing threatening to break me into even smaller pieces, it does have a name. *VICTIM.*

CHAPTER 31

September 18, 1985, Oakland, California

THEY DECLARE HIM INNOCENT. All twelve members of that jury said I was wrong, my words could not be trusted. Their verdict strips away another layer of dignity, replaces it with rage.

I imagine Aunt Bea gripping the other white-haired woman's hand as the verdict was read, crying with relief at the foreman's words, *not guilty*. Machetti slaps my assailant's back. And him. I imagine his sense of victory, his smirk, the power he felt. He had gotten away with something. Something big.

Innocence. *Innocence.* I have been robbed of mine.

◆◆◆

WORD SPREADS AT THE station. I call my mother with the news. She explodes with a "That goddamned sonofabitch!" but she has nothing else to offer. I don't blame her for this. What else could she say?

I try to go about the business of life as a student, make my lists of reading that needs to be done, finger the calendar holding exam dates.

On September 18, 1985, my assailant is a free man.

CHAPTER 32

SIX WEEKS LATER, SOMETHING unfathomable happens again. Something else, another unexpected twist pushing me back down to my knees. It is me who is accused of a crime.

It had seemed like such a small thing, a harmless favor between friends.

That fall a new policy had come down at the department: all UCPD aides were to be issued photo ID cards with their name, badge number, and date of birth. Beckman was in charge of making them. He wasn't supposed to, but he took several photos of me, snapping the camera over and over before getting a shot he deemed worthy of me. Moments later he handed over the card, still warm from the laminating machine. "You're welcome," he said, pivoting on his heel and leaving the room. I didn't want to look at it until alone, secluded inside the walls of Lost & Found. I pulled it out of my uniform pocket to examine the photo, hoping I looked better than on my driver's license. My eyes moved to the birth date. With the stroke of a typewriter key, I was a year older. Thanks to Beckman, I was now officially twenty-one.

I hadn't asked Beckman to do it but was grateful he had. Now I could go drink pitchers of beer at Kip's on Durant Avenue. I could tell the server who carded me, "I don't have my driver's license, but I have my police ID, is that okay?" It was always okay. I'd reach for my wallet, pull out the ID with confidence, enjoy the look on the waiter's face, how he viewed me differently, with respect. It was nice having something to flash. Our badges looked like toys, something purchased from a cheap drug store. I flashed the ID to waiters a total of five or six times.

It never occurred to me that this was a felony.

◆◆◆

A RASH OF SCANDALS rock the aide program. Details are sketchy, but Alfred Ling has some kind of mental breakdown. Officers search his apartment, finding thousands of dollars of UCPD equipment—radios, mace, batons, police uniforms. Alfred's arrested, charged with theft, felony possession of stolen property. Then somehow Beckman gets arrested too, charged with the same crimes as Alfred even though he only has a couple extra uniforms at home, a slim jim we all used for popping open car doors when people locked themselves out, a booklet of blank parking citations. All of us had citation booklets, using them to park our own cars illegally. We would write ourselves a cite, keep the signature and badge number illegible, slap it onto the windshield under the wiper blade. Seeing that a citation had already been written, no meter maid would ever bother to stop. It was a perk of the job.

I'm not clear why, but Sara Bertini, the sergeant who once taught me how to dust for fingerprints, the sergeant now crawling up the ass of every aide in the department, somehow has me in her crosshairs. She calls me back to her desk in the detectives' room and tells me to sit down.

She wastes no time getting to the point. "We've learned you're in unlawful possession of UCPD property."

I am pretty sure she's bullshitting, that my name has come up in her investigation because I'm friends with Beckman, but that she doesn't really know any specifics. Still, a fissure of doubt moves through my body. Someone could have told her about the ID. Beckman could have told her, someone else might have known. I stare back at her, know I have to maintain eye contact or she will smell guilt.

"This translates into three felony counts," she says. "Possession of stolen property, misappropriation of university property, and fraud." She pauses, squinting at me. "If you're convicted and get the maximum, you could go to prison." Then she pauses again for effect.

It works. My heart pounds inside me and my face feels like it's on fire.

"I need to ask you some questions. Can you do that for me?" she asks, staring at me with steely eyes.

I nod. "Okay."

She taps her open palm to her temple. "Oh," she says, trying to act casual, like she's only that moment thought of something. "This is so silly but I guess I should be formal about this."

She places a tape recorder on the desk between us, shaking her head, grinning over how ridiculous this all is, that she has to go to the bother of recording something as simple and straightforward as a friendly chat between us girls.

"I guess I have to read you your rights too." Another toothy smile at the sheer absurdity of these bureaucratic hoops.

She recites the words I have heard watching crime dramas in my parents' living room so many times, words I never dreamed would ever be directed to me. "You have the right to remain silent. If you give up this right, anything you say can and will be used against you..."

My heart pounds so hard, so fast, I almost worry Sara can hear it, that she sees it pulsing in my temples. I imagine sitting in the UCPD holding cell next to Amy's office, the same cell where they put Beckman and Alfred Ling. I think about the question on job applications that I have always skimmed by. *Have you ever been arrested?* With every ounce of effort I can muster, I manage to swallow, then speak.

"Okay," I swallow again, "I guess I'll take advantage of that right."

Sara looks surprised. I'm a little surprised myself.

"What?"

"I'll take advantage of that right to remain silent." My self-preservation instinct has kicked in again, and I feel a surge of pride. It takes courage to tell a cop to fuck off like that, especially when that cop is someone you used to admire, used to want to impress, until one day you realized that was never going to happen.

Sara pauses, appears to regroup. She hadn't expected this, I can tell. But I don't know what happens next. Do I simply get to take the Fifth and leave? It can't be that easy, can it? Sara moves to Plan B, proceeds to explain that when I was hired, I signed an employment contract, something that said in the event of internal department investigations, I agreed to waive my personal rights and cooperate fully, and that meant answering questions, telling everything I knew.

I waver now. So I don't have the right to remain silent.

I have no idea what to do and feel like I've already used up what little fight I had left in me. I can't force myself to stand up to this woman, this sergeant, anymore.

And so I fold, tell her everything. All on tape. My voice. Telling. About me, the ID, Beckman.

The moment I've finished, Sara thanks me for my cooperation, then returns to her secrets-between-girls voice and adds, "I'm not going to arrest you right now, but I need you to go straight home and wait by the phone for my call. Understand?"

I tell her I do, and I'm filled with a new strain of terror, different from what I'd known so well in the past eighteen months but equally shattering. *Arrest.* She'd said *Arrest.* I'd heard things about jail, knew I could never handle it. And best-case scenario, even if I didn't go to jail, my life was over. With a criminal record I would never get into law school, would never be allowed admission to any state bar association. Everything I'd worked for. Gone. What would I do now?

I don't go home. *I have to study!* I sit inside Doe Library, but concentrating is a joke and my eyes take in the majesty of the expansive reading room, its Greco-Roman style, white granite quarried from the Sierra foothills, Roman-arched windows flanked with paired Corinthian pilasters. Athena herself stares down from the panel above the north bronze entry doors. Athena, goddess of wisdom and knowledge, goddess of law and justice.

◆◆◆

BACK AT MY ROOM, the phone rings the moment I step inside the door. It's Sara and she's half yelling. "I thought I told you not to leave your house?"

"I had to study," I protest meekly. "I went to the library."

Later that day, I'm served with a subpoena to testify against Beckman. My head spins. This is a nightmare. It is all happening too fast. When will I be arrested? When will Beckman be subpoenaed to testify against me?

◆◆◆

183

JOHN CONSULTS WITH A professor and gets me an emergency appointment with a criminal defense lawyer in Downtown Berkeley.

I sit in her office looking at plaques, awards, and certificates when she walks in and introduces herself. Cris Arguedas. Before she's even taken off her coat, she asks me what's going on. I tell her, and she listens carefully, shaking her head in disgust.

"That Sara violated your constitutional rights."

Cris's confidence is staggering. She's unlike anyone I've ever met. She is an absolute badass and her voice, her gestures, they tell me without a doubt that she is on my side. No judgment, no questions asked, she is fighting for me, like no one else ever has.

She picks up the phone and calls a Deputy DA who takes the call immediately.

"Yeah, I represent Karen Thomas." Pause.

I can hear the woman's voice through the line. I can't make out her words but can tell from the pitch of her voice she's scared shitless of Cris.

"Do what you have to do, but my client's not testifying. She's going to take the Fifth."

Cris hangs up, turns to me, and explains that if she has to appear in court with me the next day, she will have to charge me a fee, but otherwise her services today are free, a gift. I heave a sigh of gratitude, sputter thank yous and worried questions about court tomorrow—*What if? What if?* Cris bats away my concerns, then gives me a lecture on why I should vote to confirm Rose Bird as California's Supreme Court Chief Justice. I listen gratefully. I had planned to vote to confirm anyway.

◆◆◆

THE NEXT MORNING, I walk to the courthouse again, the same old-smelling building where I testified against my attacker in front of the judge with the feather earrings. I am scared again, filled with stunned disbelief to find myself as a witness in my second preliminary hearing within the space of a year. Only this time I will be taking the Fifth. This time I am worried about landing myself in jail.

I hold Cris's card in my hand. Her parting instructions were, "Call if they try to fuck with you." I am prepared to be fucked with, feel at this point it's my birthright, a legacy. But I'm not fucked with. I step inside the courtroom, say I'm taking the Fifth on the advice of counsel. I don't even have to sit down on the witness stand. I am dismissed, it's all over in the space of a minute, and I leave, still too scared and bewildered to feel relief. I could not for the life of me understand this criminal justice system. I had no clue how to navigate it.

◆◆◆

THE NEXT DAY AT the station, I'm given the option of being fired, which would reflect permanently on my employment record, or to resign voluntarily effective immediately. I resign. On my way out, I see Sergeant McClaughlin, search her face in expectation of much-needed solidarity, the empathy she had given so freely on that night last summer. But instead she gives me the stink eye, then looks away like she can't even bear to look at me, shaking her head in dramatic disgust.

I walk out of the basement of Sproul Hall.

I never go back.

CHAPTER 33

SPRING 1986. I HAVE graduated early but linger in Berkeley, studying for the LSAT. I have long ago given up on the frat parties Kim and I went to as freshmen, drinking Everclear-based concoctions with names like Orange Fuck and breathing in the scent of Ralph Lauren Polo cologne. But in a fit of nostalgia, a flash of realization that we will soon depart the chapter of our lives known as college, Kim and I decide to check out a party promising to be populated by a handful of old acquaintances from our early years in the dorms.

I wear tight red pants and a matching sweater borrowed from Kim, tying a red-and-black plaid scarf around my neck as a finishing touch. Before I leave, I take a long stare at the mirror, and for once I like the look of the young woman staring back at me. The red pants flatter my ass, my hair looks good for a change, and my skin is clear and shines. I slick on a coat of bright red lipstick and race out the door.

Kim and I enter the party and almost immediately we're separated in the tight crowd. Music throbs. David Byrne sings, *"Strange but not a Stranger!"* I get a beer, searching the room for faces I might recognize, but those faces are gone, graduated, replaced by a new wave of eighteen-year-old babies.

It's dark and the music is too loud but my body hums with awareness, senses razor-sharp, and by some acoustical miracle I hear the voice of a young man as I move to glide past him. That voice is as clear as it might be if we were standing alone together in an empty room, the volume of each syllable transmitting perfectly into my ears.

"Watch this," he whispers to his friend, "I'm gonna grab this girl's ass."

Time does that thing it does sometimes, winding down to impossibly slow frames, and it's like I'm watching a movie, a scene featuring some other woman. I understand, naturally, that the girl he speaks of is me and simultaneously with this perception I feel his hand slide along the seam in the fabric of my pants, down my ass, and into my crotch, a hand pushing hard between my legs, grabbing with such force I feel my labia separate. And in this movie, in this scene of the woman in red, without hesitation, in one exquisitely fluid moment, she grabs his arm, wrenching it behind his back the way she'd seen the real cops do so many times. She twists that arm so hard the face of this young man—or is he a mere boy?—crumples and his friend looks on in appalled panic.

She speaks.

"Don't you *EVER* fucking do that to a woman again."

Her voice is low, calm. Powerful.

She bends his arm even harder when he doesn't respond and now his face looks like he might cry. "Understand?"

He moves his head up and down. "Yes!"

"Huh?"

"Yes!"

She drops his arm and keeps walking, not bothering to look back.

That's when I come back inside my own body, back into my hot red outfit and scarf, feeling a little bit stunned that the woman who coiled this asshole's arm was me. I smile inside, not realizing yet that this is a moment I will cherish for the rest of my life.

Somewhere inside I feel grateful to this little shit. I appreciate the moment he has given me, thankful for the proof that I could still decimate someone who violated me, for the lesson that I still possess power, even if I still so often drag myself through my days feeling like I hold no power at all.

1995
SAN DIEGO, CALIFORNIA

CHAPTER 34

April 20, 1995, Department S-9, San Diego Superior Court Felony Arraignment

STANDING AT THE PODIUM in Superior Court Department 9, I scribble out my arraignment litany on the front page of the indictment that the judge's clerk has handed to me. They're the same words I recite in this court weekly, the speech every other lawyer in this room has memorized:

Good morning, Your Honor, Karen Thomas appearing on behalf of Dwayne Sayers who is present and in custody. Mr. Sayers has been advised of the charges against him and waives formal reading of those charges. He has been advised of his constitutional rights, including his right to a speedy trial. He hereby waives that right and accepts a trial date convenient to the court.

I even write out *Good Morning* and my own name, that's how concerned I am with becoming tongue-tied, screwing up in a courtroom packed full with my peers: public defenders, other lawyers in private practice like me, DAs and bailiffs and clerks. It's a tough crowd, often snarky, gossipy, petty even, a group that calls defense lawyers who never take a case to trial "Dump Trucks" for dumping all their clients by pleading them guilty.

Dwayne appears beside me at the podium dressed in his navy-blue uniform, *San Diego County Jail* stenciled in white across his broad back. I have coached Dwayne ahead of time, outlining what he is expected to say, explaining this is an administrative hearing where he simply enters an initial not-guilty plea, that at our next court date there will be plea bargaining, that if we don't like what's on the table we will go to trial.

Speaking the litany, I stand erect, shoulders back, and I lower my voice an octave as I had as an aide on patrol at Berkeley. It's the voice of a serious woman, a woman not to be trifled with.

The moment I've finished, the presiding judge speaks. "Mr. Sayers, is this correct?"

"Yes, sir." Dwayne's voice booms. Polite, yet deep, defiant.

"And how do you plead to the charges against you: assault with a deadly weapon in the parking lot of Bank of America and armed robbery at the ATM machine of San Diego Federal Credit Union?"

"Not guilty, Your Honor."

Arraignment completed, Dwayne and I exchange nods and the bailiff escorts him through a door. The whole matter takes less than two minutes. I gather my briefcase, race out the door. I have three more court appearances this afternoon.

◆◆◆

I LIKE TO THINK the men and women who get me as a lawyer are lucky, even though most days I feel I'm in over my head. Taking a case to trial can be exhausting. I have a strong work ethic, ingrained by my parents, but I am motivated to carry the burden of fighting prosecutors by my sole driver in this life: my need to be taken seriously, to be perceived as tough, competent, fierce. I still have something to prove, though what that something is remains impossible to pinpoint. I spend all my money and then some on clothes. Suits from Nordstrom, silk blouses, designer pumps with heels high enough to flatter my calves but sensible enough to permit swift navigation of courtroom halls, walks to and from the jails. I want to project an image of success, to fool everyone into believing I'm killing it in this business. I keep the chip on my shoulder hidden.

We all wear masks, costumes, armor. We pretend, try to be who we are not. Casting a spell, creating illusion, we wear these masks to become invisible. But we also wear them to be seen, to be viewed as the person we wish we could be. Sometimes this works. Sometimes we fake it till we make it, masquerade until one day we're not imposters anymore. But living as theater also constitutes lying. And lying creates distance, sometimes an abyss, between ourselves and the people who surround us, a vast chasm inside our own selves.

CHAPTER 35

1995

IREPRESENT DRUG DEALERS and addicts. Drunk drivers and robbers and fraudsters. I represent men who hurt women. What does this say about me? How can a woman who herself was assaulted, then revictimized inside a courtroom, become a defender of people accused of crimes? What makes that woman want to excoriate victims on cross-examination the way she herself was flayed?

Few people know of the events from the summer of 1984 and the following year. Only this handful of friends can remark on the delicious irony of my specializing in criminal defense. Some of these friends hold the opinion that I chose this path because so long ago I lost my power, my assailant stripped it from me, and I remain desperate to get it back. They say I'm turning my history, my victimhood, on its head, claiming strength by violating others in the courtroom as I was violated, because there's a primal urge to injure that which has injured us. In this new role, nothing about me says *victim*. As *victim* I was silenced. Now I have a voice.

Other friends believe I'm showing everyone: *Look!* I'm so forceful I can defend people accused of the most heinous crimes.

The ugliness of humanity, manifested in criminal acts, once found me, but now I'm in control, now *I* go hunting for *it*. Others claim it's an evolved form of dissociation, of leaving my body as I had that night in the hallway, only a dissociation that lasts years. Still others argue that for me to mirror the steely force of my rescuer, Cris Arguedas, creates a way to reclaim my power.

Maybe.

If any of this is true, it was never a conscious decision. Life remains full of choice and chance and we try to reconcile all the enigmatic inconsistencies, try to thread a life together into a linear narrative, all in hope of finding meaning. The truth is, I never chose this path. It was flung on me like everything else.

During law school, I clerked for the San Diego County District Attorney's office, then worked for a federal judge whose docket consisted primarily of criminal cases. I still wanted to become a prosecutor. I wanted to make things right. Clerking in the DA's office guaranteed me an offer as a deputy district attorney with a starting annual salary of $36,000. But I was still a financial disaster with student loans to pay, so instead I took a job with a civil litigation firm ($52,000! A fortune!). The firm assigned me a "mentor" I nicknamed *tor*mentor who told me repeatedly, "We own you. And you're going to earn every last penny of that bloated salary of yours."

Miserable, I quit within the year. It was 1991 and an ugly recession triggered budget cuts and a hiring freeze for San Diego County, eliminating the job in the district attorney's office that would have been mine. Worse, there seemed to be no jobs anywhere. I had no income, couldn't pay my rent. I moved back in with my parents.

Desperate for cash, I started making court appearances for the handful of criminal defense attorneys I knew. Being on the other side of prosecutors felt humiliating. They treated me like shit. They treated all of us like shit. In the windowless room outside of court where those prosecutors conducted plea negotiations, I did my best to wheedle out a better deal for clients. But there was no negotiation. Take the deal on the table or go to trial. Those were the choices.

I began to view prosecutors differently. Every last one of them seemed so smug, so neat and clean, so in control. None of them seemed to appreciate that this task of being alive is difficult. To those prosecutors, there was right and there was wrong. They knew nothing of the messy places in between. I began to wonder, how do we distinguish between good people and bad? How can we judge anyone with such certainty?

It was never supposed to be a full-time gig, but after a few months I started making some money, moved in with a high school friend, opened my own office. I got myself appointed to a panel where private attorneys take over cases when the public defender's office has a conflict of interest. I made court appearances for more seasoned lawyers, ghostwriting their briefs to make ends meet and to learn. Sometimes those lawyers fed me cases where the client couldn't come up with the funds for their more substantial retainers but scrabble together the money for my more meager fee. I came to understand phrases like voir dire, fruit of the poisonous tree, locus poenitentiae—a place for repentance.

Walking inside jails, prisons, holding cells, felt like adventure. Proximity to criminals made me feel tough, potent. These were serious places, stocked with dangerous people, yet I was protected, untouchable. Like my days as an aide, it became a way of play-acting, brushing up against the bad but from a safe distance. Defending men and women accused of crimes became a way of rebelling, of waging war with authority, and in those battles I began to wonder: How do we uncover truth? What if people commit acts for reasons longer than their rap sheets, reasons more complex than the elements of their crimes? In my ringside seat, I see up close what goes wrong to deliver people to a jail cell. I witness all the ugly beautiful humanity. Too much sometimes. Sometimes so much it hurts.

So yes, criminal defense. Defender of persons accused of crimes. Sometimes awful crimes. Why?

Because we never have a clue where this life might take us.

CHAPTER 36

I N THE 1985 MOVIE *Jagged Edge*, Glenn Close plays Teddy
Barnes, a lawyer defending her dashing multimillionaire client
Jack Forrester, played by Jeff Bridges. Forrester stands accused of
tying up his wife and murdering her with a hunting knife. During
the course of the film, Ms. Barnes is sexually harassed by the DA,
called a bitch by a witness in open court, and falls in love with her
client. After fucking his brains out all night long, Teddy tells Jack
on the morning of trial, "Wear a blue suit."

The lovers lock eyes and Teddy adds, "Juries like blue suits."

Jack giggles, then stares at her, awed by her moxie.

Hollywood's portrayal of female criminal lawyers is laughable,
but I too have fallen in love with my clients. Not romantic love, not
sexual love, but love nonetheless because what else can you call
it when you know that decades later you will still think about the
men and women whose lives have intersected so briefly with your
own? When you wonder if they're still alive, still addicted, still
in prison, still funny and smart and wry? Or maybe it isn't love.
Maybe it's the thrill of a strange kind of intimacy with another
human being, maybe it's the thrill of being needed.

So much is an act but one part glimmers pure and true: my clients fascinate me. They're all so real, so textured, so beautifully damaged and flawed. I feel compassion in my heart for the child-molesting client I represent in his appeal. He's serving ten years in prison, where inmates have their own form of moral codes. At his tearful request, I use my letterhead to write to him of his plea agreement in an imaginary drugs-and-guns case. He hopes it will convince the other inmates he is not really a child molester, that they will stop the daily beatings. I smile inside trying to convince a judge that my client can't serve time in custody because he has Tourette's syndrome and his uncontrolled shouts of *Cunt! Motherfucker!* will earn him chronic beatdowns in jail. Then there's the woman who swears she can't go to jail because she has chronic IBS and her shit smells so bad it will earn her nonstop beatdowns. There's Edward Singh, arrested for firing his gun at the stars in the sky; Ginny Cordoba, eight months pregnant and charged with conspiracy to distribute methamphetamine only because she took a single phone message for her boyfriend. There's Tut Williams, busted with the cocaine and cash he carried inside a duffle bag filled with a dozen sticky dildos. The DA wants to admit those dildos into evidence simply for their prejudicial value: they make Tut look like some kind of perv. In chambers we fight, me arguing the jury should never see them, that the dildos have zero relevance to the crimes at hand and their admission into evidence can only prejudice my client. Judge Easton, the kind-hearted judge straight from central casting in the movies, white haired and grandfatherly, interrupts in his husky voice, "Madam Prosecutor, what's the relevance of the dildos?"

She has no good answer.

"No," the judge concludes. "No. Ms. Thomas is right. The dildos stay out."

I read thousands of police reports, their language cold, impersonal, devoid of emotion. In one DUI case I read:

The driver had urinated on himself, leaving a dark stain of wetness down his inseam. The suspect seemed unaware he had lost control of his bladder.

From my days as a police aide, I understand cops are trained in the art of report writing, tasked with restraint and avoidance of outright conclusions. An officer can't write:

He was so fucked up he pissed himself! AND he didn't even know it!!!!

With that DUI report, a photograph: an overturned Mazda, cones and evidence markers strewn throughout the street, bounded by yellow tape, *Crime Scene—Do Not Cross.* On the Mazda's back bumper, a sticker, upside down but still easy enough to read: *I Love My Family.*

Then there are the clients who chill my bones. Manny, twenty years old, charged with murdering his pregnant girlfriend in a fit of rage, then attempting to burn the body to erase what he'd done. In his wide shining eyes I see pure madness.

There's the mundane like any other job. Sitting inside the jail watching precious minutes tick by, waiting for languid guards to retrieve my clients from their cells, or waiting for slack-jawed court clerks to complete the paperwork I need to review line by line with my dyslexic client so he comprehends what must be done to comply with his terms of probation. And there's the uniquely grotesque parts of this job, like standing inside a courtroom holding cell counseling a client about his constitutional rights while another inmate takes an explosive shit on the lidless metal toilet on the opposite side of the room.

◆◆◆

THROUGH ALL OF IT I seldom think of my own assault, my own wounds, never reminisce about sipping from a Styrofoam cup while Sergeant Kistner's words floated inside my ears, stunning me with recognition that even though I was a wannabe cop, I remained clueless about this system we call justice. *What was the point in thinking about it?* I told myself. The past is the past. I had moved on.

It's with this attitude that I continue to fail to understand what happened to me that summer and in the year that followed. But how was I supposed to find meaning in a senseless act, an act that held no answer to the question *Why?* Missing from my Berkeley story is the heroine's use of the tools at her disposal to save herself, her strength and determination, what she learns about herself, how she grows, finds that thing we call redemption.

In my story there were no tools. My sole coping mechanism was staying busy, clenching my teeth, and grinding through each day no matter how bad I felt. Courage had nothing to do with it. I only went through the motions. They told me to show up for a hearing, I showed up. They told me to come testify at trial, I went and testified. They come after me? I try to fight back with my feeble little fists and the help of a kind, generous badass.

The fear stayed with me until finally, on its own time schedule, not mine, it started to fade, moving to the background until it finally stopped eclipsing every other piece of my existence. The sound of footsteps became only a rare trigger, not a terror that dictated the tone of my days.

So is that what I learned? That sometimes you just have to push through the day? That when you're in the middle of suffering, there is nothing that resembles growth? Growth doesn't come until years later. If it ever comes at all.

All I can say is I survived it.

For years I rarely think of it. I appear to transcend.

But somewhere deep inside my body—it's there.

CHAPTER 37

June 19, 1995—Department S-8,
San Diego Superior Court Settlement Division

SITTING AT THE DEFENSE table in Superior 8, I wait for the bailiff to open the door, for the parade of men to shuffle into the plexiglassed holding area of the courtroom. When they settle on the long wooden benches and I see Dwayne has arrived from jail, I say good morning to the bailiff, ask him how his weekend was, tell him I need to speak with Mr. Sayers. I step inside among the men in their matching blue uniforms and canvas slip-on shoes. The space reeks with the stench of bad breath and a dozen unshowered bodies.

Without fail, the men behind the plexiglass are polite, nodding acknowledgment, sliding down the narrow bench to give me room to sit. I reach Dwayne and shake his hand. It is smooth, dry, enormous, my own fingers and palm disappearing inside it.

I don't bother with small talk. "The DA's offer is thirty years," I say.

Dwayne's face crumples in disgust. "For a plea bargain?"

I nod.

Dwayne mumbles, "That's some bullshit."

"It's total bullshit given that we can go to trial and lose on everything and you'll likely get forty years."

Dwayne shakes his head. "At that point, what's the goddamn difference?"

For a moment we say nothing, each of us staring through the smudged plexiglass at the lawyers gathering in the courtroom.

At the visiting room of the jail the day before, Dwayne and I reviewed what he already knew: California prisons are so over-crowded that inmates generally serve only half of the sentence imposed if that inmate receives "good time" credit—credit for acceptable behavior inside. This turns a sentence of forty years into twenty, a sentence of thirty years into fifteen. "I want you to think about this." I pause to let Dwayne know I am serious, to let it all sink in.

Dwayne whispers, "I'm fucked with those pictures."

I nod agreement. At the jail, we stared at each photo, Dwayne fingering each of the glossy black-and-whites. Before the DA had produced them in discovery, Dwayne and I held out hope that the ATM photos might be blurry, indistinct. But they aren't and there is no denying Dwayne is the man holding the gun in the photos.

I tell Dwayne I've filed a motion to bifurcate, a request that the court break the case into two separate trials, one for the assault in the parking lot, one for the ATM robbery.

"We gonna win that?" Dwayne asks.

"Maybe," I say. "Maybe not."

Dwayne looks down at his hands.

"But if we lose that motion, we can plead guilty to the ATM robbery charges and go forward to trial on the parking lot assault. If we do that, the DA can't admit the ATM charges into evidence because we will have made them legally irrelevant. The jury won't ever see the photos, won't hear about a robbery with a similar gun in the same neighborhood the night before the assault."

Dwayne nods, still unspeaking.

"By pleading out you'll still do some time, but a lot less than what they're offering."

"Unless we lose on the trial of that lady."

"Right. Lose on the charge of assaulting the woman in the bank parking lot and you get the full forty."

We are wordless again as Dwayne and I contemplate our high-stakes poker game—but it's the prosecution's fault for giving us little to lose. Give in and plea: thirty years. Lose it all: forty. Like Dwayne says, at that point there's not much goddamn difference. Except the chance to wield a little power, to make the DA work for it, to flip them the bird, to get to say, *You want to take my life? Fine. But I'm going to fight you for it.* The visceral need to fight back is something I understand. Staring through the plexiglass, waiting for Dwayne to speak, I think about this man who is my client. He's a deeply flawed person. But he's a human being. And all he has right now is me.

After five full minutes of silence, Dwayne finally heaves out a heavy sigh. "Fuck it," he says. "Let's go to trial."

July 24, 1995

On Monday afternoon, we're assigned to Judge Hirsch for trial and he swiftly denies the motion to bifurcate. Dwayne then pleads guilty to the ATM robbery charges as planned.

Judge Hirsch's face is narrow, wrinkled, and it pinches in on itself when he speaks in his tight voice. "Jury selection on the remaining counts will begin day after tomorrow. That will be all." He stands and disappears into his chambers, moving so fast the tails of his black robe float up behind him into the air.

The bailiff takes Dwayne away.

◆◆◆

Every Monday night I drive straight from court to my parents' house for dinner. I can't go home first to shed my armor and change into the comfort of jeans and a T-shirt. If I go home the exhaustion of the day will grip me and I won't want to leave. Besides, it gives my parents a thrill to see me dressed up in my suit. Their daughter the lawyer. *A real lawyer,* they tell friends in their camping club. *One who goes to court, talks to juries and judges, not one of those sits-behind-the-desk-all-day lawyers.* They are proud of me, and I like it when they view me as grown up. I'm thirty years old but in my family, women aren't really grown up until they're married and have a kid, and I haven't gotten around to either of these yet.

My parents greet me at the door as they always do, and I kiss each of them hello. I'm vaguely aware my parents are aging, drifting into their seventies now. My mother had me when she was thirty-nine years old, not an unheard of age for giving birth today but pretty rare when I was born. I've never thought much about my parents' age or the gap of years between us. They always lived like old people even when they were in their forties. My parents remain in good health so it's easy to ignore the heaviness of concepts like mortality. Besides, I'm too busy to think of such things, too focused on myself, on my *illustrious career.*

We move straight to the dinner table, already set with the same dishes and flatware I'd eaten with in this house while growing up, the same brand of paper dinner napkins folded beneath our forks.

My mother brings serving bowls and platters to the table, waving away offers of help. They hold my favorite foods, meatloaf filled with bread stuffing, mashed potatoes and gravy, fresh green beans. We dig in.

Rarely does our dinner conversation dwell on the details of what I do for a living, but I share that I'm starting a trial on

Wednesday so I'll be busy, too busy to call. My mother asks what kind of case, and when I tell her she falls silent, staring at her food. I think my choice of specialties perplexes her and I can't blame her. Sometimes it perplexes me.

My mother shifts topics, asks about a public defender I've dated off and on, a man for whom she hasn't tried to hide her dislike. "Seems like he gives with one hand, takes away with the other," she said once. I ignored her but inside felt stunned by the accuracy of her perception.

Tonight she asks about John as well. My mother met John at my college graduation and on a visit to San Diego and liked him, liked him enough to ask about him on occasion. *Did I ever hear from him? What's he doing now?*

I cut into a piece of meatloaf, remind her we haven't really stayed in touch.

That's a shame, she says, asking if he ever left DC after we'd moved there together for internships.

I nod, respond through a mouthful of mashed potatoes, tell her I think he's working in the Senate. Senate Judiciary Committee maybe? I know he works for a Democrat. Warranted or not, I had always given myself credit for nudging a man with a Ronald Reagan poster on his wall toward the nobler party.

I shrug to my mother, signaling I have nothing more to say on this topic, and the conversation drifts elsewhere.

July 26, 1995—Superior Court Department 12

FROM BEYOND JUDGE HIRSCH's courtroom, I hear keys scraping against metal, finding a heavy lock, turning. Then the smaller clicking of handcuffs releasing, the weary groan of a door. Dwayne appears, transformed by the clothes I bought for him at Target.

He settles into the chair beside me at the defense table. "You look nice," I say, picking a piece of lint from the shoulder of his sweater-vest.

Dwayne grins, suddenly shy. "Thanks," he says. He had balked at my choice of clothing until I made him understand: appearances matter.

◆◆◆

"*VOIR DIRE*" TRANSLATES FROM French, "to see to speak." It's the questioning of prospective jurors by a judge and attorneys, the process of selecting twelve strangers and trusting them with the task of deciding a person's fate.

The defense and the prosecution each receive ten peremptory challenges—the right to kick a person off the panel for any reason or no reason at all. Each side also receives an unlimited number of opportunities to excuse a prospective juror "for cause," where the juror flat-out admits he can't be fair and impartial, or something he's let slip gives the prosecution or defense the chance to argue that even though this juror won't admit it, there is no way this person is fit to serve. A lawyer tries to argue dismissal "for cause" as much as possible so she can save her peremptories. You never know what sits in that sea of faces. Retired cops. Probation officers. People you can't afford to let on your jury no matter what. If your client is black, you pray for at least one black face in that crowd.

Jury selection is a crap shoot. Jurors lie. Some lie to get on a jury. Some lie to stay off. Walking into court, a defendant is presumed innocent. But people carry assumptions. Half of potential jurors believe, *Well, he must have done something. Otherwise why would the cops arrest him?*

Like most things in law school, no one teaches you how to pick a jury. It's a learned skill. There are obvious land mines, personal biases to avoid. A standard question in voir dire is, *Have you or anyone close to you ever been the victim of a crime?* If the prospective juror says *Yes, my sister was raped*, there will be follow-up questions. *Was a suspect arrested? Did the case go to trial?* The answers to these questions prove critical to the decisions that follow. *Yes, he was arrested but he pleaded guilty* constitutes a potentially good answer, a response that serves to subtly educate every juror in the room. See? Guilty people plead out. Innocent people fight and go to trial. That's why we're all here! My client is innocent! But the response, *He was arrested but they let him go* proves more fraught. Further probing might be necessary but facial expressions and body language may forbid it, leaving a lawyer with difficult choices: waste one of your precious peremptories on this person to get him out of the room? But who knows what lies ahead further down the list of jurors? If the prosecutor is savvy she will ask a follow-up question, maybe even prefaced with a sycophantic, *I'm very sorry.* She will ask, *In spite of that outcome in your sister's case, can you still be fair and impartial in these proceedings today?* If a juror swears he can be fair and impartial, he will likely not be excused for cause and a defense lawyer is faced with using one of her peremptories. The problem is that no one wants to cop to their prejudices. Everyone views themselves as fair. And even if they have the self-awareness to know they're not, that they're human and burdened with prejudices and biases like every other person, who's going to confess to that in a courtroom full of strangers?

Jury selection reminds me of what I learned in my days on patrol at Berkeley. We're all constantly assessing our surroundings. We size people up, sort them, categorize them. It's an unconscious information-management system, and we judge by race, sex, job, clothes, car, haircut, makeup, speech. We work hard to make sense of things, but we know only a small fraction of what holds true about this universe. We make assessments and often we are wrong. Sometimes I keep a juror on the panel for unscientific reasons: our eyes meet and we share a smile, or a woman's face reminds me of my mother. It sounds silly and maybe it's an odd thing to admit, but sometimes these human components help me connect to these strangers tasked with deciding the fate of my client.

Today, I ask my questions, I do my best. Dwayne winds up with a jury comprised of eight white women, three white men, and one black man. Not an ideal mix given that my black male client is charged with assaulting a white female. But there's only so much I can control in this system we call justice.

July 27, 1995

I'M ALMOST FINISHED CROSS-EXAMINING the petite blonde victim in this case. I've elicited her admission that while she spoke several times to detectives to assist in prosecuting this case, she refused to speak with the investigator for the defense. It's her right to refuse, but a decision I will use to my advantage in closing argument: *Why?* I'll ask the jury. Why speak to the cops and not the investigator examining the case from the defendant's point of view? Bias? Is she hiding something? I can't remember if a defense investigator contacted me when I was the victim so long ago. But I know I too would have refused to speak to that person.

As I learned in my role as victim in Alameda County, there are kind judges (feather-earringed judge from my assailant's preliminary hearing) and asshole judges (the Honorable Donald P. Masters presiding over my assailant's jury trial). Judge Hirsch falls into the latter category. He chews me out in front of the jury for taking too long in showing the victim photos of items recovered inside her purse, the purse found on the passenger seat next to

Dwayne two hours after her assault. I'm making a list—a lengthy list—of all the items absent from that purse when it was found in Dwayne's possession. I want to belabor this point so I can raise the question later: Maybe someone else had this purse before it fell into Dwayne's hands? Why would Dwayne keep the hairbrush but toss the wallet? Maybe this poor schmuck Dwayne simply wound up with the purse somehow? What if he stumbled across it? What if someone else pistol whipped this woman with the gun that was never recovered by the police?

But Judge Hirsch has cut me off. "Ms. Thomas, wouldn't it make more sense to ask her about what *was* in her purse instead of wasting time listing what was *not* in her purse?" His voice drips with disdain.

No goddamn it, it wouldn't, Your Honor. And thanks for fucking up the whole rhythm of my cross-examination. I'm sure the prosecution appreciates your help. And by the way, my client's facing forty years. Forty years! And you can't spare me five minutes to make my point in a way the jury might remember?

But I can't say this, can I? Instead I say sweetly, maybe with the lightest sprinkle of sarcasm, "Thank You, Your Honor. Actually, I have no further questions for this witness."

Asshole.

My body still carries the anger of not being allowed to speak the way I want to speak in court—it still quakes inside me with rage when I am not allowed to be heard. But today it doesn't matter. I've elicited enough testimony to make my point. I will drive this message home in closing argument, making sure to get in a dig at the judge. "Now before Judge Hirsch cut me off, we were learning that at least fifteen items that had been in the victim's purse were no longer inside that purse when it was found in Dwayne's possession hours later. Why?"

July 31, 1995

DWAYNE'S JURY COMES BACK deadlocked—eight guilty votes and four holdouts, three of them women. In the criminal defense world, a hung jury is almost the same victory as a flat-out win. Dwayne and I are ecstatic.

Outside the courtroom, I speak to two of the women who voted not guilty. It's 4:00 p.m. and the normally crowded halls are nearly empty. As one of the women compliments me on my closing argument ("You explained everything so well!") a lawyer with whom I once shared office space turns the corner just in time to overhear her comments. It's Mike McCabe, one of the lawyers who represented Robert Alton Harris in his failed appeals from a sentence of death. In 1992, Harris was the first person to be executed in the state of California in twenty-five years. I respect Mike deeply and to have him witness this praise from two holdout jurors feels like a stroke of unspeakable luck. After the jurors leave, Mike mimics them in falsetto voice, "Oh, Ms. Thomas! You explained everything so well!"

I punch him in the arm, unable to stop the grin from spreading across my face. For this legal legend to be standing in the courthouse hall giving me shit is the ultimate form of flattery, of belonging, and I savor it as he leans in to peck the high bone of my cheek, wishing me congratulations.

◆◆◆

AFTER A HUNG JURY, the case starts all over again. We are back in Department S-9 to get dates for a new settlement conference, a new trial. Inside the plexiglass box, Dwayne is buoyant, so buoyant I feel certain he has gotten hold of some of the drugs known to find their way inside the county jail.

He stands, the sudden movement earning a glance of concern from the bailiff. But the bailiff turns away again when he sees Dwayne pumping my hand and smiling. "You were Perry fucking Mason in there!" Dwayne squeezes my shoulder with his other Mr. T-sized hand, then adds, "Goddamn!"

The inmates surrounding us on the hard, narrow bench are all grins too, nodding in agreement as if they had witnessed Dwayne's trial themselves, and again I find myself bathing in the glory, glory in the approval of all these felons.

◆◆◆

AT THE SETTLEMENT CONFERENCE three weeks later, Dwayne ends up pleading out—to the same deal offered before trial, no deal at all really, thirty years in state prison (of which he will serve half if he can manage to stay out of trouble). I told Dwayne, "I just don't think I can pull it off again." The prosecution knew my case now, knew all the tricks I would pull, and this time they would be ready. Dwayne signed the deal readily, almost gratefully, his demeanor that of a man refueled by pride.

It's as if all he ever wanted was someone to fight for him.

2014

CHAPTER 38

April 2014, San Diego, California

THE REST OF THE world is pulling itself out of a crippling recession, licking the wounds of economic trauma, but the local legal market remains stagnant. A few years back I needed a break, quit my high-paying, pressure-cooker job, but now all the jobs are gone, now I can't find enough work to support me and my husband, whose earnings selling real estate have been dismal. We have worked, saved, invested, misjudged, lost everything. At night I can't sleep. I worry—literally—about homelessness. I'm a JD/MBA who worked hard her whole life, who a few short years ago drove a Porsche 911, made $280,000 a year, lived in a $2 million ocean-view home, and was shortlisted to become a federal magistrate judge. What the fuck happened? How could every single thing go so wrong?

Nearly thirty years since Berkeley, since the night in the hallway, and that nineteen-year-old girl is a ghost. Her life in those years? Move to Washington, DC with John, work for a Congressman on Capitol Hill. Break up. Return to California for law school at UC Davis. Graduate. Through winding twists of fate, specialize in criminal defense.

The problem with criminal defense is that a lawyer hungers for, her ascension on the career ladder depends upon, taking bigger and better cases. But "bigger and better" means uglier. More violence, more death. Facts bizarre and bloody enough to make heart and head both ache.

After eight years I left the specialty, moved on to a national class-action plaintiffs firm pursuing securities and consumer fraud cases. I worked long hours and got paid handsomely. I went back to school again, got an MBA, moved to Silicon Valley for a few years working for a firm wed to the tech boom. There may be crime in those parts too, but in Silicon Valley the criminals wear Brioni and Ike Behar.

My clients continued to live their lives too. For several years I received Christmas cards from Dwayne, a gesture treasured by lawyers earning their living defending persons accused of crimes. I learned something unexpected in my criminal defense days: that I wanted to fight for these people, that fighting for them empowered me too. Beneath the narrative of our days there is another story, a story we don't get to write. In my days at Berkeley and in my days in court, I learned: justice is not something clearly defined.

Somewhere in the middle of it all I meet a new man, fall in love. We share our lives together. I suffer through his betrayal with another woman. I dive deep, back into the well of anxiety and depression. Once again, I lose my way.

◆◆◆

I LIE IN BED on a Tuesday afternoon, one pillow tucked between my knees, another over my head. I'm desperate for sensory deprivation but the San Diego sun insists on glaring through the curtains straight into my face. San Diego is a city without seasons and one long scorching summer has stretched through two full years, launching California into its worst drought in history.

The next-door neighbor isn't helping either. Since losing our house in 2010, my husband and I have rented a townhouse with a shared pathway to our front door and that of our neighbors. The neighbor I have unimaginatively named Douche Bag now stands on that shared path talking loudly into his cell phone. He's not even thirty years old, a budding venture capitalist, and he is everything phony. I detest the grating sound of his voice, his rich parents who bought him the townhouse, his arrogance and privilege. It's the mere sight and sound of the perfect normal life of him and his young wife that often fuels the spiral of my panic. Unable to block out the sound of his voice on his incessant calls, I know far more about him than I would like: Debbie at the office wants to undermine him. The founder of a promising new startup got popped for a DUI. Douche Bag owns a pedigree dog complete with handler and dog show competitions. Sometimes this dog shits on our front steps.

I always believed that if I learned a man had cheated on me I would hit an eject button, springing that man immediately and completely out of my life.

I always believed this, yet here I remain.

My husband and I are now nothing more than roommates, living in our parallel hells. For the past six years I have lived in this marriage with one foot in, one foot out, existing by straddling two possibilities, not living fully in either of them. Our marriage is a broken promise, our days together an enslavement. The stiff silences last weeks, so much of this time spent sleepless, an elephant sitting on my chest. I'm miserable yet can't bring myself to leave. I can't leave because I love this person. I love him in spite of all the shitty things he's done. I love him in spite of the fact he has proven himself untrustworthy.

Pulling the pillow tighter to my ears, my mind loops with all we have shared. Homemade pomegranate mojitos. The houses we flipped. Roasted chicken. His affair. Fourteen Thanksgivings. The house we built together. The death of our fathers. Resentment. Punta Mita. Turkey chili and Veuve Clicquot. The baby we tried to have but couldn't. Madrid. Anger. Losing everything. The yelling. Napa. Fourteen Christmas Eves. Auckland. Tears. All the moments which make up a life with someone.

◆◆◆

SIX YEARS AGO, MY husband raced out of the house to meet a prospective client, leaving on the laptop he always turned off, always kept guarded. Outlook was open and emails sat there, begging to be read, promising to confirm the suspicions that had rooted inside me for months. Telling myself it was okay to break the rules to learn if someone else was breaking the rules, I rushed through a split second of guilt as desperation trampled ideals. My stomach clenched, and I thought of Bluebeard's wives as I held my breath and my hand curved over the mouse. There were many emails to choose from. They told a story, a story that shattered me. The person I once trusted most with my life had lied, over and over.

Still, I stayed. I stayed because of my visceral belief I was not strong enough to live in this world without him. Even as dysfunctional as things have become, our lives remain inextricably woven together. Yanking those two lives apart seems impossibly violent. And yet the prospect of staying with this man feels like a life sentence. So here I am, paralyzed by indecision, having no clue how to un-knot all these tangles.

It was ten days after reading the emails that I had my first panic attack. Driving down the hill from our La Jolla home headed to visit my mother, I became dizzy, started to feel out of control, had the sensation the car was moving without me, that it wasn't turning down rolling hills but was instead rolling *over*. I couldn't breathe, pulled over, struggled to regain control, but couldn't. I turned around and headed back up the hill, still shaken but calmed in the knowledge I was moving toward home. I called my mother and told her I was sorry, I couldn't come visit that day. I told her I was dizzy, maybe sick. She had dizzy spells too, so it was something she could understand.

The days feel unbearable again. I am stretched over the edge, terrified. I am losing my grip, losing myself, and I want—no need—to scream, a primal wail. I feel it rising inside, consuming me, even as I fight to press it down. I feel my skin won't contain me. It's like the Berkeley days. Everything I thought was true in this world isn't true at all. You are safe. You are not safe. Your husband loves you. Your husband fucks other women. I have a life. Everything in my life is a lie. I don't know how to be anymore.

Thirty years since the night in the hallway and I am at the bottom again. The chapters in between, chapters telling a story of a woman in control, have been erased. All around me is in ruin. Another emotional undertow, followed by unspooling, a sense of certainty that what's left of me is vanishing, that I am losing myself for good. I have slid down the sinkhole, down a broad black throat that swallows me whole. The sky swells with my disbelief. I let go of the pillow, sit up to a slouching position, pick up a book from the nightstand. Maya Angelou. Hell is internal, she says.

Hell is internal.

Hell is internal.

Hell is internal.

CHAPTER 39

April 2014, San Diego, California

A LMOST DAILY I GO for a run. Nothing crazy, just four miles. It's how I break up my day. Running brings a brief calm, quiets the incessant chatter of my mind. Running, if I'm honest, is my only source of pleasure.

On these little jogs I wear my tattered Cal Bears cap, the navy blue worn and faded, the thread of the gold scripted *Cal* loose and frayed. At least once a week it earns a shout out from some passerby of "*Go Bears!*" Because that's what one Cal Bear says to another Bear by way of greeting. Usually I forget I'm wearing the cap and as my brain fumbles, I've already passed the person before I can muster a meek "*Go Bears*" in return. If my husband is with me, a man who spent the period that made up my college years playing bass in heavy metal bands on Sunset Boulevard in Los Angeles, he will cringe with embarrassment over the nerdiness of this exchange.

Today I am alone and I try to be conscious, to connect with my surroundings, to feel a gratitude I rarely register anymore. I follow the winding concrete paths of Balboa Park, trying to focus on beauty. Sun filtering through trees bending in the breeze.

Black crows cawing. Happy dogs trotting along on flex-leashes. I am trying simply, desperately, to be present in my own life.

Running along, the ball of my foot rolls over concrete in rhythmic steps and sweat soaks the nape of my neck, wetting the edges of my tattered cap. I pass the Parks & Rec men, waving as I always do, envying them for their jobs. Maybe not a lot of money but a steady paycheck, minimal hassles, a good night's sleep, and a tidy pension from the city after thirty years. Not bad.

The path twists and I reach the place where I am all alone in the thick nest of trees where the grass flanking the path becomes invisible, covered in fragrant beds of pine needles. All around me is silence. I focus on my connection with the path beneath my feet, rolling forward, shifting my weight from foot to foot, grounding me to the earth, repeating in a tempo that feels like a song.

The breeze startles the leaves and I search side to side, making sure I am still alone.

Then another sound intrudes. Ten yards behind, the taps of another's jogging footsteps, pace steady, growing louder as they near. A runner's breath exhales in beats matching the sound of shoes hitting concrete.

Panic flutters in my chest and my mind fights. My brain knows with near certainty that this person means me no harm. It's a runner. In a park. Just like me. But my body refuses to listen and as it takes control, I am seized.

Something inside begins to choke me, squeezing my lungs. The ground beneath turns unsteady, the horizon starts to swim and the tingling, visceral as nails scraping chalkboard, starts at the base of my spine. It begins slowly, above the tail bone, a tornado of nerve endings rippling, rushing up the base, swelling at the middle of my back. Like a shiver of a tambourine, it rattles, transmitting a message from the deepest place, tumbling into a spasm of panic, meaning spilling across flesh. *I own you*, it says.

The tornado keeps rushing, rolling, all the way to the base of my sweating skull where it pulses. A surge sends pinpricks to my hands, and I can no longer fight the urge to swing around, to set eyes on the person making the footsteps sound, to make eye contact, to satisfy my body, to calm this storm.

As I relent, permitting my head to whip around, I strain to appear casual, knowing I have failed miserably the moment I see the look on the other runner's face. He's a twenty-something man with a buzz cut, sweating in his Navy cadet uniform of blue shorts and a T-shirt. He raises a palm in apology. "Sorry to frighten you, ma'am," he says, then continues past, giving the crazy panicked lady a wide berth. And it's only as he runs on in front of me that the air begins its return to my lungs.

◆◆◆

THE BALL OF A foot colliding with concrete, a simple slapping sound. How can that evoke fear? How can something that happened so long ago hold so much power? And how can it wield that power after lying dormant for so many years? Every day pieces of memory fade away and die. But not this. It's an involuntary memory, a madeleine of terror, an ingrained sensation of *before* and *after*.

It makes no sense. In nearly fifty years on this planet, I have heard footsteps slapping pavement behind me—What? A million times? Only once has that sound led to terror. *Once.* That night is just something that happened, something to catalog as I tally the unexpected things I've experienced in this life: Sitting in a Manhattan conference room preparing to take a deposition, then watching a plane fly into the World Trade Center. The betrayal of a spouse. Losing a home and life savings. A car accident unfolding in slow motion, a crash certain to have killed me if a city light pole had been situated only seven inches farther east.

There is something unique about the sound of footsteps. His were the slap of rubber-soled tennis shoes hitting concrete as he jogged along the sidewalk toward the entrance to my building, inscribing a message into the ground, like writing one's name in wet concrete. Perhaps it's his own special way of reminding me, of promising he'll always be with me, even if it seems he has disappeared for some years. Could I have known I would never forget? That he would arrive again and again at times of his own choosing, forever lodged inside my body? Each time it happens my body speaks to me, telling me the shadows of my past have not disappeared. Our lives intersected so briefly, but he has stayed with me. His footsteps inhabit my body. How do I get them to stop?

For years it came and went, and I dismissed it as a minor annoyance. But as the triggers keep coming, triggers that attack when I'm at my weakest, I start to think. What if I'm missing something? Missing a piece to the story of my own life? What if that incident had transformed me even if I've refused to allow myself to believe it? If this still happens thirty years after the fact, what if my body is in revolt? What if it's responding because I insisted on blocking the trauma, refused to allow myself to process the impact of my assault, betrayed myself by lying, by insisting I was *fine*? Maybe the more we try to forget the wounds of the past, the tighter they grip us. Perhaps my body is shirking my mind's refusal to do something with these memories. Perhaps it's time for the mind to finally come around.

◆◆◆

In 1984, THE TERM "post-traumatic stress disorder" or "PTSD" was not in common use. It first appeared in the DSM-III in 1980 and its definition was limited. In 2014, it's everywhere, a label for veterans of yet another war, for the millions of people in this world who have suffered disaster.

The American Psychiatric Association defines PTSD as a reaction to an extreme traumatic event. Primary symptoms include increased arousal in the form of insomnia, impaired concentration, or persistent hypervigilance. Factors that predict development of PTSD include personality traits of high neuroticism and poor self-confidence. Another factor is family characteristics, and yet another is the environment for recovery. Lack of support from family, friends, and community can make a victim feel alone and helpless. There is also considerable impact where a victim is disbelieved and where there is "secondary victimization" such as when the police or lawyers or jurors or prosecutors or an entire criminal justice system make a victim feel like a chump.

Psychologists say that when people live through trauma, the memories get connected in their minds with what they saw, heard, smelled, or felt at the time. Anxiety and fear become linked to sensations that occurred during the event. These sensations become cues that evoke anxiety when they are experienced again later, bringing the memories and emotions flooding back.

In other words, the texture of memory is smooth, slippery.

A traumatic event is not remembered and categorized in a person's past in the same way as other life events. Instead, trauma continues to invade the senses and a person experiencing PTSD will relive the life-threatening experience, reacting in both body and mind as though the traumatic event is still occurring.

In other words, the past makes the present ache.

CHAPTER 40

April 2014, San Diego, California

I CALL MY MOTHER every evening at 6:00 p.m. on the dot. If I'm more than three minutes late she worries something awful has happened to me and says so, and this saying so floods me with irritation, and I don't want to feel irritation toward this woman who is my mother, the woman who brought me into this world, who raised me, shaped me, trained me to fear everything in sight, and so it's easier just to do things her way, to call at precisely the same time every night.

On these calls she gives me news of the day inside her assisted living facility. Bingo. Someone fell and had to go to the hospital. Somebody died. Her mind resets every two minutes, and so she repeats these events at least three times. Then she asks if I'm cooking dinner.

"Nope."

"I don't know how you get away with that!" Her voice holds its typical edge, but it's sprinkled with genuine bewilderment that I am not cooking dinner for my husband.

Given the fabric of my days, I have little to share with her either, and so we have the identical exchange every night. As we wind up the call, she punctuates the close of her side of the conversation with fear. "I just hope we don't have an earthquake."

She says this every time we talk.

◆◆◆

FOR THE PAST SIX years, my mother has moved in and out of sense, drifting further and further into nonsense. After my father died in 2006, she sold her home of forty-three years and moved to a senior "independent living community." As her health deteriorated, she moved to assisted living. The woman I once knew as my mother is gone and I miss her terribly. A sadness strangles me on these phone calls, a sorrow steeped in the understanding that we don't know each other anymore. Being unable to share anything real with her makes it difficult to breathe. I long for the mother of my childhood, the mother I'd known before I left for Berkeley. Someone who took care of me, who stood at the stove for hours cooking her roasts, scalloped au gratin potatoes, homemade cherry pies. I yearn for someone to fold my laundry, place it neatly on my bed, for someone to ask when I walk through the door, *Honey, how was your day?* Though that woman disappeared years ago, I wish I could speak to her, wish she could offer soothing words on how to deal with this woman who has replaced her, a frail, wobbling woman who can no longer hold her own body straight.

I didn't save my mother's letters from my time at Berkeley. It seemed unnecessary. I believed she would stay the same forever, in that house on Hugh Street, just as she had always been, so what was the point of keeping mementos of a woman who would never change? The salutation and tempo of the few letters I can scrounge up grieve me now. Her familiar handwriting, the recipes I asked for and never made, her warnings to *bundle up, it's cold up there!*

Her perky, *Hi love!* The money she sent, saying, *Hope this check gets there on time!* They reflect the mother I once had, a woman who began to fade years ago, a woman who, so imbued with the habit of worry that she persists in it now, even when on balance there is nothing in what's left of her life to worry about.

My mother is living proof: fear is a habit.

CHAPTER 41

April 27, 2014, San Diego, California

SUNDAY. MY DAY TO visit my mother. I can be a good daughter and drive to the mobbed grocery store on West Washington Street, fight for a parking place, wait for the hungover deli clerks to notice me standing at the counter shifting my weight from foot to foot, watch as they *oh-so-slowly* scoop the foods my mother loves into a container: coleslaw, macaroni and cheese, fried chicken. Or I can save myself the frustration and call in a BLT to the market one block away.

I call in the BLT.

◆◆◆

STRESS SIMMERS INSIDE ME and with all that has gone awry, I grip tighter, desperate to maintain control in a world that cannot be controlled. I am compensating for recent catastrophes by living my life with extreme caution, acutely aware of all that can go wrong. Driving in particular suddenly seems an absurdly irrational act of trust in my fellow humans, those texting while careening down the lanes of a freeway, those steering with one knee, drifting into my lane while applying mascara in a rearview mirror. I must be that much more vigilant to prevent disaster.

Driving onto the Martin Luther King, Jr. Freeway heading east toward the neighborhood where I grew up, my body fills with dread. I start the deep left turn onto the on-ramp where the attack always starts, rippling its way through me the same every time: senses pulsing like a strobe light, twinge of shaking in the knee, alarm in the knowing: I am losing control.

I fight back, gripping the steering wheel so tightly my fingers turn white. Then my palms sweat so much my hands seem to slip. I try to focus, tell myself to breathe. But it's no use. My head swims, I feel dizzy, like I'm going too fast, like the tires are rising from the concrete and I know I'm going to lose control of the car, am going to flip over and crash. The twinge in my knee graduates to tremors that course through my leg until it's bouncing of its own accord. I feel it all with horror, my own body defying my will. I slow to forty-five, then forty, and when the road straightens out I try to tell myself, *You made it. You made it! Hard part's over, just steer straight ahead!* But the panic's got me. All I can do is move forward, hoping for the best even while expecting the worst.

Exiting the freeway, I start to calm down. I hate myself for these panic attacks. I feel weak, crazy, out of control. I don't even recognize myself. Powerful women aren't terror-stricken by something as routine as driving a car. But then again, I'm not feeling so powerful these days.

I have a therapist, a man I've seen off and on for years. He is gentle, helpful, knows my history, my struggle with anxiety, depression, my inability to feel I am *enough*. But he couldn't seem to help me conquer the panic attacks, so I was referred to an EMDR specialist. This woman was sharp, confident, certain of her craft. She was no blank-faced grad student in a corduroy jacket with elbow patches. The theory behind Eye Movement Desensitization Reprocessing therapy is to find out what's behind your fear, to conjure the root of it as a strategy for overcoming it. The woman showed me coping skills to try to navigate my way out of the attacks—tapping around the bones of my eye sockets, above my upper lip. *Do you know why news photos of people who've witnessed tragedy always show them covering their faces with their hands,* she asked? *They're not ashamed or hiding their tears, they're comforting themselves. The act of cradling our own faces is rooted in our biology, rooted in our need to soothe ourselves.*

Then she got down to the nitty-gritty, putting me into a hypnotic trance, taking me back to face whatever trauma might come up. But the memories didn't transport me back to Berkeley and Blake Street. They brought me to childhood moments with my mother—distant drunk relatives of hers showing up uninvited to our home, expecting to be fed, triggering her anxiety and hence mine; a sixth-grade bowling event where I threw nothing but gutter balls and bawled with shame, where my mother's words in response left me empty, not consoled. The EMDR therapist told me that when a mother holds her infant in her arms, she transmits to that baby her beliefs about the world. The beliefs my mother transmitted to me? That the world is dangerous, random, cruel. That a person has to watch out, be careful. As a child, I hadn't fully realized how anxiety ruled my mother's life. It suddenly became clear that if I didn't make some serious changes, it would also rule mine.

◆◆◆

I KNOCK ON MY mother's door and enter to the drone of an oxygen machine. Her lungs are shot, and even with the oxygen she makes a soft grunting noise with the effort of each breath. Sixty years of smoking will do that to you. She sits in her chair with an afghan covering her legs even though it's ninety degrees outside. The day is bright and sunny but she has the blinds closed, curtains drawn across them. It occurs to me that she had always done this in our house when I was growing up: shutting out a beautiful day. It's one of the million questions I had never bothered to ask my mother: Why? It's one of the million questions that, because of her descent into dementia, will never be answered.

The room is spare but comfortable. In her dim cave, she has the same twin bed I curled into as a child when I feared that, like Linda Blair, I too was possessed by Satan. Next to the toilet is a call button in case she can't get up and back into a standing position. A white piece of paper is tacked to the wall: *DO NOT RESUSCITATE.*

I try to get her to eat. She is ninety pounds and looks impossibly small, preciously frail, her frame so stooped it seems to curl into itself. Her whole body shakes and her head wobbles on its neck like she has Parkinson's, though the doctors say she doesn't. When I hug her it's like wrapping my arms around a wispy paper doll. I study her liver-spotted hands, thick green veins sagging inside her thin skin. Without makeup, her face is the color of ash.

The room is infinitely quiet. We sit at her tiny table playing Kings in the Corner, exchanging whatever small talk we can muster. Time with my mother is like the days spent that summer in Berkeley: everything moves impossibly slowly.

Studying my mother, I feel something zinging through every cell. It is love, deeper and more palpable than anything I've ever felt for another human being. I have not lived one day on this planet without her existing for me and can't imagine the loneliness of the world without her in it.

She looks up from her cards. "What?"

She is blind in one eye, seeing only shadows, yet her gaze bores into me. I can't look into those eyes, can't hold their rheumy richness with mine. They will take me too far, to a place I can't bear to go. If I swim in those eyes too deeply, she will see inside me. She will see everything I try so desperately to hide.

"Nothing," I say.

◆◆◆

My mother likes to walk me out to my car when it's time to go, to stay with me as long as possible. This takes forever. She removes her "inside oxygen," the long tube that coils from the machine, winding in ropes at her feet. As she pulls that tube off her face it tangles with her hearing aids, popping them out of her ears and onto the floor. I scoop them up and hand them to her. She puts the hearing aids back in, then loops the long oxygen tube over the side of a chair. Then she fumbles toward her walker, pulling away from me as I try to hold one arm to steady her. She trips over the oxygen tube she has worn for the last nine years, over the flatness of the carpet, over her own feet. I hover close, ready to catch her, to break her fall. This rankles her.

"I'm fine!" she snaps.

She is more child than mother, a cranky toddler, quick to take issue. She still sees me as five years old, not the nearly fifty-year-old woman that I am. Sometimes this makes me feel an ache inside my chest and sometimes I just feel irritation.

She finally reaches her walker and leans onto the handles gratefully, pushing toward the door.

"Don't forget your outside oxygen," I say.

"Oh." She stops, reaches into the basket of her walker, pulls up the hose of her portable oxygen, placing it under her nose and sliding it over her ears, knocking out both hearing aids again.

Each time she says goodbye at my car, she says it like she fears it may be the last time. She has been saying it this way for the past nineteen years. "Goodbye, sweetheart. I love you *veeerrryy* much." The words are drenched in sadness.

I start the engine, turn toward home, and for a few beautiful moments feel the relief of freedom. But the sensation flits past and exhaustion sets in. This visit has drained me, my panic attack has drained me, and though I have plans with Janice and a whole Sunday afternoon ahead of me, I know that I will call and cancel, will spend the rest of the day with my own curtains drawn, curled up in bed with a pillow over my head.

CHAPTER 42

I N 1984, MY ASSAILANT had no prior record, and since that night in the hallway I have often speculated I was his first. For reasons I can't really explain, I have also suspected I was his last, that the whole tribulation of arrest, arraignment, hearings, handing his fate to twelve strangers, made him lose his taste for hunting women.

From the moment I laid eyes on him, I'd seen a graduate student, someone brilliant studying bioscience or metallurgical engineering, but a person with poor social skills. I picture him still living in the Bay Area, a professor now, an academic milquetoast, pale and soft, his hair thinning further over the years, a credit-worthy homeowner, a man who commutes to campus, keeps regular office hours, who drives home at the end of the day to a single glass of wine. I envision a wife, someone smart and quiet and plain. I wonder if he has told her about his arrest, his "ordeal" he will call it if he lies to her, his "close call" if he tells the truth. I wonder if he has children, if these kids think they know their father, what he is capable of. I wonder what books he keeps on his shelf, whether there are any we share.

I had seen him a total of five times. The night he attacked me, less than thirty minutes later when I identified him, in the

Park N Shop aisle, at the preliminary hearing, and at the trial. I knew nothing about him, still know nothing. We had spent so little time together but if I were to list the most significant, mind-altering moments of my life, the minutes spent with him would rank at the top, because I finally understand that for those few staggering minutes my body internalized the knowledge that he might be the last person on this earth to ever hold me.

I wonder sometimes if he ever thinks about me. It seems impossible that he could have forgotten, but perhaps I didn't matter to him as he mattered to me? Maybe he didn't sense what I sensed—the pure intimacy of it. His hand touching my mouth and nose, the skin on my face. Our bodies pressed together, hearts pounding, the shared moments of visceral uncertainty—mine whether to scream, his whether to run.

In my mind, we are bound together forever. He is mine. He is my assailant.

So as I had back then, in that other time, that other life, I think about him. A little at first, then a lot, then the word for my thoughts becomes *obsession*, an inability to let go, an inherent need to simply *know*. If I dig up that other time, face it head-on, maybe I can stop the tambourine of panic from shivering up my spine; maybe I can kill this thing inside me.

I was blinded by the trauma of the attack, by my ignorance of the criminal justice system, and my own psyche. Now I comprehend that justice system. Now I am finally ready to see. In my journey to become sane, I need to know the truth about this man.

But I can't even remember his name anymore. I had clung to it for so long and then through the years my mind released it, let it go, choosing to move on, trying to take back my life.

Now I want that name back.

It's a thirty-year-old pre-Internet event, but I am going to find him.

EXCAVATION

CHAPTER 43

May 2014, San Diego, California

THIRTY YEARS IS A long time to let pass between trauma and the compulsion to examine it. And so, I begin inside the place I have always avoided: myself.

I pull out my journal from that time, a book of unlined pages bound by a cover of tangled wildflowers. Flipping through, I brace myself for the pain of reading the open frightened feelings of my nineteen-year-old girl-child self.

The Spring 1984 entries read as I would expect:

April 24, 1984

"School sucks. Housing sucks. But I'm in LOVE and life is bitchin' anyway!!!"

May 21, 1984

"I love John soooo much. He's perfect in my eyes, so complete. There's nothing about him I don't love."

But the first entry after my July 19 assault shocks me:

July 22, 1984

"I'm so depressed right now it's unbelievable. It's that same old hopeless, scared, intense feeling I've been getting a lot lately."

A lot lately? What does that mean? Had I felt that way even before my assault? There's not even any mention of the attack, just a pep talk to myself to be more independent, not to be so clingy with John. At the close of the July 22 entry, I direct myself with a clear mandate: *GIVE JOHN MORE SPACE!*

The words feel so dishonest. Could this have been how I really felt? Why didn't I write about what the sound of footsteps now triggered in my body? My fear of the dark, of what lurked outside, of how I wanted to move but couldn't, of how I needed my mother but couldn't bring myself to tell her what had happened? Why didn't I write about that? Was I afraid that simply putting words on the page would end what little grasp I had on sanity? Was I too ashamed to admit my terror—even to myself?

Saturday, July 28, 1984, 10:10 p.m.

"I'm feeling a little scared right now. I'm all by myself & feeling very paranoid & edgy. I'm like that now ever since that guy attacked me. It's a terrible feeling. I'm afraid that someone's crawled in through a window & is hiding, waiting to get me. It's hard to concentrate on Econ."

Sunday, July 29, 1984, 10:30 p.m.

"Econ sucks! I'm so behind & I don't understand this shit & I have a problem set due tomorrow! Fuck!"

Then more about John, John, John.

August 3, 1984, alone in my apartment:

"John and I were together Mon–Weds nights because I've been feeling really scared to stay by myself lately...I hope I don't get scared tonight. I feel like I'm going insane."

I want to hold this poor girl in my arms, cradle her, say, "Oh Baby Doll, it's okay to be scared! This world, it's beautiful, but it's crazy and awful and terrifying too. What happened to you would upend anybody. You're still a badass, you're just not going to feel like yourself for a while, I'm afraid. And frankly, yes, you should be scared. Look at this place for fuck's sake! Listen. I'm going to figure this out. I'm gonna get you out of here. Just sit tight for a minute. And fuck that guy John. He's a good guy but if he can't handle you being clingy right now then fuck him. And Econ? Sweetie, it's hard. And it takes focus, concentration, and you just don't have it in you right now. Shhhhhh. It's okay. We'll figure all this out. We always do, don't we?"

August 4, 1984

"I'm about to go up to John's—I'm going to study & sleep there tonight so I don't have to worry about being scared."

In subsequent entries, not a word about my talk with Kistner, not a word about my failed bout with therapy. I guess it makes sense. It had been the last resort, the final thread of hope. Who could endure the task of writing that what you felt was your last chance had failed, just like everything else?

November 6, 1984

Holds no mention of Bibi Lee, how I worried for her.

December 18, 1984 11:15 p.m., the terror's back—just like I remembered:

"Kim's gone home for vacation & I'm alone in the apartment again. Yes, I'm terrified."

It hurts to read these pages. I feel such devastation for the corrosive pain this girl is suffering. I feel devastation that this girl was me.

Like most people who have suffered some kind of trauma, my understanding and reaction to my assault and the attendant anxiety has shifted and changed over time. During my criminal defense days, the trauma inexplicably seemed to disappear. Since then, I've struggled to understand what it has meant to me as a being, how it has impacted me as a person, how it has shaped who I am today. For years I questioned whether I was a "real" victim, whether I deserved to speak of this event. I continued to cling to the internal mantra, *I wasn't even hurt!*

Only with the distance of time can I see my self-betrayal. Back then I minimized my assault, insisting I was *fine*, denying, even to myself, how this event had shaken me to my core. To think that I stayed in that apartment for an entire year is ludicrous. Things could have been so much easier if I had simply moved. It sounds so obvious, such a simple fix, but there was a housing crisis in Berkeley. In spite of rent control, affordable housing was scarce and finding a place even remotely close to campus proved no easy task. And I had studying to do, classes to attend, a job to work. Plus there was the matter of a lease—I didn't know you could break a lease—and coming up with first and last month's rent and a security deposit. These were insurmountable obstacles for a person of my means and resources.

Only in the wake of thirty years can I see it as it was: a young woman, a child really, shocked and traumatized, stripped of the little bit of power she was scraping to develop. A young woman who thought she was starting to become worldly, who saved herself only through her own vigilance and believed she had to be that much more guarded to ensure nothing like this ever happened again. A young woman who felt contempt for her naivete in ever having trusted in her own safety.

How I wish I could have been kinder to myself, more gentle, more loving, more honest. "Of course you feel this way, sweetheart, of course! It's okay. You're not crazy. You'd be crazy not to feel this scared." How I wish I could have given myself a break, taken better care of myself.

Then a question rears its ugly little head.

Have I *ever* learned how to do that? Don't I wish I could do that for myself now?

CHAPTER 44

May 2014, San Diego, California

A ND THEN. MORE QUESTIONS.
Why am I so anxious and afraid? So obsessed with all that can go wrong? Is it, in equal parts, a devastating assault, a husband's betrayal, losing everything, being imprinted by a mother's anxiety? Or is the answer that it's just plain good sense after trauma?

What is trauma? What is the meaning of victimhood? How does one adjust? What if courage is dull? What if courage means getting up each morning, dragging yourself through the day, clinging to the hope that things will someday, somehow get better, even though you can't yet see how that can ever be possible? What if healing only comes in little pieces of success over time? What if healing is painstakingly slow, achieved only in increments of hundreds of thousands of baby steps which, strung together, propel us forward to change? What if recovery only occurs over the course of a lifetime?

Why is it so hard to ask for help? Why did these things happen? Why does anything happen? What does it mean to feel safe? Is safety a state of mind? But surely it has objective factors as well? What if security, safety, control are all illusions? Innocence is always betrayed eventually, isn't it?

Does fear have limits? Can it grow exponentially larger? Or do we force it to stop at some point, to time out, to dissipate and fade? I'm so afraid of losing control, so afraid of something bad happening, but bad stuff has already happened, right? And I'm still here, I've survived so far, right? What if gripping so hard to maintain control is what makes us lose control?

What does it mean to suffer? Does suffering only degrade and diminish? Or is it the opposite? What if it makes us evolve into more empathetic beings? What if that thing called the Shattering is really something else? What if that Shattering transforms, becomes something new, becomes an Awakening?

Why have I lived my whole life trying to prove something to the world? Why do I have so much self-doubt? How do I cast aside my lifelong belief that I'm not good enough, that I'm somehow not worthy?

Why do we feel ashamed of our fear? Why are we not merely scared, but ashamed of what we're scared of? Why do we flog ourselves this way?

Why do I have these panic attacks? What makes my body do this? Why does the body take over for the mind? What kind of woman can render herself a badass in court, then some years later become panic-stricken by the sound of footsteps again, panic-stricken with the simple act of driving a car?

Why has it been so hard to let my mother know me? Why is it so hard to let anyone know me?

How could a woman who identifies as a feminist represent men who hurt women? Why does an assault victim choose to spend years of her life defending people accused of crimes? What if we simply accept that nothing happens in this life the way we expect it to, that we are complicated, layered, conflicted beings who are loaded with inconsistencies? What if we accept that our paths are jagged? That they lack a single clear trajectory? That we are messy?

What if this life is one long journey of losing our power, striving to get it back, losing our power, striving to get it back? What if it's me who has to take the first tiny huge step in reclaiming my power, reclaiming my life, ending my victimhood? Maybe when you've lost, when you've been victimized, the only person who can help you is you. Maybe it's that once you take that leap, you are empowered again.

Who would I be without my fear?

What if I'm not as powerless as I've led myself to believe?

I long to be, in the words of the Buddhist Pema Chodron, a "compassionate warrior." I want to lean into the places that scare me, to embrace them, and in so doing, steal back their power over me.

I want to die with no regrets.

Only I can end my hell.

The next afternoon I go out to look for an apartment.

My hands are shaking.

But I'm doing it anyway.

CHAPTER 45

May 8, 2014, San Diego, California

A BERKELEY PD CLERK has given me a court case number and at 2:30 p.m. on a Thursday I call the Alameda County Superior Court to see where this leads me. I reach a recording informing me that the court is now closed. The voice instructs me to please call back during normal business hours.

I call back the next morning, careful to call before noon because California courts, in addition to being closed by two thirty on a Thursday, also close at noon on Fridays, fallout from the chronic California state budget crisis. Stupidly I have written *People vs.* _____ on a yellow Post-it beside me, stroking its soft surface as the line rings and rings.

I brace myself mentally, knowing from experience the clerk will be surly. Who wouldn't be? It's an awful job: court clerk in the criminal division of one of the most crime-ridden regions in the country, spending all day every day speaking to victims, to criminals, to their respective families, none of whom could be happy about why they are calling, all of who are ready to unleash their anger at the voice on the other end of the line.

Finally a clerk answers. I explain that I was a victim in a criminal case and want to obtain a copy of the case file, but need to make sure it still exists since it's thirty years old. I give her the case number.

"Defendant's name?" she asks.

"I don't remember his name. That's what I'm trying to find."

"You don't have the name?" She sounds incredulous that I could lack such a basic piece of information.

"No. All I have is the case number."

"Hang on." Her voice disappears from the line, then she is back. "There are seven cases with that number. Case numbers get recycled over time. I need the name."

"The trial was in 1985," I say.

"I need a name."

"Can you read the list to me? I'll know it when I hear it."

"No," she snaps. "That's a privacy issue."

Irritation skitters across my skin. Why does *his* privacy need protection?

"Can you at least tell me if the file still exists?" I ask.

The clerk doesn't even try to hide her irritation. "Listen. I can't help you until I have a name. You don't have a name."

My throat tightens as it always has when I feel I'm being treated unfairly, as it does when I'm about to cry. I realize how ridiculous I'm being, how irrational and emotionally over-charged, but I can't help it. Maybe it's a symptom of too much focus on this old awful chapter of my life. Maybe it's a token of the chapter I'm experiencing right now.

After a few more futile rounds of questions and no answers, the clerk sighs and gives me the number for the Alameda County District Attorney's Office. She tells me to ask them for the missing name. I know what she is doing. She is shuffling me elsewhere, getting me off the phone. I will be someone else's problem now.

◆◆◆

I CALL COLE, THE Berkeley PD clerk who gave me the case number. Through a softly cadenced lisp, he explains there is some mistake, the report number doesn't match the incident I have described, and he can't locate the report without more information. He too needs a name.

Cole is kind, patient, not like the woman from the clerk's office, and his tender lisp renders his voice beautifully gentle. But I also sense something about him that is languid, slow-moving. Perhaps he doesn't really want to help. Or maybe he wants to but can't because of my assailant's privacy rights and the rights of all the other people who did something bad enough to be written up in a Berkeley police report. Cole asks what type of incident it was, though he has just told me my incident didn't match the case number I had provided. But I don't point this out. I don't want to be difficult.

"Assault with a deadly weapon," I say. The words sound serious. It feels strange after all these years to hear my own voice say them out loud, to speak them as a participant in the incident, to speak them not as lawyer but as The Victim.

"Try homithide," Cole says.

"What?"

"Try calling the homithide division. They handle athhaults, too. They might be able to help."

◆◆◆

I DON'T CALL RIGHT away. Instead, I wait and call at 4:00 on a Friday, reasoning this is a less busy time, that weekends are probably the big murder days. I wait for a surly detective to answer, someone overworked, exhausted from investigating too many incidents in which one person took the life of another.

I reach voice mail. I leave a message, trying to explain I need an old police report, trying to be concise, trying not to sound like a complete and utter wack job, but hanging up I don't believe I have succeeded. I also feel like an asshole. These people are busy. They are working current cases, cases that need their attention, and I am stealing time from an overworked detective, infringing on the effort to help people suffering right now, today. I am doing this because I am self-absorbed, obsessed with something that happened thirty years ago, and as my thumb lingers on the shiny smooth surface of my phone, I know somewhere inside that I won't receive a return call, that this homicide detective will have no sympathy for me.

◆◆◆

FRIDAY, MAY 23, AND the trajectory of my life is finally improving. I've found work again, found an apartment. I am frantically packing because in only a few short days the movers come. My brain is mush and I've given up all hope of lawyering any more today, of billing the hours to earn the money I so desperately need to survive this journey of leaving, of starting my life anew. My phone rings and when the 510 area code brightens the screen, a flicker of anticipation lights up my body.

The man on the phone identifies himself as Sergeant Paul Nguyen of the Berkeley Police Department Homicide Division. He is placid, soft-spoken, nothing like what I expected. I explain again who I am, what I'm looking for, as the sergeant waits, silent on the other end of the line. When I stop speaking there is a pause, a beat in time where I imagine him assessing me, sizing me up. Berkeley cops deal with a lot of crazies, after all. When he finally speaks, he presents the precise question I'd dreaded.

"May I ask why you want the report after all these years?" His voice is kind, yet it's the voice of someone used to asking probing questions, someone used to listening not only to what's being said, but to the bits left out or glossed over.

I touch the cardboard box at my side, feel the friction of the corrugated edge of the lid beneath my fingertips. Why? A perfectly reasonable question, but the truth is I don't know why. *Why* does not exist. Because what do I hope to achieve in dredging up this past when there is so much that needs my attention in the present? Why do I need to once again know my assailant's name? Why do I need to know about the rest of his life when my own is in such desperate turmoil? *Why?*

I stammer out words, staggered syllables to approximate a response to a seemingly simple question. "I still have PTSD from this incident. I'm curious. I want to know what happened with this person, what happened during the trial, what made them believe him and not me."

It's one of those moments when you speak without really being certain what's going to come out of your mouth, but I'm satisfied with what I've said. A schoolgirl's response, disarming in unadorned honesty. These are my reasons. These and a simple desire to know myself better, a need to understand how much of that ordeal is responsible for making me who I am today and how much of it is on me. Or maybe it's all on me? Aren't we ultimately, fundamentally responsible for who we become?

I pause, waiting for Sergeant Nguyen to tell me my reason isn't a reason, that I need to give a better response to the question, *Why?*

Instead he sighs a trained, practiced coo of sympathy, then asks for information about the incident, what type of crime, what was the date?

"And what was the address?" he asks.

"2330 Blake Street."

For a long moment there is only silence on the line.

"2330 Blake Street?" he asks. Something in his voice. He has slipped out of character. He is no longer the detached stony detective whose job it is to witness human atrocities, to thread together the details of those horrors, to piece together the *whys*.

"Yes," I say, jittery now. "What is it?"

Another long pause. "I lived at 2330 Blake Street in 1991 when I was a student at Cal."

We lapse into silence as each of us processes this astounding parallel in our lives. *Holy shit*, I think. What are the chances? The city of Berkeley has a population exceeding one hundred thousand people. Its streets hold nearly fifty thousand units of housing at an average density of three thousand units per square mile. If we were talking about each of us having lived at Putnam Hall in the campus dormitories, we wouldn't have given the shared address another thought. But the odds of Sergeant Nguyen and I having lived in the same Berkeley apartment building during our respective times at Cal are astronomical and it feels big, significant, something not to be brushed away.

"Oh God," I finally say. "This is unbelievable."

The word feels useless in my mouth. *Unbelievable* doesn't come close to describing what this is. It feels more like a miracle, like fate, and I feel a sudden kinship with this man on the other end of the line. I feel like this has happened for a reason, that in showing me connection, my connection with another human being, a person who might be called a stranger, the universe is telling me I'm in exactly the place I'm supposed to be on my journey through this life. I am precisely on schedule. I don't need to worry so much. I don't need to feel so alone.

I want to tell this man more, want to tell him everything, and the words spill out. Honest words. "I was an aide for UCPD. Do they still have aides? The attack happened after a shift." I babble, pause, add quickly, "I wasn't in uniform or anything."

"I am so sorry," he says. The trained part of his voice, the part that sets a barrier, is gone. These words are entirely sincere. "Let me talk to Cole," he says, "Let me see if we can figure something out."

I thank Sergeant Nguyen profusely, and after we hang up I sit down on the carpeted stairs leading to the bedroom that will soon no longer be mine. I look at the scene around me as if I'm seeing it for the first time. Half-filled boxes, paintings pulled down from the walls, rolls of half-unraveled bubble wrap. It's a scene of chaos, a scene of breaking apart, but in the middle of my turmoil I am suddenly overwhelmed with gratitude, stunned by how the universe can astonish me with its crazy beautiful surprises, surprises that make me feel connected to something bigger, a force at work in this universe, something larger than we can all fathom. Maybe moments like these are a glimpse into the mystery of so much depth and beauty, something so powerful that if we were to view it head-on it would blind us, like staring into an eclipse.

CHAPTER 46

May 24, 2014

A NOTHER MIRACLE. AN EMAIL from John. He'll be in Orange County visiting a client the following week, do I want to connect for dinner?

John and I have stayed in touch only sporadically over the years. After we broke up, he stayed in DC working in the Senate, then attended Georgetown Law School and joined a prestigious firm. I know he's successful professionally. I know he has an ex-wife, kids, a dog. But of this person who was once so central in my life, I know little else.

I say yes in spite of the lousy timing, knowing this dinner will occur right after I have moved, a time when my heart will be scraped raw. I say yes not for the comfort of an old friend. I say yes for one reason only.

I want to explore this person's memory.

I crave new insight to this distant time about which I'm obsessed.

What does *he* remember of that summer thirty years ago?

CHAPTER 47

May 25, 2014

Sunday again, but I'm lucky today. No panic attack on the left looping on-ramp delivering me onto the freeway. With the extra energy this leaves me, I suggest to my mother that we play Yahtzee, a break from our usual game of cards.

I have to walk her through each play, placing the scorecard in front of her. "Okay, what do you need? You need sixes. Want to go for sixes this turn?"

She nods, rolls the dice again. From the wide smile on her face it's clear she is having a blast.

I continue to coach her, explaining that she gets one more turn, then help her add up points for the three sixes she has rolled. "Six, twelve, eighteen. You get eighteen points. Write down eighteen in the slot next to sixes. No, not that one. Sixes. There you go."

She slides the oxygen tube from her nose, leaving it to rest like a necklace at her bony clavicle, then wipes her nose with a crumpled tissue, stuffs the Kleenex back into her sweater pocket, and forgets to replace the oxygen.

"Don't forget your tube," I say.

"What?" Her initial response to everything is *What?*

I tap below my nose. "*Oh!*" she says, grabbing frantically at her neck, pushing the tube into her nostrils, then finally settling back in to focus on the dice.

It's so rare that I can make her happy and I try to permit myself to feel satisfaction, to feel pleasure in doing something right for her. But eventually I spoil it as I always do by announcing I need to get home.

"I wish you didn't have to rush off," she says.

I linger, trying to soften the betrayal of leaving. I show her the YouTube video of Pharrell Williams singing "Happy," the number one song in America right now.

"Can you see?" I ask as she squints at the screen of my iPhone.

She nods, still squinting. "This must have taken a long time to make."

"Isn't he cute?" I ask as Pharrell dances and claps his hands.

When the video comes to its end, she turns to me, smiling. "Did he record that just for you?"

CHAPTER 48

June 2, 2014

I'M ALONE IN MY apartment, still unpacking, still working to put things in their place. I have a different emotion every three seconds. I am proud, expectant, weak, terrified. I am certain I have done the right thing in leaving my husband. I am certain I have made a horrible mistake.

I muster the courage to share my news with my mother on our 6:00 p.m. call. I keep my voice upbeat, wanting as always to protect her. I emphasize how amicable the split is, how it's the best possible thing, that separating from the man with whom I've shared fourteen years of my life is a blessed event, a cause for nothing but joy.

"Well—" she hesitates, her voice suspicious, "you *sound* happy."

"I am," I assure her.

After a long pause, she sighs. "Well, you're probably better off." Then she adds, "He'll probably find a new one right away."

"A new one?"

"Yeah."

"A new what?"

"A new woman!" Her voice snaps at my naivete.

Her reliably wry pessimism makes me smile. Yet I also know my mother is a wise woman in many ways, that the man I loved so long and deeply is the type to move on quickly.

I tell her where I'm living. She doesn't recognize the neighborhood, though she and my father had come here often when I was a child. I explain that it's near downtown.

"Just be careful," she says. "There's a lot of bums down there!"

I promise her that, yes, I will be careful. I promise my building is safe, secure.

"I hope you're not paying some outrageous amount of rent!"

If I told her what I was paying, she would keel over. "All rent is expensive these days, Mom."

She settles back down, feathers smoothed again. "Well. Just so long as you can afford it."

My therapist has taught me to look at the good intentions behind the things that come out of my mother's mouth. My mother was anxious and fearful and nervous for good reason. She knew firsthand how bad things could get and she had taught her lessons to me. And though I am desperate to unlearn her teachings, I finally understand that her chronic negativity is her way of protecting me. The words may be wrong and misguided, but the intention fueling them is love.

◆◆◆

THE FIRST PIECE OF mail to arrive at my new address is from the Berkeley Police Department. Holding the thick envelope in my hands, I study the crooked handwriting, wondering if it belongs to Cole or to Sergeant Nguyen. I hesitate before opening it, questioning now the wisdom of my pursuit, my obsession. I don't want my assailant here, don't want the energy of that ancient event, the grotesque agitation of Blake Street, to permeate my new sanctuary. What if my quest was only a symptom of my insanity, my fog-like depression, my need for a new life? For a long minute I stare at it, considering whether I should throw it away.

But curiosity wins. I want to know, I tell myself. My body needs to know.

The envelope shreds in my hands. Holding the report, fingering the pages, eyes scanning words, I'm transported. Here before me in the crooked scrawl of a cop's handwriting is the person I used to be, nineteen-year-old Karen of 1984; and like the photographs of that time, depicting a young girl wearing purple eyeshadow and a cop uniform, I barely recognize her.

Stapled to the front of the report is a handwritten note card: *245 via knife. Attempted 261.*

I still know these codes by heart, and like any bilingual person their meaning registers automatically without even a beat for transition. Assault with a deadly weapon. Attempted rape.

In the space for "Victim" my name appears: *Karen Thomas.*

Arrested: Peter D. Kostenka—white male, 27 years old. Height 6'2." Weight: 180. Hair: blonde. Eyes: blue.

Location of arrest: Blake and Fulton. On foot. Frontal attack. Dragged female toward ground via jackknife.

Evidence: one jackknife, 8" long.

Boxes checked indicate distribution of the report to Berkeley Homicide Division, Sex Crimes, the district attorney's office.

Suspect arrested? YES.

Sergeant Westinhoff prepared a report describing the "Scene":

The area surrounding 2330 Blake Street is an area often victimized by residential burglaries occurring while the occupants are at home, including attempted rapes.

Reading these words, my brain stutters one rapid-fire question. What the fuck?!

What the fuck?!

What the fuck?!

Thirty years after the fact, I'm learning I was right? That I wasn't crazy but justified in my terror that someone sneaking into my shithole apartment with me inside it, helpless and alone, had been a real possibility? A frequent occurrence for my neighborhood, even? And how is this supposed to make me feel? Satisfied in having been right all along? Satisfied in the wonder of learning three decades later that my fears were amply justified? Or should I feel something else? Something like pure horror?

But this all begs the question: Why couldn't I have trusted my feelings then? Why is it still so hard to trust myself now?

The entrance to the apartment building is a cement walkway. It is illuminated by lights but is somewhat dim close to the adjacent sidewalk of Blake Street. Entrance leads to the first-floor apartments. A row of mailboxes lines the west wall of the entranceway.

Victim's Statement:

Victim states that she was walking up the entranceway of the apartment complex of 2330 Blake. Victim heard rapid footsteps of someone running west on Blake approaching the start of the entranceway. Victim turned and saw suspect moving up the entranceway toward her. She initially thought it was another tenant returning to the complex, so she turned her back to the suspect and began walking in. Victim felt "something wasn't right" and turned around again to confront suspect.

I know this can't be what I said. "Confront" is the wrong word. I had turned back around to make eye contact, to simply let this person know I was aware of his presence. That's when I saw the knife.

He had what appeared to be a "jackknife" in his left hand and was about five to six feet away from victim. Suspect lunged at victim, moving in front and then behind her. His right arm encircled her neck, choking her as he attempted to cover her mouth. Victim screamed as suspect pulled her back almost all the way to the ground. Suspect fled west down Blake Street. Victim ran to her apartment, #1, located directly around the corner of the entranceway, and phoned police immediately.

Blood pounds inside my ears as my eyes move across the page. It's happening all over again, the tremors inside my body, the sound of the dispatcher's voice telling me to CALM DOWN.

Investigation:

I was on patrol when the initial broadcast was dispatched concerning the occurrence at 2330 Blake Street. Description of the suspect was released as a white male, about twenty-five years of age.

As I approached the victim's residence, Officer Gusterson #91 advised me he had stopped a possible suspect on the 2500 block of Fulton Street. I contacted the victim at her residence, advising her that we would be conducting a "drive-by." Victim was admonished that the person she was going to look at "might" or "might not" be a suspect, and that she was only to see if she could recognize the individual.

Victim looked at the suspect from the patrol vehicle, with proper illumination for a good look. Her immediate response was to jump forward in her seat, saying, "Yeah, Yeah, I think so."

This is nothing like what I recall. The words on the page reflect nothing of the turmoil I felt, the hesitancy, the naïve fear of identifying the wrong man, and how could they? I understand that a police report is intended to serve as a sketch, a mere outline of what happened, setting forth the elements of a crime so the district attorney's office can then decide what to formally charge. I know this, and yet the lack of detail still frustrates me. I want to read how the smooth leather upholstery of Sergeant Westinhoff's car felt beneath my palms. I want the pages to capture the panic in John's voice when he called. But only I have held onto those moments. Those pieces of the story matter to no one but me.

Victim leaned forward to get a better look at the suspect. After a long look at him, victim stated that the suspect was the man who assaulted her.

Officer Gusterson searched the suspect for weapons, finding a jackknife in his front left pocket that matched the description provided by Victim. Suspect was arrested.

OFFICER E. GUSTERSON'S REPORT tells the story from a different point of view:

I heard the report of a possible attempted rape in front of 2330 Blake Street and responded to that address from Shattuck Avenue. As I approached the intersection of Parker and Fulton Streets, I noticed a subject matching the suspect's description as given by the victim.

I pulled my car up next to him and asked him to stop. I explained that an incident had occurred in the area, and a possible suspect was seen fleeing the area who was described as he was. I then asked him for identification, of which he said he had none. Officer Oncianas then arrived to provide cover on the stop.

The subject asked if he was under arrest and I informed him that he was not. I informed him that he would be detained until the person reporting the crime could be located and brought to the scene of the stop so he could be eliminated from the investigative process. Subject seemed disturbed by this but offered no resistance. I noticed during the time I was filling out the stop card that the subject was perspiring heavily and appeared to be very agitated. His appearance was disheveled and while I was completing the stop card he rearranged his clothing by buttoning his shirt and tucking it into his pants. I asked the subject where he was going while walking on Fulton Street, and he said that he was on his way home to his residence on Derby Street. I then asked him where he was coming from and he said that he was coming from his place of employment on Wheeler Street near the intersection of Wheeler and Ashby. He related that he was a self-employed carpenter and was working on a house in that area. It then occurred to me that if he was walking home, he was taking an unreasonable route, since he had passed Derby Street two blocks south of the location where he now was.

Sergeant Westinhoff and Officer Lantow appeared with the victim. The identification took several moments, and after Officer Oncianas realized that the subject had composed himself before the viewing, Officer Oncianas and I then returned the subject's appearance to what it was like when he was stopped, with his shirt untucked and partially unbuttoned.

Following positive identification, I conducted a brief pat-down search for weapons. All of the suspect's pockets were empty except for the left front pants pocket, which contained an 8-inch-blade Buck-style knife with brass tips.

I advised Kostenka that he was under arrest for assault with a deadly weapon and that his bail would be $5,200 with the inclusion of an outstanding $200 traffic warrant. Other than the traffic warrant, no other criminal history was found.

Prior to booking, photographs were taken of the subject standing in the squad room, wearing the clothes he was arrested in. Another photograph was taken of the subject's right knee, which showed a small fresh abrasion below the kneecap. Subject was then booked without incident, and made several phone calls which were recorded on the booking sheet.

CASE CLOSED.

◆◆◆

I read the report a second time, then a third, struggling to see Karen, not merely *Victim*, but she is barely visible on these pages like she is barely present in the pages of her own journal. It's a bizarre sensation to read, to see through the lens of objective responders, an incident that has held on to your body for thirty years. Some of it I remember exactly as it reads. For the rest, it's like reading about something that happened to someone else. It's strange and I try to let myself sit with that strangeness, to simply feel, to not fight to give it a name.

And though I had read thousands of police reports in my criminal defense days, it feels so sanitized. The *Just the facts, ma'am* writing style captures none of what that night left inside me, none of what my body experienced. It was thirty years ago, but those minutes in that dusty hallway remain vivid, as if recorded on a video I have rewound and replayed until the memory is indelible, simply part of my brain matter. I see his cunning, his manipulation in the simple act of pinching a button inside its hole, in tucking in a shirt, an effort to make himself look different, to interfere with my ability to identify him, an effort that, due to my own self-doubt, my own concern for someone else's rights, had come close to succeeding.

But I finally have something I had held on to for years, then let go of: my assailant's name.

CHAPTER 49

June 8, 2014

WHEN I ARRIVE AT her room, my mother greets me with the question she has asked more than a dozen times in the past three months, "Karen, how old are you going to be this year?"

When I tell her she startles back in her chair like I've smacked her. "Fifty?!" she says. "That's hard to believe." She narrows her eyes at me, suspicious.

"It's true," I say, "and I'm thrilled." She stares with her rheumy eyes, absorbing my words. "It feels like a badge of honor," I add, amazing myself that these words are entirely true.

She nods resigned agreement. "Yeah," she says, "it's kind of a relief."

"A relief?"

"Yeah, you have to think that all the bad stuff that's happened in your life isn't going to happen again."

◆◆◆

BACK HOME. SAFE INSIDE my beautiful apartment, I type my assailant's name into Google, preparing to click on links to his name, like gifts to unwrap. I'll find him on Facebook, LinkedIn.

There will be an academic bio. All of it a revealing, an unveiling of this person who impacted me so acutely but who for thirty years has remained a mystery.

His name pops up immediately.

But it's not a LinkedIn profile, not a Facebook page, not an academic bio. It's a link to an opinion issued by the State of Minnesota Court of Appeal.

I click on it. What appears on my screen is a full written decision by the state's appellate court, dated December 14, 2004:

Defendant appeals from his jury trial convictions of kidnapping and child enticement. Defendant was sentenced to life imprisonment for both counts. We affirm the convictions and sentence of life imprisonment.

Life imprisonment???

I read quickly, scrolling to the court's summary of the facts supporting the conviction and two concurrent life sentences for Peter David Kostenka:

On April 19, 2002, while the seventeen-year-old victim was walking home from school, defendant pulled a white car into her path and grabbed her as she tried to pass around it. She fought defendant while he put her in the front seat of the car. He pinned her, face up, on the passenger-side seat and floorboards, but she continued to struggle. She screamed, bit his gloved hand, and eventually escaped. She described defendant as a tall, lean, balding man with a long, squared beard. She told police he was wearing a white tank top, tan shorts, and tan work gloves. A bystander who saw her escape and run away screaming memorized the car's license plate number. Police traced the license plate number and found defendant at the registered owner's apartment. The car's owner was defendant's friend and neighbor down the hall. Defendant had borrowed her car because his was broken down. Police identified defendant by the victim's vivid description of his blue eyes and distinctive beard. The defendant also had an abrasion on his hand near his wrist, which was consistent with the victim's description of where she bit the culprit. Police arrested defendant. While his clothes were different than the victim described, defendant's friend explained that defendant had changed his clothes since the time he left his apartment earlier that day. Following his arrest, defendant gave conflicting accounts of his whereabouts during the time of the kidnapping.

Five days later, the police investigation had failed to unearth the pair of tan shorts and white tank top that fit the victim's description of the culprit's clothing, despite a search of defendant's apartment. However, police had a phone conversation with one of defendant's neighbors indicating that defendant often parked his gray Mazda near the neighbor's residence. Police discovered that this area was a few blocks away from defendant's residence. The neighbor mentioned that he occasionally saw defendant carry packages of beer from it. Another neighbor indicated that he often saw defendant going to and from the vehicle, but he also saw defendant driving a white car around the neighborhood. An officer found the gray vehicle parked where the neighbors had indicated, and the police impounded the car, obtained a warrant, and searched the car. During this search, police found a sleeping bag, a blanket, and a backpack containing clothing, duct tape, drop cloths, rope, unused condoms, body lubricant, a razor, surgical gloves, and a knife.

I feel a stomach-lunging drop, like I have jumped off a bridge into darkness and I'm free-falling, a long gravity-defying moment before plunging into a vast body of water below, then sinking, sinking into utter silence.

Duct tape, drop cloths, rope, unused condoms, body lubricant, razor, surgical gloves, and a knife. **DUCT TAPE, DROP**

CLOTHS, ROPE, UNUSED CONDOMS, BODY LUBRICANT, RAZOR, SURGICAL GLOVES, AND A KNIFE!

I emerge again, head above water, gasping for air, every sense buzzing. *Holy shit*, I whisper over and over. *Holy shit.* My mind roils, attempting to process, but also fighting, not wanting to comprehend the physical objects these words represent. What does one do with duct tape? What purpose do drop cloths serve? What can one do with a knife? How much evil can a person accomplish with all of these items combined?

Other witnesses identified defendant as someone who often cruised streets near the victim's school in a white car, and another neighbor later came forward to confirm that he saw defendant moving a backpack from the gray car to the white car before the incident.

In this appeal, my assailant raised a myriad of issues, errors during trial that he claimed rendered his conviction unlawful. All of them were dismissed by the Court of Appeal. The court also considered Mr. Kostenka's claim that the trial court abused its discretion by sentencing him to life imprisonment, a range beyond the ordinary sentencing guidelines for his crimes. The Court of Appeal stated that a trial court may depart from the sentencing guidelines range if it has a compelling reason for that departure. The court concluded:

The trial court departed from the guidelines range and sentenced defendant to life in prison on two grounds. First, the court considered the items found in defendant's car as evidence of defendant's intent to rape and murder the victim. Second, the trial court opined that the guidelines did not adequately reflect the extent of defendant's mental illness underlying his obsession and depravity. The court concluded that the extent of his obsession resulted in no likelihood that defendant can be rehabilitated to the extent that he can ever be allowed to live in society. These factors are objective and verifiable, because the existence of the physical objects and defendant's history of severe mental illness were empirically supported by the record. Furthermore, these factors provided a substantial and compelling picture of a seriously dangerous and depraved individual who has not been and most likely never will be reformed or deterred by the prison system. Therefore, the trial court did not abuse its discretion when it sentenced defendant to life imprisonment.

CHAPTER 50

*D*EFENDANT'S INTENT TO RAPE *and murder the victim...*
        A seriously dangerous and depraved individual...
Sitting in a new apartment, in front of a computer, alone, safe, freed from a shattered marriage, staring at a whole new life ahead, a barrage of emotions rains down. Shock. Utter disbelief.

The seriousness of my assailant's intentions that long-ago night are no longer debatable. Something I had fought so hard to dismiss as nothing, as a mere minor incident in my life, could no longer be denied. I think about the connection between me and this man, how he changed my life, how, as it turns out, he had wanted to end it.

As I read and reread the opinion, I wonder, ask myself over and over, what did it reveal? What did it tell me about my life? What am I supposed to feel learning thirty years later how close I came to a tortuous death? Validation? A child's reaction: *Seeeee? I told you so! (Goddamnit!)* Satisfied he will die in prison? Enraged he was permitted the opportunity to traumatize more women after me? Grateful my encounter with him was not so much worse? Lucky to be alive?

A note rings out in that room, a beautiful tone that resonates somewhere inside me even if I can't name it right away. In those fleeting minutes in that hallway this man intended grave harm. Something primal in me had known this. Something instinctual inside me knew to be deathly afraid. Now I understand I was right to have felt so terrified. *I was right.* I felt his intentions, his serious, serious intentions, and my body remembers. How it felt to be overtaken. It intuited. It *understood.* My body got it right. My body refuses to forget.

Sometimes fear is justified and perhaps the worst part of victimhood is the self-blame, the refusal to trust yourself, of adding the weight of shame to the burden. To be given the knowledge that I can trust my own instincts and feelings because those instincts and feelings are spot-on, is a gift.

What I learn in this moment:

Trust. *Self*-trust. In terms of regaining power, trusting oneself means everything. Everything.

And there's something else too. If you're ever faced with the fleeting decision: Fight or submit?

Fight.

◆◆◆

I THINK OF THE girl in Minnesota, how she will never forget that day, how she might not fear footsteps but cars, viewing every man as a threat, ready to jump out and grab her and stuff her inside with the backpack holding its death kit, tools of torture, rape, an agonizing end. I imagine the terror she must have felt once he got her in the car. I think of her fight, the sensation of teeth piercing skin. I imagine her testimony, how her jury had believed her. I think about the validation of a sympathetic jury, just verdicts, being believed. That is what I have always wanted most of all.

I glean from the opinion that my assailant went on to have a long and glorious career as a sexual predator, but there is little I can find online. All I can pull up is his 1995 registration as a sex offender following conviction for some unlisted offense and a 1997 conviction for misdemeanor sexual assault. I enlist the help of a private investigator, but the trail goes cold.

Still I think of the others, know there must be some girls who weren't so lucky, that some nights he must have gotten it right. How many bodies did he leave behind undiscovered? How many young girls lost the struggle and disappeared? I think of them, their own eyes widening with realization as mine had. *This. Is. Happening.* I see them bloodied and ruined, knowing they won't be going home ever again, that they will feel peace only in death. And him. His pleasure, his power, his perfect control. Laying out the tools from his death kit one by one, lining them up, each waiting to fulfill its own special purpose.

If I met him, would he describe the feeling? The exhilaration, the thrill of catching his prey? How it's everything he'd imagined yet entirely different? How it feels to be freed, unbound, to rush up and take what he knows is his? Would he describe the sensation of watching the life leave another human being?

I fantasize about writing to him. *Hi,* I'll say, *remember me? How many others were there? I know there are dead bodies somewhere. Wait. I know you are smart enough to not respond to that. What were your plans for me? Why did you choose me? Remember when we saw each other at Park N Shop?! How awkward was that?! Remember when the jury believed you and not me? I am still pissed about that, BTW. I've spent a goddamn lifetime trying to understand why that happened, how it happened, how I could rewrite that script, how I could become the one in control. I've spent a lifetime shuddering at the sound of your goddamn footsteps.*

But of course I don't write. What would be the point? What would he say in reply? *Of COURSE I remember you!!! Thanks for thinking of me. How ARE you??!!!!*

I Google further, learn about his family. They are wealthy, smart, prominent in their community. His father is a well-known engineer, another stunning fact given that I had always imagined my attacker as someone with the sensibilities of a scientist. How had my senses intuited engineering sciences in the genes of my assailant? How does a body glean such exquisite detail in a brief intimate encounter with a man and his knife? We are such intuitive creatures. We instinctively know so much about our surroundings, about our fellow beings, and yet so much of it we brush away, deem it unworthy of attention.

Google can't answer the most important questions. What kind of childhood, what kind of home, what kind of world produces such a man? What went wrong to deliver him to his jail cell? What sustained cruelties did he endure? Or was it a single incident that sealed his fate? I think about this family, how horrifying these crimes must have been for them, how chilling it must all still be. Do they know what happened to turn him into a monster? Or was he always this way? Do they visit him in prison? What do they talk about? Or perhaps they have simply tried to ignore his existence, a black spot on a family's record, something shameful, something to be buried away. Forgotten.

◆◆◆

I OBTAIN A COPY of the court file from my own case, desperate to peel back layers, to discover all that had been hidden from me, to learn what happened while I was barred from that courtroom so many years ago.

Reading the file feels strange, like overhearing someone talk about you behind your back. It tells me he testified, and I imagine him on the witness stand, seated in the same chair where I had sat, and I can almost hear his lies. He was just walking home from work, an innocent guy in the wrong place at the wrong time, carrying no wallet, no identification. And that knife in his front pants pocket? The knife identical to the one described by Karen Thomas? Well hell, as expert testimony has already established (thanks to my family's money and their ability to get me all the justice money can buy) knives like that are available in any one of a hundred sporting goods stores within a fifty-mile radius of beautiful Berkeley, California!

Two women sharing his last name testify. Character witnesses, as I'd suspected. A lease agreement is entered into evidence, an effort to corroborate his story that he lived nearby and the route taken home from his 11:30 p.m. carpentry job made perfect sense. I read the names of the jurors, wonder which names match which sets of eyes that rested on me as I testified, which eyes rolled, which eyes judged me. I wish I could find each one of them, shake them by the shoulders, tell them, You got it wrong, motherfucker. Dead wrong. You should have listened to *me*.

There's no transcript, only an entry by the clerk noting what time closing arguments occurred, when the judge instructed the jury on the law. Even without a transcript, I know my attacker's lawyer would have hammered home reasonable doubt, that all of the little inconsistencies had to raise doubt in any person's mind as to Peter David Kostenka's guilt, and how if such a doubt existed, the jury was obligated, morally and legally *obligated*, to return a verdict of not guilty. I had made the same argument to juries myself, dozens of times.

◆◆◆

THEN FEAR SKITTERS ACROSS my skin. Does a life sentence really mean life? What if he's been paroled? What if he finds me? Suddenly I am grateful again for choosing my fortress of an apartment with its doorman, locked elevator, security cameras. I am safe, I tell myself. Safe.

I Google Minnesota Bureau of Prisons. On the homepage is an "Inmate Locator" search function. I input his name, age, race, and up pops the details of his incarceration.

Sentence: LIFE.

Earliest possible parole date: LIFE.

Convicted at jury trial. Date sentenced: May 2003.

Date conviction affirmed: December 2004.

I click on the name of the prison where he is housed, a "special" prison for inmates so mentally ill they can't function in a "normal" prison environment. A link for his Identification Number tells me he is Inmate #234359. Without hesitating I click on it.

The speed of the website staggers me with his image, his torso against the white cinder block wall of a prison, and I jump back in my chair. "Jesus!" I shout to the empty room.

It's him. Older and heavier, but him. Just as I have, he has aged. Time, the prison-prescribed meds, the paste of processed prison food have caught up with him. His blue eyes look more puzzled now.

But those eyes. Those bright blue eyes, staring, locking onto mine even from a photo. I scroll away. *It's just a photo*, I tell myself. *He can't see you.* But I can't stop myself. I return back to them. After all these years they are still so intent, still as I have always remembered.

CHAPTER 51

June 9, 2014, San Diego, California

FIVE DAYS LATER, I walk to the restaurant to meet John. We have only seen each other once in the last twenty-something years, when I visited DC in 1999 to run a marathon. I'm still half crazed from the emotional tsunami of my move, from all I have unearthed. My jaw clenches so tight my throat is constricted, and if I try to force myself to eat, I gag on anything I attempt to chew. I haven't consumed more than three hundred calories in the past two days and I am starved, woozy with unease.

I arrive first, sit at the bar, order a glass of wine. As I raise it to my lips, I'm grateful to see that in this moment my hands are not shaking.

When John walks in, we hug hello. As he settles beside me, I notice the top button of his shirt is open, revealing a glimpse of that patch of chest hair I'd known so well but forgotten entirely until now. Something unexpected ripples inside, a hint of some ancient spark, and I can't help but smile, astounded once again by what the body remembers.

We move to a table and suddenly I'm ravenous. Beef carpaccio infuses my blood with iron, arugula and parmesan and bread fill me, make me feel whole again. I'm so eager to spill my news that before we even review the standard life inventories (How's your mom? How's your job? How old are your kids now?) I blurt out my question: "Do you remember when that guy with the knife attacked me?"

Of course he does.

In a feverish blur of words, I tell him all I've discovered. I detail the duct tape, the rope, knife, drop cloths, and he swallows, shaking his head in silence. When he speaks, his vocabulary seems as impoverished as mine. All he can say is, "Holy shit."

He remembers how upset I had been with Willa, how the verdict had gutted me all over again. He remembers the voice of the Berkeley PD dispatcher putting out the call of a 245, attempted 261, hearing the location, feeling the ice-cold comprehension that this voice on the radio was talking about me.

I tell him of my plan to visit Berkeley, to retrace my steps on Blake Street in two months on the thirtieth anniversary of my attack. I tell him I'm not sure, but I think this might be something I want to write about, perhaps an essay, maybe a book.

John asks how it all feels and I tell him, honestly, that I don't yet have an answer.

I ask him questions. What else does he recall? But he has nothing else to give me, he has shared all he knows. The conversation shifts to the department, the aide program, how it felt to be pretend cops.

"We were cool, right?" I ask, worry in my voice. Could it be that we were just a bunch of mall cops?

"We were totally cool."

The certainty in John's voice quells my concern, reassures me. The same way it always had.

CHAPTER 52

June 2014

WHEN CHELSEA CLINTON ANNOUNCED her pregnancy, the media blustered over whether Hillary Clinton should not run for president because she will be *a grandmother*. It's a question never before posed to a male grandfather candidate and the hypocrisy infuriates me. Thirty years have passed since Geraldine Ferraro was nominated as the first female vice-presidential candidate in US history and so much has changed. So much has stayed the same. The rules for men and women remain different.

As a woman, I'm fed a constant diet of contradictions. At any moment I can flip open a magazine, snap on the television, open a new tab on my screen, and every one of these sources will tell me: Smell good, have soft skin, be beautiful, be sexy. But not too sexy. Not slutty, but don't be a frigid bitch. Get into the best schools. Be nurturing. Give a spectacular blow job. Work hard. Be fierce. Accept that you will earn less than your male peers.

In 1951, Sylvia Plath wrote, "Being born a woman is my awful tragedy.... All is spoiled by the fact that I am a girl, a female, always in danger of assault.... Yet God, I want to talk to everybody I can as deeply as I can. I want to be able to sleep in an open field, to travel, to walk freely at night." As a woman living decades later, the risk of sexual assault still forms the rules I must follow: how I should dress, how I should behave, how I should physically get myself from Point A to Point B. Because I am female, I do not have the same freedom as a man. I do not have the same freedom of safety. There are inherent difficulties inhabiting a female body. Those difficulties are exacerbated when that female body wears a police uniform, when that body attempts to exert authority of any kind.

◆◆◆

UNLIKE WOMEN IN SOME countries, I can vote, drive a car, divorce a husband. But I can't walk alone in darkness with any certainty I won't be attacked. And so, much of the time, I play it safe and stay inside. But at some point, the fear percolates, hardens into anger, defiance. If a man can walk home alone at eleven thirty at night, why can't I? It's an undeclared war against women.

My story is such a common one, it's timeless: A man overpowering. A woman's will defied. Sexual violence against women permeates our culture. In the years it took me to write this book, it was stunning how often, in casual conversation with other women about what I was working on, I heard, "Yeah, something like that happened to me too."

So many women have been assaulted, raped, worse. Maybe you are one of them. If not, you can count yourself lucky, but certainly you have a mother, a sister, a friend who has suffered this trauma. Even if they've never told their story.

We carry our wounds in our heads, our hearts, our souls. Where is the outrage? Why aren't we protesting? Rioting in the streets? Where are the vows by our government to combat crimes against women? Where are the vows from our representatives promising to create a world where women are finally safe? Why do the incessant news stories of violence against women fail to rock this nation? Why do they fail to leave it teetering on its edge?

We need to speak up and tell our stories. We need to riot in the streets. We need to reclaim our power any way we can. We need to stop letting ourselves be victims.

CHAPTER 53

July 5, 2014, San Diego, California

I CALL MY MOTHER. It's Fourth of July weekend but she thinks it's Thanksgiving, and when I gently correct her, she gets upset. I hear the bewildered terror in her shaking voice as she apologizes, stammering, "I just don't know what's wrong with me!"

I can't even imagine how this must feel, to know you're losing control of your own mind yet being incapable of doing anything about it. Or maybe I can imagine. Maybe I understand exactly how this feels.

I do my best to soothe her, tell her it's all right, that she's doing great. I tell her I forget things all the time. All of this is true. Sometimes I wonder, what is the point of memory?

The line goes silent for a moment and then my mother speaks again.

"Someone keeps doing something wrong," she says.

"Who?" I ask.

"I don't know!" The edge to her voice is razor-sharp.

"Well, what are they doing?" I'm wary now, worried I have missed something, that my mother's caretakers are harming her somehow.

She pauses, hesitating, and I sense her holding back, unsure whether she can share the news of what torments her. Then she blurts it out. "Someone keeps stealing my Irish Spring soap!"

Sometimes there really are no words. I feel lame, useless, utterly disarmed.

"I'm sure everything will be all right," I say, my voice thin, weak. Then, in benign effort at redirection, I try to steer the conversation elsewhere.

With the space of thirty years, I can reexamine why I couldn't tell my mother of my assault sooner, why I couldn't reach to her for help. What I believe now is what I suspected then but couldn't bring myself to admit: I was afraid her reaction would only fan my own anxieties; that she would make me feel worse; that she would encourage me to come home, to give up, to retreat back into the safety of the house I'd grown up in. I worried she would make me endure even more shame than I already felt for being so stupid, for putting myself in a position to let this thing happen to me. I feared she had no other help to give, and that the act of reaching out to her and coming back empty-handed would destroy me.

What I don't know—what I'll never know for certain—is whether my belief is correct, whether this fear was justified. Much of the evidence points to the conclusion that it was. Because of the traumas of her own life, my mother evolved into an anxious, nervous person with a hyperawareness of all that could go wrong. But in all my years on this planet, I saw her cry only twice: once at the airport saying goodbye to an uncle (a warm spot in the otherwise cold front of her childhood), and, decades later, the night my father died.

And beyond her refusal to crumple, I'd also witnessed a woman with a fierce hatred of injustice, a woman angry and watchful over how "the little guy always gets shit on." She didn't take the life path to fight that injustice formally, didn't become a political leader, didn't write laws or argue them. Instead she simply took the best path she could find for herself and that path included creating me, doing the best she could for me, even if I've sometimes felt that wasn't good enough.

One of my fondest memories of her stems from a post office employee picnic we attended when I was twelve. It was a Sunday afternoon in a public park. Kids played in the grass bordering the asphalt parking lot. Employees and their spouses sat around scattered wooden picnic tables eating hamburgers, tossing back a few beers. Everything felt peacefully dull until a van rumbled through the parking lot, traveling at an absurdly unsafe speed given that kids played all around. One of the mailmen whose small children were among those playing wiffle ball at the edge of the lawn yelled at the driver, "Slow down, asshole!"

The van braked, lurched into park, and a bearded, tattooed biker type slid out of the driver's seat and stalked toward that mailman, a skinny redhead who looked frail next to this angry man in his leather vest and thick hairy arms. It was clear to me and everyone watching that this biker dude was going to kick the shit out of this little mailman and he was going to do it right in front of all of us. Everyone in the park stood frozen, stunned silent, unsure what to do other than maybe run to a pay phone and call the cops who most certainly wouldn't arrive in time to save the little mailman, a man who was now holding up his palms, backing away and apologizing.

That's when my mother moved in, stepping between the two men, placing her body squarely in front of the mailman, shielding him from the biker. The leather-vested man shook with rage, yelled at her to get out of the way, that this had nothing to do with her, that she should mind her own goddamn business. My mother refused to budge and within a minute the biker retreated to his van and took off, winning the last word only with the gunning of his engine and the squeal of tires.

What does this memory have to do with why I couldn't ask my mother for help, with how I've always judged her? Maybe it's a slice of her I like to remember, a bit of her badass self, a self she didn't get to show off too much, a piece of her that had shriveled up inside from the sheer act of surviving all that she'd suffered through in her younger life. Maybe the memory reflects my mother's sense of justice, a sense she passed on to me. Maybe it shows her as a tangling of contradictions, anxious and fearful but willing to put herself in harm's way if the situation warranted. Maybe my mother is like all of us, flawed human beings who are walking coils of contradiction, so often struggling to simply survive.

I'll never know how things might have been different had I asked my mother for help, had I thrown myself on the floor at her feet and begged her to make it all go away, which was exactly what I'd wanted to do that summer, and through that trial, and again when I nearly went to jail myself. I'll never know how things might have been different or how they might have been the same. And I'll never be able to ask my mother: What would you have done had I told you sooner? What would you have done had I told you the whole truth? What would you have done had I flung myself before you and cried and cried? I'll never be able to ask because that woman who was my mother is gone.

ANNIVERSARY

CHAPTER 54

July 17, 2014

THE YEARS LIE STACKED up behind me. All thirty of them. I pack, check email, and marvel to find a message from John. He remembers I'm going to Berkeley this weekend, empathizes with all it will raise. He gives me his cell number in case I want to talk. His thoughtfulness touches me.

The cab is late. I'm nervous. I'm excited. I'm questioning why in hell I am taking this trip, what this attempt at time travel will accomplish. My jaw clenches, giving that familiar strangling feeling in my throat when the anxiety percolates close to the surface.

The cab arrives and the driver smiles broadly, apologizing. He is chatty, smart. He asks what airline, where am I going?

"Berkeley."

He asks if I'm in the educational field, if I'm affiliated with the university. He is from a country in East Africa that I've never heard of. He explains that it became an independent nation in 1991.

I tell him I'm researching a book. What kind of book? he wants to know.

The cab smells as all cabs do, a mingling of BO and cigarettes. It's hard to understand this man because of his accent and the volume of the music coming from the speaker behind my head.

Creative nonfiction, I say, hoping to discourage him, to throw him off the trail. I still can't bring myself to say "memoir." It sounds so pretentious.

"What kind is that?" he asks, staring at me in the rearview mirror.

"Memoir," I say. "Things that really happened," I add.

"What is yours about?"

Suddenly I feel the familiar sting in my eyes that tells me I'm going to cry. It's the intimacy I'm sharing with this fellow human being. It is so pure, so beautiful. It's strange and wonderful and feels like one more miracle, one more gift from the universe. I know this man honestly wants to know, that he will understand and appreciate whatever I tell him. It's so rare to connect with someone on this level. My own mother doesn't listen to me like this, doesn't relate with me this way.

Still, I hesitate. "This weekend is the thirtieth anniversary of the night I was a student at UC Berkeley and was attacked by a man with a knife."

He lets out a low whistle.

"So this weekend is about revisiting what happened?" he asks.

Then I say something I don't realize is true until the words leave my mouth. "It's about releasing. It's about letting go."

He nods thoughtfully. "That must be the kind of thing you remember forever," he says.

I pause for a moment, absorbing this remark. "It is," I agree.

"Did they catch him?"

"Yes, but he was acquitted at trial."

"He was AK-quitted?" He squints, still looking at me in his rearview mirror. "What this word mean?" He widens his eyes. "They let him go?"

I nod and he lets out another low whistle.

I tell him he should write.

"I know, I know," he says.

"Just your story of living in Africa, how you came here, your life now. A publisher would snap that up in a second." He smiles at this and asks me what I think about Amazon's self-publishing platform.

◆◆◆

ON THE DRIVE INTO Berkeley from the Oakland airport, my second cabbie is silent, oblivious to the thrill of memories his ride gives me. We pass the Oakland Coliseum where my Mills College friend and I saw The Clash open for The Who in 1982, then, Alta Bates Hospital, Telegraph Avenue, the Park N Shop at Telegraph & Derby now metamorphosed into a CVS drugstore. We stop for a red light at Sixty-Second & Telegraph and as the smell of KFC permeates the cab, I think about how I flew into Oakland after trips home to San Diego during college, taking a shuttle from Oakland airport to the BART station, then dragging my suitcase nearly two miles home from the station on Shattuck Avenue, all because I couldn't afford the twenty dollars for cab fare.

We turn right onto Durant Avenue from Telegraph, pause for a sea of students crossing. With a red marker someone has crossed out the word FREE on a metal sign reading DRUG FREE ZONE.

"Be very careful here at night," the driver warns, his tone fatherly. The warmth in his voice, the genuine caring for my well-being, it is nothing less than precious.

He drops me at The Durant Hotel, a place I'd always dreamed of staying, infamous now for the 1990 siege when Mehrdad Dashti, a thirty-one-year-old paranoid schizophrenic, had a psychotic break. He went to Henry's Publick House and Grille in the hotel lobby, bringing with him a revolver and two pistols, one of them a fully automatic MAC-10, a 9mm assault weapon that fires a clip of thirty rounds all at once. Dashti took thirty-three hostages at the restaurant, terrorizing them, forcing male hostages to rape female hostages with carrots, ordering the females who were blonde to strip below the waist as he taunted them, calling them sluts and whores. The siege lasted seven hours, leaving one student dead and others wounded before Berkeley police killed Dashti with a hail of bullets to the head and chest.

◆◆◆

I CHECK IN, RUSH back outside, eager to explore. Campus is my own private time capsule, a museum packed with all the memories of the phase that ties for the worst of my life.

As I pause at the curb deciding which way to enter campus, a Prius sneaks up beside me and I can't help but smile at all the incongruencies of past and present. In 1984, there were no hybrid cars, no GPS, no Uber, no Lyft. Mark Zuckerberg was in diapers. A company called Apple had just unveiled the first Macintosh desktop computer, people were only just learning a new meaning for the word "mouse." No one blogged. No one thought about recycling. There were no paninis, just sandwiches. Reagonomics was gospel. The Berlin Wall was still intact. Nine Eleven hadn't happened yet. Lots of things hadn't happened yet.

Michael Jackson, Princess Di, Geraldine Ferraro, my father—they're all gone. Today it's Nicole Richie in the tabloids, not Lionel, and in line at a grocery store, the cover of *People* magazine features a montage of photos of Bad Boy Prince Harry, speculating he may finally be settling down. Nineteen eighty-four is a place that exists only in my imagination.

Still, I find myself searching faces, hoping in vain to see one of the handful of people I knew, seeking out students with Sony Walkmans, headsets bobbing on their heads. But all around me people wear buds in their ears, stare into tiny screens, bang fingers across the surfaces of phones, oblivious to what's around them. In 1984, to talk on the phone was expensive, even on Sunday after 5:00 p.m. There was no Facebook, Twitter, Instagram. No email, texts, FaceTime. No easy, instant, effortless interaction. With the crutch of these technologies would I have felt less lonely, less desperate? Do people feel any less lonely today?

A UC police car cruises by me and I stare inside hoping to see Kistner or McClaughlin or Chris Galan, but I find only a stranger's face, peering back at mine with suspicion. Even the street people are different, Orange Man and Polka Dot Man replaced by a new assortment of human oddities. A tall beefy black man walks down Bancroft screaming to some invisible foe, "YOU IS A PUSSY! PUSSY! PUSSY!" The street echoes with *Pussy* until he finally drifts out of earshot. No one even blinks. Another man pushes a Top Dog cup toward me as I pass, calling, "Come on! Throw me some cash here." Then he adds, "Cheer me up."

One thing hasn't changed in thirty years: the people on the streets of Berkeley still have panache.

◆◆◆

As of 2014, Berkeley faculty, alumni, and researchers have won seventy-two Nobel Prizes, nine Wolf Prizes, seven Fields Medals, fifteen Turing Awards, forty-five MacArthur Fellowships, twenty Academy Awards, and eleven Pulitzer Prizes. In 2013,

UC Berkeley was ranked as the number one public university in the world by *US News & World Report*, marking its sixteenth consecutive year as the top public university. Even so, the campus seems less intimidating, less enormous than I remember it.

Only now do I realize how much I missed. I'd never had the time to see the beauty of the sky, to appreciate the stunning leaves of all the lush trees. What I see now is magic, intelligence, creativity, sunshine, the most beautiful architecture in the world. Campus is vibrant, alive, so different than what I recall. My eyes were so clouded by the fear, the tedium, the weight of needing to study, study, study, to work, the heaviness of always feeling behind, of always feeling I wasn't enough. Gazing around, there are no more relics of anger, no signs of fear. The fog that brought so much gloom seems mystical now, and I feel like I'm floating.

It's true I'm still scared, but I'm finally learning that everyone in this world is scared, that the definition of courage is being afraid and doing it anyway. I know this because I have different eyes now, older eyes, bleary at times, but growing ever more bright and clear. I'm not the same girl of thirty years ago, lugging her sad scared shadow all over campus, across the seedy city streets. That girl is gone, replaced by a woman with a lifetime of experiences, a woman who has faced juries not as victim, not as accused, but as advocate, finally possessing some control. She's been replaced by a woman who has written, who has practiced law for more than twenty years, a woman bruised by the heartbreak of a failed marriage, a woman who somehow found the strength to leave that marriage to forge a better life, a woman who has fallen down many times, yet who has still managed to climb back up onto her feet every time.

I got more of an education here than most students. I didn't learn the lessons I'd hoped to learn, but that doesn't make what I waded through any less valuable, does it?

◆◆◆

THE TIME. THE PLACE. The senses. So many have faded. Others remain strong. John placing both hands on my waist, pulling me against his warm flesh, the taste of a latte from Café Roma, icy cold beer sliding down my throat, Dan Rather's voice on John's television.

I snap photos on my iPhone: Sather Gate, the Campanile, the Top Dog sign on Durant Avenue. I text them to John, grateful to be in contact with someone on the other side of time, someone who appreciates these memories as much as I do.

I walk the incline past Wheeler Auditorium, turn left, passing South Hall, its brick still embraced by tangled vine, straight toward the face of a building where I'd rattled a well-meaning grad student trying to masquerade as a therapist. I couldn't have known it at the time, but I suppose what I'd wanted was to simply deposit my burden of fear and walk away lightened, dusting off my palms, feeling like my old self again. Paying to go to a real therapist never entered my mind. With the space of thirty years and having now reaped the benefits of a good therapist, I wish I could have gone to someone who knew how to help me. It's a sad fact, but money stood between me and therapy during the most vulnerable time of my life, the time I needed it most. Money stands between hell and freedom for so many people still.

I float along, stop, lower myself onto a concrete slab of bench in front of Moffitt Library, remembering the time spent in that spot, Bike Bureau, exhausted afternoons debating whether I should go to Psych class or blow it off, go home and try to nap. I conjure the vision of a board covered with fliers for statistics tutors, FMLN demonstrations, posters of Bibi Lee's face, words imploring me to help, pleading, *What if she were your lover, your sister, your friend?*

♦♦♦

I DROP BY THE police station, still in the Sproul Hall basement where I haven't set foot since the day I was forced to resign. I stare at names on plaques. Sara Bertini, Amy Bryant, Rachel Stevens. All of them have left this place.

The university is more frank now about the reality of violence, and UCPD has grown to sixty-four officers, forty-five full-time civilian personnel, and sixty student employees. The aide program is now the Community Service Officer Program and the khaki police uniforms John and I wore are long gone. CSOs wear navy blue pants and gold shirts. They carry radios and flash lights, but there is no way they could ever be mistaken for "real" cops as we so often were. The Berkeley Police Department has also evolved. Its website brands the department as transparent and community friendly, posting photos of smiling uniformed officers, listing names, badge numbers, beat assignments. A link to crimemapping.com shows clusters of cartoon-like images reflecting 130 crimes around campus in the space of a single week. A mask reflects a robbery on the 2300 block of Shattuck, at San Pablo & Bancroft a cartoon gun reflects "weapons," a white fist against a red background shows an assault on University Avenue, and there's a new crime we didn't have in 1984: video voyeurism. The 2300 block of Blake Street appears crime free this week.

♦♦♦

AGAIN WITH THE BLISTERS. Forming on the backs of my heels as they always have from the friction of my own wandering. But I have so much more to do, to see and feel.

I retreat to the Durant Hotel, hunch down in bed, allowing my body to regroup. I watch *American Beauty* on my laptop even though I've seen it dozens of times. I watch the character

Lester Burnham speak the line I've used often lately to answer the question posed by so many loving friends, friends who gently inquire since I left my husband, *Are you okay?*

The line is, *I feel like I've been in a coma...and I'm just now waking up.*

CHAPTER 55

July 18, 2014, Oakland, California

MY LATEST CAB DRIVER punches the address of the Renee C. Davidson Courthouse into his GPS and we're off. On the 24 West, moving toward Downtown Oakland, my jaw clenches, leaving my throat raw, and again I'm asking: What the hell am I doing? What can I possibly be hoping to find?

◆◆◆

WANDERING THE LOBBY OF the courthouse, all around me are men and women wearing lined, tired faces and rumpled suits, each clutching frayed files and battered briefcases.

I'm not sure where to begin.

Moments later I text John: "*Sitting outside Department 22.*"

But Department 22 is not the place I remember and this bothers me. I want to exist within the spot I inhabited so many years before, to move inside its space with a power and strength I then lacked.

The door is locked and I peer through its small square window at a dark courtroom that is half the size of my memory. I am convinced I recall it correctly, that the courtrooms have been renumbered at some point over the years, but after asking three different clerks in surrounding courtrooms, each giving me a look that says I'm a crazy person, I give up.

It chafes me to think that everything might not be exactly as I recall.

◆◆◆

I RIDE THE ELEVATOR to the district attorney's office on the ninth floor. The narrow wooden bench where John and I sat waiting for Willa Esposito to prep me is gone, replaced by a wide lobby holding a battered couch on one side, a worn table and chairs on the other. The room feels shabby and sad, reeking with the grief of the thousands of victims who have passed through it.

A skinny black woman sits at the table hissing into her phone. "I didn't answer 'cause I was texting you, goddamnit!"

Her whole body tenses as she listens to the response on the line. "I am not going to argue with you in this motherfucking courthouse! I am trying to get my motherfucking shit together!"

Something about this woman fascinates me, the way each of my clients always had. I sense she has had a hard life and this sparks thoughts of my mother's hard life. I want to sit down beside this woman, ask why she's here, what's going on that brings her here today, who is this person she's arguing with? But I don't dare. I'm afraid even to gaze too long in her direction, worried my glance will invoke her wrath, but I steal peeks as I wait in line at the reception window. From where I stand now, simultaneously victim, witness, near felon, defender of persons accused of crimes, someone who has seen the criminal justice system up close, too close at times, I feel an overwhelming compassion for this woman. In addition to everything else, I have received the middle-of-the-night call from a friend in jail, felt the bolt of electricity as the brain fights the cobwebs of sleep to force sense out of the voice on the other end of the line. I have called upon clients' family members to serve as character witnesses, have seen the frustration and shame and fear in their eyes. I've made the visits to jails to confer with clients, have breathed in the scents of defeat and despair. Every last one of these moments, every last one of these beautifully flawed beings, still make my heart ache with empathy, even in spite of my own victimhood. How can this be?

From behind a thick plate of glass, a woman with almond-shaped eyes and lustrous magazine-worthy hair asks how she can help me. Her perfect eyebrows rise as I explain I was the victim in a case stemming from an incident thirty years ago, that the case went to a jury and I am trying to determine whether there is any chance of obtaining a trial transcript.

I know this is unlikely. The court reporter is most certainly retired, if not dead, so the chance of retrieving her raw notes is improbable. And because my assailant was found not guilty, there was no conviction from which to appeal and therefore a transcript was probably never even generated. Still, I need to give it a try. I want more than what I've been able to uncover. I want to know what was said in my absence, to read the lies my assailant told, to read the testimony of his *Andy Griffith Show* character witnesses, people still fuzzy and colorless in the shadows of my memory. I want to hear Peter David Kostenka's lawyer make his closing argument, to know precisely how he stitched together all I had gotten wrong. I want to read Willa's argument, to learn whether that jury ever heard about the shirt in the photo, about its magic trick, how it transformed itself in the light.

The woman behind the glass is polite, helpful. She sends me to the Superior Court clerk's office, but the clerk's office tells me to go to the DA's office, and so I ride the elevator again back to the ninth floor.

The skinny black woman is off the phone. She sits, legs crossed and swinging her foot, reading some crumpled court papers.

"You're back," says the pretty woman as I approach her window. She is not perturbed in the least and offers to have the chief deputy DA come out to speak with me. I sit in the armchair next to the skinny woman and her papers, hoping she will strike up a conversation with me. She doesn't.

A gray-haired man in glasses steps through a door into the lobby. He looks between me and the woman, his face uncertain. "Karen…?"

I rise and explain what I'm looking for. He tells me what I already suspected was true. The reporter would not have retained any notes for this long and due to the acquittal, no transcript would have been prepared for appeal. I describe where my assailant is now and why, and the chief deputy nods his head, face arranged to convey understanding, and then he explains what else I already know: how tough on sentencing California courts have become since 1984, how items such as those found in Mr. Kostenka's backpack would earn a life sentence here too. His voice is apologetic, gentle, and though this assurance is empty and pointless, I appreciate it anyway, feel a deep gratitude for his effort to soothe. It seems to him perfectly sensible that I am here in this lobby asking questions about something that happened thirty years earlier, and I feel something I don't feel often enough: I feel understood.

"I'm so sorry we didn't get it right for you."

His empathy triggers the clenching in my throat and I feel my mouth twitch as tears sting into my eyes. I allow myself to accept this man's kindness, letting it hold me like an embrace.

No one ever asked me, What do you want? What do you need? If they had, I wouldn't have known what to tell them. But now I know that my answers to those questions were simple. Validation. Justice. To sleep. A safe place to live. And now this chief deputy is giving me what else I needed then but never got. Acknowledgment. Recognition. Respect. The pieces of the puzzle needed to help me claw back my own power. Somewhere deep inside that black place in my heart it dawns on me: this is what I've always needed most of all.

CHAPTER 56

July 19, 2014, Berkeley, California

A NNIVERSARY. A DATE THAT means nothing to anyone but me. The thought of setting foot back on Blake Street, of facing that building again, even from the other side of thirty years, fills me with dread. When I locked that apartment door for the last time, I slammed it shut as hard as I could, reveling in the violence of the sound it made, how it echoed through the building like the night of my screams. I ran to John's car, gunned the engine, peeled out like I was being chased. It had been my own private hell and I never wanted to see that place again. Until now.

As with every other piece of this excavation journey, I don't know why I'm going there. A desire to reclaim that space? A desire to say FUCK YOU to the past? To retrieve that part of myself that was lost there so long ago? All I know is that the need to return is physical, something alive inside my cells, and this visceral need is not only about what happened that night in the hallway. That night is simply one piece, one finite part. Going back is just as much about all the rest: the pretending, the sleeplessness, the chronic state of terror, the loneliness, the physical sense that everything inside me had been scraped raw.

Retracing the steps I took thirty years ago, a sense of alarm rises and I worry the mental focus on this attack has been too much, that there's no such thing as catharsis and I'm wreaking physical harm to my own body by dredging up this past. But as I move down Dana Street approaching Blake, I feel an odd sensation of my present self inhabiting the past, of my body conjuring alchemy, pulling off a sorcerer's trick, of inhabiting two places in time simultaneously. It's with this sense that I suddenly want to see it all: the bathroom where I jumped at the sight of my own shadow in a blackout, the bedroom facing an alley, the windowless kitchen, the cinder block walls, the pale pink refrigerator.

I walk purposefully, intentionally, greedy to soak up my surroundings with full awareness, yet also wanting to retrace not only my steps but my thoughts of that night. What could I have been thinking before my life changed forever? What floated through my nineteen-year-old mind the night a piece of me died?

When I reach the building, I study it from across the street. Suddenly all the gloom of that summer, all the lonely terror, flies back and hits me in the face. I'm untethered again, sensing the old familiar fear that I will float away, will lose myself for good. I sit on the curb and continue to stare, afraid to get too close. The building is even uglier now, older, more run down, and to anyone else it's just a dump in a crap neighborhood of a dangerous city. To me it's sacred, a burial site where one part of me died but another was born.

Eventually I stand, dust myself off, and walk across the street. I stand at the spot on the sidewalk where I first saw him, trying for a moment to feel what he must have felt in that moment our eyes met. I peer inside the hallway. The threshold is barred now by a locked ice-blue steel gate that looks like the door to a cage.

Every window of the basement apartment that had been mine is covered with thick iron bars, further evidence that I had always been right, that I was as vulnerable as I had felt, that my worst fears had been spot-on.

Looking back, I know I was wildly ignorant, dangerously naïve. With the clarity only time can give, I see it was nothing less than insanity for me to keep putting on that uniform, to keep pretending, hoping against hope that nothing bad would happen every single time I wore it. I know now I betrayed myself by adopting the mantra *I'm fine I'm fine I'm fine*, betrayed myself by not talking about it, by pushing it down even as it swelled up so big it threatened to consume me. There is a word I should have spoken then, a word that might have made things better. That word is *Help*. I see how crazy it was to stay in this shithole excuse for an apartment. But when we are "in it," we always feel stuck, always believe we have no choices, no options. What I finally know is that this is seldom true and just as it's unfathomable now that I stayed in this apartment, stayed in that job, it feels equally unfathomable that I stayed stuck in my marriage for as long as I did.

Instead of self-flogging, instead of denial, I offer tenderness to that nineteen-year-old sleepless girl lying stiff and scared on the thin used mattress that came with her rent. I offer sympathy, empathy, wisdom, self-love, and all the power that comes with it. I send her a message that she is stronger than she knows.

That night in the hallway wasn't my end. Thirty years to the day later, I stand in front of it with a sense of awe. Awe for what a beautiful mystery this life is.

And as I take one last look, at that hallway, at the wall I scraped up against, I feel the enormity of the gift I have been given. A life to live any way I choose.

CHAPTER 57

July 19, 2014 10:30 p.m., Berkeley, California

IN THE HOTEL LOBBY at Henry's Publick House and Grille, I sip champagne, silently toast my assailant, silently thank God I'm alive. What I feel is gratitude. I am ready. Ready to let go, to feel the grace of release. Ready to step forward into this next phase of my beautiful life.

This is how it ends. The heroine keeps moving forward.

I now believe there is an invisible order to things. Anonymous figures positioned to come together in the most inexplicable ways, inflicting cruelties upon one another, inflicting kindness upon one another, creating a web that makes up our lives. It's only from a brutal assault, from the betrayal of a spouse, from losing everything I spent a lifetime working for, from watching a beloved and beautifully flawed mother start her slow, painful descent into dementia that I've become the person I am today: a woman capable of seeing the contradictions of human existence; who sees that we are all much more alike than we allow ourselves to perceive; who sees humanity in everyone; who feels a little too much; who needs a little too much quiet time; who still suffers from panic attacks and shaking hands; who cannot stand to be late and consequently arrives early for everything; who self-medicates with a bit too much wine each evening; who, if she has her druthers, is in bed by nine. And while I still slip into phases of outright war against myself, I am also learning to show myself tenderness.

Experience teaches us all kinds of things we didn't want to know. These pieces of my story—they were all trauma, and though I didn't choose for any of them to happen, though I still suffer in so many ways, I wouldn't change any of it. The dark nights of my heart have taught me things.

In the aftermath of upheaval, the focus is on getting through, on simply surviving the crushing emotions that follow you through each day. But after enough struggle, something shifts. The pain becomes less raw. What happened cannot be undone, what happened will always be part of you, but you come to understand that you're a better person not in spite of it but because of it. And talking openly about our loss is what heals.

I am damaged. I have flaws. I will always be working toward becoming my best self. It will be a lifelong process for me and I have accepted that. For some people, being happy just happens. For others, it takes work. Today I commit to that work. I want to release the anxiety that has dictated my life and how I live it and how I experience everything and how I relate to everyone around me. I am sick of living in a constant state of fear and I want desperately to stop.

For so much of my life, I have not known who I am.

I have lived a lifetime believing I am not good enough. But I'm finally beginning to see this is a lie.

This is a project. One I've been avoiding, struggling against all of my life. But I'm ready. Ready to fight, ready to fail, ready to begin my life once again.

I am a work in progress.

Aren't we all?

EPILOGUE

2018

Peter David Kostenka took something from me, but he also gave me a great gift. It took me thirty years to name and understand what I experienced that night, what I experienced as a "victim," what I learned evolving out of victimhood.

But could he have turned out to be even more?

Did he push me back into a life with John?

I'm not one to ponder divinity, but humor me for a minute.

A man tries to abduct me with the likely intent to rape, torture, mutilate, and murder. He fails. His attempt leaves a lasting mark. I attempt to excavate the roots of that mark, to understand it, if not escape from it. In the process of investigating the truths of that time so long ago, I receive an email out of the blue from John, with whom I've had virtually no communication over the span of thirty years. He suggests we meet for dinner. I'm reluctant because I'm lazy, because I'm emotionally wrecked from having left my husband, and I don't see the point. Except I do see the point because I am desperate to hear John's recollection of events, desperate to share how close I came to dying, if not that night in the hallway, most certainly in the days to follow.

So I meet him. We rekindle a friendship.

◆◆◆

SHORTLY AFTER MY BERKELEY Anniversary, I rebooted the mourning of the end of my marriage. I learned that my mother's prediction that my husband would "find a new one right away" had proven prescient, and for reasons I didn't understand, the fact that he had moved on so quickly triggered the heartbreaking loss all over again. I tortured myself with my thoughts. Thoughts like: He replaced me so easily. This proves he never loved me. This proves our fourteen years together were a lie. Thoughts like: She must have less cellulite; she must have no wounds; she must be more fun than me. I couldn't stop the tormenting.

During this anguish, John returned to San Diego. We had dinner again, and I was such a mess I couldn't help myself from crying at the restaurant.

Hot, right?

But through the course of that evening, John somehow managed to guide me out of my funk. Suitably cheered, he walked me home and at the lobby of my building, in a gesture worthy of a Hollywood romance, placed his palms on each side of my face and pulled me in for a single stunning kiss.

Is something at work in this universe that's beyond our comprehension? A fate, a direction not of our own choosing? A destiny that plays out not because of our choices and actions, but in spite of them? I can't help but wonder at the mystery of this life. There are times I know I'm being pushed and prodded by a divine force, a force that sees paths different from the ones I wanted to follow, the routes I've clung to so tightly my knuckles turn white with my need to control.

◆◆◆

BECAUSE OF THAT FIRST dinner with John, a dinner I would never have bothered with were it not for my assailant, a relationship formed. A relationship that has changed the course of my life.

John helped me overcome the crippling sadness of the end of a marriage. He showed me I could love again, provided much needed support of all kinds to help me stabilize again. Much of this book was written in his DC home, inside the beautiful writer's room he helped create for me.

John and I are a couple again, partners in this strange and beautiful life, working daily on our happily ever after.

ACKNOWLEDGMENTS

THANK YOU TO THE awesome team at Rare Bird, especially Tyson Cornell, Julia Callahan, Jessica Szuszka, and Hailie Johnson. Working with you has been an honor, and I am privileged to be in such excellent literary hands. Thanks also to Angelle Barbazon, publicist extraordinaire: your commitment to me and this book has been unwavering, and from day one working with you has felt like working with a dear friend.

My deepest thanks to the amazing writers who endorsed this book with their blurbs: Rene Denfeld, Susan Henderson, Samantha Dunn, Antonia Crane, and Chuck Sevilla. You inspire me deeply, both as writers and as human beings.

Profound gratitude to early readers of these pages: Robert P. Kaye, Donna Trump, Gregg Temkin, David Ulin, Samantha Dunn, Nicole Polizois, Cheryl Jacobs, Christina Simon, Helen Malmgren, and Natalie Eaton. Your suggestions, notes, and critiques were invaluable—as were your votes of confidence.

I owe so much to my writing friends: Sara Lippmann, Aleida Wahn, David Rocklin, Melissa Chadburn, Bud Smith, Nancy Stohlman, Tony Press, Sara Fitzpatrick Comito, Amy Wallen, Jim

Ruland. And to my beautiful muskateers: Meg Tuite, Len Kuntz, and Robert Vaughan (also early readers of this book before it was a book)—so much gratitude and love. Always.

Writing is lonely and this book was difficult to write. I couldn't have made it through without the love of Katie Gonzalez, Jena Waid, Jeff Floodberg, Judy Combs, Darlanne Mulmat, Mary Jo Boring, Joe Bratsky, Kathy Hearn, Serena Suarez, Brandy Antunez, Dede Dulaine, Greg Vega, and Glen and Donna Gross. Thanks for showing me the way when I felt lost. And to Kim Baldonado: thank you for sharing this crazy journey with me—both then and now.

Janice Deaton and Blake Harper, you are my forever family. I'm a writer, hence supposedly good with words, and yet I can't even begin to express what you mean to me.

Finally, applause to Jack, Thomas, and Olivia Bentivoglio for giving me the benefit of the doubt even when you weren't entirely sure what I did all day—always locked up in that room, always sitting at that desk. And finally, finally, so much love and thanks to John Bentivoglio for being there from the beginning, for living through all of this with me, for loving me then, and especially for loving me now.